W9-ACG-016

12/
26

Southern Literary Studies

Louis D. Rubin, Jr., Editor

*Caroline Gordon as Novelist and
Woman of Letters*

PS
3513
.O5765
Z63
1984

Caroline Gordon as Novelist and Woman of Letters

Rose Ann C. Fraistat

Louisiana State University Press

Baton Rouge and London

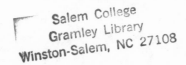
Salem College
Gramley Library
Winston-Salem, NC 27108

Copyright © 1984 by Louisiana State University Press
All rights reserved
Manufactured in the United States of America

Designer: Barbara Werden
Typeface: Linotron Galliard
Typesetter: G&S Typesetters, Inc.
Printer and Binder: Vail-Ballou Press

Publication of this book has been assisted by a grant from the Andrew W. Mellon Foundation.

Quotations from *The Cocktail Party*, copyright 1950 by T. S. Eliot, renewed 1978 by Esme Valerie Eliot, reprinted by permission of Harcourt Brace Jovanovich, Inc.

Quotations © 1959 by Richard Wilbur reprinted from "Advice to a Prophet" in his volume *Advice to a Prophet and Other Poems* by permission of Harcourt Brace Jovanovich, Inc. First published in *The New Yorker*.

Quotations from Dudley Fitts and Robert Fitzgerald (trans.), *The Oedipus Rex of Sophocles: An English Version* (New York, 1949), reprinted by permission of Harcourt Brace Jovanovich, Inc.

Quotations from John Crowe Ransom, *Selected Poems*, 3rd edition, revised and enlarged, copyright 1924, 1927, 1934, 1939, 1945, © 1962, 1963, 1969 by Alfred A. Knopf, Inc., copyright renewed 1952, 1954 by John Crowe Ransom, reprinted by permission of Alfred A. Knopf, Inc.

Quotations from Robert Penn Warren, *Selected Poems, 1923–1975*, copyright 1936, 1940, 1941, 1942, 1943, 1944, © 1955, 1957, 1958, 1959, 1960, 1963, 1965, 1966, 1967, 1968, 1969, 1970, 1971, 1972, 1973, 1974, 1975, 1976 by Robert Penn Warren, copyright renewed 1964, 1968, 1969, 1970, 1971, 1972 by Robert Penn Warren, reprinted by permission of Random House, Inc.

Quotations from "Green Centuries," "Loss in the West," and "O Pioneers" are reprinted from *The Collected Poems of John Peale Bishop*, edited by Allen Tate, with the permission of Charles Scribner's Sons. Copyright 1948, 1976, by Charles Scribner's Sons.

Quotations from Allen Tate, *Collected Poems, 1919–1976* (New York, 1977), Flannery O'Connor, *Mystery and Manners: Occasional Prose*, ed. Sally Fitzgerald and Robert Fitzgerald (New York, 1969), and Flannery O'Connor, *The Habit of Being*, ed. Sally Fitzgerald (New York, 1979), reprinted by permission of Farrar, Straus & Giroux, Inc.

Quotations from the Chattanooga *News* reprinted by permission of Lee Anderson, Editor, Chattanooga News-Free Press.

Quotations from Dante Alighieri, *The Inferno*, trans. John Ciardi (New Brunswick, N.J.: Rutgers University Press, 1954), reprinted by permission of John Ciardi.

Library of Congress Cataloging in Publication Data

Fraistat, Rose Ann C., 1952–
    Caroline Gordon as novelist and woman of letters.

    Bibliography: p.
    Includes index.
    1. Gordon, Caroline, 1895–   . 2. Novelists, American—20th century—Biography.
I. Title.
PS3513.O5765Z63   1984   813'.52   83-19963
ISBN 0-8071-1151-1

To my mother and father, Ann and Bill Cleveland

Contents

Preface

The final years of her life Caroline Gordon spent working on a novel, and it was primarily as a novelist that she regarded herself, though her impeccably crafted short stories and her years of college teaching and assistance to younger writers were enough to secure her literary reputation. The aim of this book is to illuminate and evaluate Gordon's contribution to the history of southern letters. Her short stories have been closely read and appreciated, but her novels have not received comprehensive critical attention. Nor has the scope of her achievement as critic and teacher been adequately examined. With her lifelong dedication to what she termed "the mysteries of the craft," Caroline Gordon well earned the accolade of "woman of letters."

*

My thanks to Robert Lucid and Robert Regan, both of whom read the manuscript at an early stage and made many helpful suggestions. Thanks, also, to Stuart Curran for his assistance in translating Greek. Brainard Cheney, Louis D. Rubin, Jr., and Robert Penn Warren all kindly responded to written queries while I was researching the book.

For his continual thoughtfulness and counsel, my special appreciation goes to Arthur H. Scouten, who from the first encouraged me to undertake this study. And to my husband Neil, who read and reread every page and offered such valuable advice and assistance, my many thanks and love.

Caroline Gordon as Novelist and
Woman of Letters

Chapter I / A Woman of Letters

The Role of the Man of Letters in the Literature of Revolt

The artist must . . . be willing to be both a seer and a revelator; . . . he must know how to transform his private vision . . . into something that is essentially public.
—WAYNE BOOTH, *The Rhetoric of Fiction*

The men of intellectual duty, those who should have been responsible for action, have divided themselves into two castes, two cults—the scholars and the writers. Neither accepts responsibility for the common culture or for its defense.
—ARCHIBALD MACLEISH, *The Irresponsibles*

Addressing an audience gathered for a Flannery O'Connor symposium at Georgia College in April, 1974, Caroline Gordon recapitulated her career with these words: "I am . . . a novelist by profession, and . . . I am *not* a critic. But one of the greatest pleasures authors enjoy is talking about their craft. And I have not been able to resist this opportunity to discuss some of the mysteries of the craft as exemplified in the works of a master craftsman."[1] One of the important fiction writers of the Southern Renaissance, a well-known teacher, and, despite her modest protests, a significant interpreter of literature, Caroline Gordon showed the breadth of talent, the command of literature, and the sense of social and moral commitment that one might well attribute to a "woman of letters."

Although the term *man of letters*—designating someone devoted to scholarly, critical, and "creative" or fictive writing—has become uncommon in the twentieth century, a number of literary historians and critics have found it the most appropriate and revealing description for the major figures in the Southern Renaissance: Allen Tate, John Crowe Ransom, Donald Davidson, and Robert Penn Warren. Allen Tate, who was married to Caroline Gordon for over thirty years, consciously placed himself in line with Matthew Arnold and

---

1. Caroline Gordon, "Rebels and Revolutionaries: The New American Scene," *Flannery O'Connor Bulletin*, III (1974), 43.

T. S. Eliot, as he intimated even in the titles of some of his essays, such as "The Present Function of Criticism" and "The Man of Letters in the Modern World."[2]

Whereas Gordon thought of herself primarily as a novelist, she also supported herself, like Tate, by teaching and writing critical articles. Her literary career exemplifies the transitional course of many modern writers who have relied on the university for support but have professed an allegiance to a community larger than the purely academic one. Certainly Gordon's sense of vocation was reinforced by her close associations with the leaders of the Fugitive and Agrarian groups, by her friendship with Ford Madox Ford, as well as by Tate's belief in the importance of the realm of letters.

For Gordon and Tate, the man of letters was connected with the European tradition, the French *homme de lettres*. So Caroline Gordon portrays their friend Ford Madox Ford: "Breadth of view, immense knowledge of many literatures, and an unwavering loyalty to his great profession marked Ford as perhaps the last great man of letters in the nineteenth-century style. Whatever concerned the vitality of letters was within his province. He was one of the few great editors of this century. In reckoning his value one must not forget that as editor of the *English Review*, founded in 1908, he brought what we know now as 'modernism' to England." Similarly, Tate calls Ford a man of letters "on the French model of the mid-nineteenth century: a man of enormous 'culture' who had survived into an age that no longer assumed the autonomy of the arts but had gone off into varieties of neo-primitivism or into 'politics.'"[3]

Empathizing with this friend and his somewhat anachronistic beliefs, Tate and Gordon felt at the beginning of their vocations that art and its disciplining technique promised, as it had in the nineteenth

2. Tate, Ransom, Davidson, and Warren are described as men of letters in Louise Cowan, *The Fugitive Group: A Literary History* (Baton Rouge, 1959); Louis D. Rubin, Jr., *The Wary Fugitives: Four Poets and the South* (Baton Rouge, 1978); and Lewis P. Simpson, *The Man of Letters in New England and the South: Essays on the History of the Literary Vocation in America* (Baton Rouge, 1973).

3. Caroline Gordon, "The Story of Ford Madox Ford," in Francis Brown (ed.), *Highlights of Modern Literature: A Permanent Collection of Memorable Essays from "The New York Times Book Review"* (New York, 1954), 114–15. See also her "Dedicatory: Letter to Ford Madox Ford," *Transatlantic Review*, n.s., III (1960), 5–6. Allen Tate, Contribution to "Homage to Ford Madox Ford—A Symposium," in *New Directions in Prose and Poetry*, No. 7 (Norfolk, Conn., 1942), 487.

century, a câche of spiritual values. Not surprisingly, Tate's description of Ford's fiction is just as applicable to Caroline Gordon's early work; her first published novel, after all, was written under Ford's tutelage. Continuing his homage to Ford, Tate writes, "As the heir of Flaubert and the avowed disciple of Henry James, Ford believed passionately in the novel as work of art, a distinct *genre* to be explored and developed in terms of form, not of social ideas or of mere subject matter." Gordon's admitted respect for the Impressionist novel and her frequent references to the tenets of Flaubert, James, and Ford further link her with an older European tradition of letters, in which the authors' own experiences as novelists have shaped their preferences for certain techniques and their sense of the novel's historical development.[4]

While her affinities as critic and fiction writer lie with a basically nineteenth-century European tradition, Gordon resembles such moderns as T. S. Eliot and the Fugitive poets, who assume that great writers participate in an international tradition that preserves in literature much of the best of human feeling and thought. Her own dedication to letters she evidences in her numerous critical writings, the anthology of short stories that she edited with Allen Tate, her classroom teaching, and her many novels and short stories. Her early newspaper work, though only indirectly related to her career as author and critic, shows us a woman already concerned with a cultural and intellectual world whose boundaries extend well beyond regional limits.

One of Gordon's first responsibilities at the Chattanooga *News*, for which she worked from 1920 until 1924, was reviewing new books. For the early months of 1920, her column appeared weekly under the by-line "Carolyn Gordon." Written in the more casual tone and with the brevity expected in newspaper reviews, her criticism reveals, nonetheless, that appreciation of craft which marks her later essays. In her assessment of a novel by Nalbro Bartley, for example, Gordon writes, "'The Gorgeous Girl' disappoints on every page, yet manages to hold the reader's attention to the end by the vividness of presentation and facility of phrasing which are this writer's most striking characteristics." Again, in a discussion of Francis Lynde's novel, Gordon's

4. Tate, Contribution to "Homage to Ford Madox Ford," 487.

final praise focuses equally on craft and plot: "'The Wreckers' is that somewhat rare thing—a book which combines dramatic action with finished workmanship, and as such ought to find a wide and varied audience."[5]

Clearly, Gordon's column does more than recommend the best new romance or adventure story; it expresses a concern with the world of letters as a whole. Thus, the death of Mrs. Humphrey Ward occasions a tribute to the novelist and an appraisal of her literary career. And in evaluating the *Southern Review*, published in Asheville, North Carolina, Gordon welcomes the new magazine as a sign of the growing consciousness of the South's responsibility to its writers: "The south has always made generous contribution to American literature. . . . Yet New York has ever been the mecca of southern writers. There seems to be no reason why the south should not be able to afford a recognition of literary talent which would preclude the possibility of southern ideals and traditions being lost in the writers' adaptation to a changed environment. It seems to be the desire of the editors of the Southern Review [*sic*] that this magazine should meet such a need." Three years later, Caroline Gordon was among the first southern reviewers to recognize the calibre of the *Fugitive*, calling it the best of the little magazines then being published in the South. Louise Cowan records in her history of the Fugitive group that a subsequent letter from John Crowe Ransom mentioning Gordon's praise introduced to Tate the name of the woman he was later to marry. As William Stuckey observes, "though the kind of writing she did for this newspaper was of little value to her as a fiction writer, the association was responsible for a significant change that both her personal and professional life were to take."[6]

Indeed, the direction of Gordon's career changed importantly as a result of her marriage to Allen Tate. Her relationship with him involved her in the main phalanx of the Southern Renaissance. Over the course of their careers, John Crowe Ransom, Donald Davidson,

5. Carolyn [Caroline] Gordon, "New Books," Chattanooga *News*, May 1, 1920, p. 12, April 10, 1920, p. 9.

6. Carolyn [Caroline] Gordon, "New Books," Chattanooga *News*, April 10, 1920, p. 9, February 28, 1920, p. 8. Louise Cowan quotes from "U.S. Best Poets Here in Tennessee" (Chattanooga *News*, February 10, 1923) in her *Fugitive Group*, 98. William J. Stuckey, *Caroline Gordon* (New York, 1972), 13.

Robert Penn Warren, and Allen Tate promoted the profession of letters in the South and, by travel, study abroad, lectures, and their own
writings, introduced the region to an international intellectual community. They developed and made popular a useful method of criticism. Through their textbooks and classroom techniques, they helped
to reform the teaching of English literature in American colleges and
universities. As editors of and frequent contributors to little magazines and journals, they encouraged the growth in the South of periodicals of high quality. They solicited the work of talented southern
writers, including Caroline Gordon as well as Katherine Anne Porter,
Eudora Welty, Peter Taylor, and Andrew Lytle. And through their
own critical essays, they helped to bring proper recognition to these
authors and such others as William Faulkner and Flannery O'Connor. Moreover, by the example of their own excellent fiction and
poetry, these men fostered a southern literature of a high quality.

Caroline Gordon's development as a writer was surely affected by
these leaders of the Southern Renaissance, but her husband's ideas
and writings most directly influenced her. With Allen Tate, she
shared a concern for agrarian ideals, an interest in fictional and poetic
technique, and a preoccupation with the role of the man of letters in
the modern world. Their agreement and collaboration was so extensive that Caroline Gordon's work can often be illuminated by examining Tate's prose and poetry.[7]

In listing Caroline Gordon with other writers who began a "literature of revolt" in the twentieth century, Ellen Glasgow suggests some
essential attributes of the history of southern letters. This literature of
revolt was an effort to establish a vital literary community in a region
that had long ignored its writers. The men who began the Southern
Renaissance defined themselves in opposing the predominant literary

7. The Agrarian influence on Gordon's writings is discussed throughout Frederick
P. W. McDowell, *Caroline Gordon* (Minneapolis, 1966), and a number of other critics
point to its importance. More particularly, Richard Gray examines Gordon's interest in
the old plantation myth for literary rather than social or political purposes, mentioning
her affinity with Tate's position. See Richard Gray, "Acts of Darkness, Ceremonies of
the Brave: Caroline Gordon," in his *The Literature of Memory: Modern Writers of the
American South* (Baltimore, 1977), 153. For Tate's influence on Gordon's writing, see
Frederick J. Hoffman, *The Art of Southern Fiction: A Study of Some Modern Novelists*
(Carbondale, Il., 1967), 175; Danforth Ross, "Caroline Gordon's Golden Ball," *Critique*,
I (Winter, 1956), 68; and Stuckey, *Gordon*, 13, 142.

fashions—particularly the very popular maudlin romance and hackneyed local-color writing. Calling themselves fugitives, a group of Nashville poets—including Ransom and Donaldson and, later, Tate and Warren—identified themselves, albeit somewhat ironically, with the concept expounded by their friend Sidney Hirsch of the poet as a wanderer and possessor of secret knowledge. The Fugitives were later to comment that their opposition was possible, paradoxically enough, because they were united by their strong sense of common background and community ties, but the effect of this constructive antagonism towards the South was to orient them towards the community of letters in Europe as well as in New York. Interestingly, when William Van O'Connor offers a historical context for Caroline Gordon's work, he does not mention the Southern Renaissance but includes her among "the generation of writers who spent at least a part of their youth in Paris" in the worship of "*ART.*" Like the Fugitives, the expatriates viewed themselves as voluntary exiles forming their own new community.[8]

With their protest against sentimentality and affectation, the Fugitives truly were, as Willard Thorp remarks, "establishing the profession of letters in their region." Allen Tate, who introduced the group to the poetry of T. S. Eliot and Hart Crane, strengthened the ties of the southern writers with the international literary world during his years of living in New York and in Europe, where Hemingway, Fitzgerald, Malcolm Cowley, Crane, and others of the expatriates became friends and colleagues of the Tates. If, however, the Southern Renaissance began as a rejection of the existing literary life in the region, it grew and matured when the same leaders of the Fugitive group felt compelled to defend the strengths of the agrarian tradition in the South. Although the hierarchical order of the Old South had provided "no place for the writer," after the Civil War writers such as Thomas Nelson Page helped to portray the South as a redemptive

8. Ellen Glasgow, *A Certain Measure: An Interpretation of Prose Fiction* (New York, 1938), 147. Louise Cowan, in *Fugitive Group*, 44, discusses the name of the group and its magazine. On the Fugitives' strong ties to the community, see Donald Davidson, "The Thankless Muse and her Fugitive Poets," in his *Southern Writers in the Modern World* (Athens, Ga., 1958), 5, and Allen Tate, "*The Fugitive*, 1922–1925: A Personal Recollection Twenty Years After," *Princeton University Library Chronicle*, III (April, 1942), 83. William Van O'Connor, "Art and Miss Gordon," in his *The Grotesque: An American Genre and Other Essays* (Carbondale, Il., 1962), 168.

community—a center of civilization not based on materialism. That same image of the South was fully developed and promoted after World War I, as the Fugitive poets became increasingly aware of the menace that industrialism posed to their region. The patronizing, even abusive, publicity that the Scopes trial brought to the South strongly moved Ransom to oppose the antireligious stance of the liberals; before long, Tate, Davidson, and Warren were also defending the South against the advocates of progress for its own sake.[9]

The literary revolt that Ellen Glasgow describes is exactly this protest against "the uniform concrete surface of an industrialized South." Industrialism came rather slowly to the region, with the result, as Lewis Simpson explains, that the South was late in joining "the Great Literary Secession." This secession Simpson defines as "the struggles of the man of letters to represent the imperatives of the Word" in spite of "the pressing medley of demands" exerted upon him by this complex political, commercial, and technological age. For the South, the form of this literary secession became Agrarianism. Tate and Ransom were the first to express concern and to propose action, and by 1929 a group, including the four major figures of the *Fugitive* magazine, was at work on the collection of essays published as *I'll Take My Stand.*[10]

In that manifesto of the Agrarian stance, Ransom and others declared that the Old South had been a community based on an eighteenth-century model, which had fostered such social arts as manners, oratory, and the hunt. Although this depiction of the South may be historically inaccurate and misleading, it is valuable as a literary image. Lewis Simpson, looking specifically at Tate's "The Profession of Letters in the South," analyzes the necessity for such an image: "Tate as a modern writer—as a writer educated in the literary world in which a reactionary poem like *The Waste Land* had become the major cultural symbol—needed to believe in the legend of the South as a traditional European community. The need grew out of the literary drama in which he was involved; it was a requirement of

9. Willard Thorp, "Southern Renaissance," in his *American Writing in the Twentieth Century* (Cambridge, Mass., 1960), 235. For the effects of the Scopes trial on the Fugitives, see Louise Cowan, *Fugitive Group*, 206–208; John L. Stewart, *The Burden of Time: The Fugitives and Agrarians* (Princeton, 1965), 109f.; Rubin, *Wary Fugitives*, 194–95.

10.Glasgow, *Certain Measure*, 147; Simpson, *Man of Letters*, 235.

the poetry of his role as a man of letters in the modern world." Initially, some of the Agrarians conceived of their anti-industrial argument as a program of reform, so much so that John Crowe Ransom studied economics and traveled about the country to debate the merits of the system. Years later, Donald Davidson, who had continued to think of this defense of the South as practical and political, complained to Tate when Ransom renounced his Agrarian position. Tate replied, "You evidently believe that agrarianism was a failure; I think it was and *is* a very great success; but then I never expected it to have any political influence. It is a reaffirmation of the humane tradition, and to reaffirm that is an end in itself."[11]

In truth, Agrarianism did provide the South with a necessary image of its past, and largely because of the efforts of Ransom, Tate, Davidson, and Warren, the region accepted this myth. In Caroline Gordon's fiction, as in the fiction of William Faulkner, Katherine Anne Porter, Eudora Welty, and other southern writers, this agrarian ideal is examined. Whether deplored or longed for, the myth of the Old South helped to form the region's sense of identity.

Influenced not only by T. S. Eliot's pronouncements on the roles of the artist and critic but also by the Agrarian movement, Tate and others like him came to believe that the writer was responsible to his community through his art—not through political action. Although by 1955 Tate no longer claimed to believe that man can find salvation by being an artist or by holding on to a historical or social tradition, he still insisted that the man of letters must continue to "recreate for his age the image of man, and he must propagate standards by which other men may test that image, and distinguish the false from the true." The poet's responsibility, more specifically, is "to write poems, and not to gad about using the rumor of his verse, as I am now doing, as the excuse to appear on platforms and to view with alarm." And criticism, as Tate explained it, keeps alive the knowledge of our-

11. Lewis P. Simpson, "The South's Reaction to Modernism: A Problem in the Study of Southern Letters," in Louis D. Rubin, Jr., and C. Hugh Holman (eds.), *Southern Literary Study: Problems and Possibilities* (Chapel Hill, 1975), 52; Tate to Donald Davidson, December 4, 1942, in John Tyree Fain and Thomas Daniel Young (eds.), *The Literary Correspondence of Donald Davidson and Allen Tate* (Athens, Ga., 1974), 328. Thomas Daniel Young, "A Prescription to Live By: Ransom and the Agrarian Debates," *Southern Review*, n.s., XII (1976), 608–21, offers a concise account of Ransom's part in the debates.

selves, which literature continually gives, and distinguishes that mode of knowledge from others.[12]

By conceiving of their protest as essentially literary and not political, southern writers have united aesthetic and ethical concerns in their art. Whereas the good artist does not make narrow moral preachments, he or she is responsible for portraying a world imbued with spiritual values. This acceptance of the artist's responsibility is, in part, an inheritance from the nineteenth century as well as a reaction to the contemporary situation of letters, where the "creative" writer and the critic infrequently joined together in an aesthetic criticism of life. In *The Rise and Fall of the Man of Letters*, John Gross analyzes the introduction of *The Sacred Wood* to show how T. S. Eliot sanctions the duties of the "second-order" critical mind: namely, to analyze the artist's works closely and to provide the intellectual climate that nurtures "first-order," or creative, endeavors. By thus encouraging a specialization already evident in the literary world, Eliot "cast out the old-fashioned man of letters," asserts John Gross, only to call "into being the New Critic."[13]

Since the author, or "poet," as Eliot calls him, primarily creates, Eliot focuses in "Tradition and the Individual Talent" on the conflict between the artist's personality and the objectivity he must command as the "medium" or "receptacle" in which "feelings, phrases, images" are stored and synthesized. Correcting Matthew Arnold, Eliot restricts the business of the critic to the preservation of tradition: the critic is "to see literature steadily and to see it whole."[14] In the South, however, the concept of the man of letters still flourished. There, the artist and the critic were often the same individual, and the first New

12. Tate, "The Man of Letters in the Modern World," in his *Essays of Four Decades* (Chicago, 1968), 3; compare with his remarks in the preface to his collection *The Man of Letters in the Modern World*, in *Essays*, 624. Tate's remarks on the poet's responsibility are found in "To Whom Is the Poet Responsible?," in *Essays*, 26. Tate distinguishes between criticism and literature in "The Man of Letters in the Modern World," 4.

13. See Robert B. Heilman's analysis of Agrarianism as protest in "The Southern Temper," in Louis D. Rubin, Jr., and Robert D. Jacobs (eds.), *Southern Renascence: The Literature of the Modern South* (Baltimore, 1953), 12. Rubin discusses *I'll Take My Stand* as protest literature in *Wary Fugitives*, 237–50. John Gross, *The Rise and Fall of the Man of Letters: A Study of the Idiosyncratic and the Humane in Modern Literature* ([New York], 1969), 236, 237.

14. T. S. Eliot, *The Sacred Wood: Essays on Poetry and Criticism* (London, 1920), 55, 56, xv.

Critics, despite Gross's implications, combined close analysis with broadly moral considerations.

Though Tate perceived that creative and analytical skills are shared by both artist and critic, like Eliot he did not believe that the writer should be distracted from his literary tasks to take practical action. This view markedly contrasts with that of Archibald MacLeish who, in outrage at the events that had led to World War II, published *The Irresponsibles* in 1940, asking, "Why did the scholars and the writers of our generation in America fail to oppose these forces while they could—while there was still time and still place to oppose them with the arms of scholarship and writing?" MacLeish deplored the specialization that had divided "men of intellectual duty" into two classes— "the scholars and the writers" and harkened back to the concept of the man of letters, which had been obsolete for most Americans since the nineteenth century. Reminiscent of Carlyle's exalted claims for the profession, MacLeish's description attributes heroic stature to the man of letters: "He was a man of wholeness of purpose, of singleness of intention—a single intellectual champion, admittedly responsible for the defense of the inherited tradition, avowedly partisan of its practice." [15]

Caroline Gordon also depicts the man of letters as a possible hero but not as a man of action nor as a propagandist. Her "intellectual champion" acts as a seer or prophet of culture, preserving and creating the forms of archetypal truth by which civilization lives. Like Tate, who answers MacLeish in the poem "Ode to Our Young Pro-Consuls of the Air," Caroline Gordon suggests in *The Women on the Porch*, for example, that the writer best serves his community by remaining an artist. In a scene apparently influenced by the imagery of Tate's poem, the scholar and poet Jim Chapman meets a soldier on a train, and his vision of the young man as a living bomb prophesies the downfall of the violent and dehumanized society that has fostered the war. Yet this seemingly simple contrast between the man of action, who is a product of and an agent for his culture, and the man of intellect, who evaluates that culture and delineates images of proper heroic action, becomes a more complex issue in the total context of *The Women on the Porch*. Before Jim Chapman can become a "prophet,"

15. Archibald MacLeish, *The Irresponsibles: A Declaration* (New York, 1940), 3–4, 21.

he must correct his own faulty vision; thus the novel records the conflict between his overdeveloped critical abilities and his repressed intuitions and emotions. As modern society has separated the man of letters' role into those of the scholar and the creative writer, so Jim has permitted a division within himself between his reason and his spirit.

Similarly, when Allen Tate entitled his 1953 collection of essays *The Forlorn Demon,* he seemed to invite a conception of the modern man of letters as an outcast, tormented, and despairing intellectual. Eliseo Vivas, examining Tate's own career as a man of letters, offers this explanation: "In one sense, I suggest, 'the forlorn demon' is the modern man of letters, doomed to inhabit Baudelaire's *fourmillante cité.* He is a demon because he has aspired to become an angel, and by doing so plunged himself into hell. But the title suggests another interpretation, according to which the demon is now the Socratic daimon, who is forlorn because we citizens of the swarming secularized city of today disregarded his prohibition and attempted to do something we have no business attempting." As Vivas reminds us, Tate's writings censure the "angelic imagination," which presumes to understand the mysteries of life solely by means of the intellect. Tate's example, Edgar Allan Poe, represents the doomed angelic imagination of the modern intellectual—the same artist *manqué* we view in Caroline Gordon's *The Women on the Porch, The Strange Children,* and *The Malefactors.* However, each of the writers in these novels matures, becoming the kind of Socratic daimon Vivas describes, a voice calling to civilization to reject its own damning secularism.[16]

Literature and Knowledge

If literature does not give us knowledge, it ought to be recognized that it is prior in the order of logic to all knowledge, since it is constitutive of culture, which is one of the conditions of knowledge.
—ELISEO VIVAS, "Literature and Knowledge"

Whereas Poe's thought exemplifies the improper habit of mind for a man of letters, Dante, for both Gordon and Tate, provides a model of the richest, most fulfilling imaginative response to human experience. The 1960 edition of *The House of Fiction* quotes at length

16. Eliseo Vivas, "Allen Tate as Man of Letters," *Sewanee Review,* LXII (1954), 143.

Salem College
Gramley Library
Winston-Salem, NC 27108

Dante's exposition of the four levels of meaning in literature: the literal, the allegorical, the moral, and the anagogical. In adding this material to the anthology, Tate and Gordon stress the importance of symbolic naturalism in fiction. Though Gordon concedes that the "anagogical level is not ordinarily the concern of fiction writers, who write of events that take place in this world, not the next," both she and Tate hold that the supernatural infuses this world and actively affects human lives. In fiction they look for depictions of the world that are compatible with their belief.[17]

In Tate's essay on the "symbolical imagination," he identifies Dante as an artist possessing a visionary knowledge that "does not reject" but "includes; it sees not only with but through the natural world, to what may lie beyond it." An earlier essay, "The Hovering Fly" (1943), develops this idea by analyzing Dostoevsky's description of a fly in the final chapter of *The Idiot*. Tate concludes, "We shall not know the actual world by looking at it; we know it by looking at the hovering fly." In other words, fiction illustrates a principle Tate introduced in "Religion and the South" (1930), where he posits that the human mind, unable to grasp reality with reason alone, needs images to present the ineffable and capture a sense of life's complexity.[18]

Tate's essay on religion, originally included in *I'll Take My Stand*, is in part an attack on the claims of science in the twentieth century. So, too, the insistence on literature as knowledge is a reaction against the cult of progress and materialism. Because reason, as the tool of science, and industrialism, as the product of scientific advancement, are perceived as threats to the imagination and the human spirit, writers like Tate and Gordon emphasize the appreciation of mystery and nonrational experience as necessary balancing forces. R. P. Blackmur attributes Allen Tate's notion of poetry as knowledge to "the assaults of science on belief," for Tate, along with John Crowe Ransom and Ivor Richards, "suffered the same monstrous growth of the possibility of consciousness without conscience."[19]

17. Caroline Gordon and Allen Tate (eds.), *The House of Fiction: An Anthology of the Short Story with Commentary* (2nd ed.; New York, 1960), 455, hereinafter cited parenthetically in text as *HF*.

18. Tate, "The Symbolic Imagination," "The Hovering Fly," "Religion and the South," all in Tate, *Essays*, 446, 117, 558–76.

19. R. P. Blackmur, "San Giovanni in Venere: Allen Tate as Man of Letters," *Sewanee Review*, LXVII (1959), 619.

Caroline Gordon also believed that literature offers a more complete knowledge than science, as Danforth Ross indicates in his account of her opening lecture to his writing class. Ross explains that first Gordon divided the writing of fiction into the part which could be taught and that which could not, then remarked: "'There is a mystery to the writing of fiction. . . . There is an irreducible something that you can't put your finger on.' She would leave it to us to discover the mystery if we could. She spoke boldly, as if scornful of a scientific age that had systematically sought to eliminate mystery from the world, to make man the measure of all things, to refuse to admit the existence of anything that was not tangible." Gordon, Tate, and many of their contemporaries conceived of the individual as "a culture building animal," to use Eliseo Vivas' words, and saw that the artist's task was to discover the archetypes and ideals that structure civilization. Vivas concludes his essay "Literature and Knowledge" declaring that literature "gives us an aesthetically ordered picture," which, if not strictly knowledge, is "prior in the order of logic to all knowledge, since it is constitutive of culture, which is one of the conditions of knowledge." [20]

Gordon and Tate, especially in their joint endeavor *The House of Fiction*, endorse the techniques of symbolic naturalism for recording the experience of mystery in this world and suggesting the archetypal patterns of human existence. They see the technique in its historical and literary context as the fusion of two separate traditions—symbolism and naturalism. Elsewhere Gordon examines Baudelaire's sonnet "Correspondances" to show how he presents details so that the objects and experiences of everyday life "lift us from the natural level to the supernatural level." [21] To clarify their use of the term *naturalism*, Tate and Gordon distinguish the impressionist tradition, on which they focus in *The House of Fiction*, from the branch of naturalism exemplified by the works of Zola, Dreiser, Sinclair Lewis, and Dos Passos. Writers such as Flaubert, Chekhov, James, and Joyce "perfected the art of dramatizing the Enveloping Action [the social background or the life from which the story comes] without offering

20. Ross, "Golden Ball," 69; Eliseo Vivas, "Literature and Knowledge," *Sewanee Review*, LX (1952), 591–92.

21. Caroline Gordon, *How to Read a Novel* (New York, 1957), 164, 166, hereinafter cited parenthetically in the text as *HRN*.

it to the reader in large chunks: the art of making the inert detail move" (*HF*, 451–52). For further lifting "the objective detail of his material up to symbolic level," as he does in "The Dead," Joyce receives the highest tribute: "If the art of naturalism consists mainly in making *active* those elements which had hitherto in fiction remained *inert*, that is, description and expository summary, the further push given the method by Joyce consists in manipulating what at first sight seems to be mere physical detail into dramatic symbolism" (*HF*, 183).

As the term *symbolic naturalism* implies, Gordon and Tate evaluate fiction according to two fundamental principles: how masterfully the illusion of reality is created and how well the work fuses levels of meaning. To encourage both well-crafted and morally responsible works, they dictate certain practices for fiction writers. For example, they favor a story without auctorial comment, one that "renders" rather than "tells." Consequently, Hawthorne is faulted for commenting on the issues in "Young Goodman Brown" and is accused of moralizing because he was unable to solve the technical problem of authority—that is, point of view (*HF*, 37–38). Not unexpectedly, Crane's concealed narrator, like Flaubert's, is preferred to Hawthorne's intruding commentator, and Henry James's method of the central intelligence is held in greatest esteem.

As Wayne Booth points out in *The Rhetoric of Fiction*, using a third-person narrator and excluding direct commentary by the author (or the author's fictional projection of himself) may enhance the dramatic quality, but these techniques do not eliminate the author's moral perspective. The author's judgment, of course, is involved in any selection and ordering, though it may require a more attentive reader to interpret a work told by an impersonal narrator. Caroline Gordon and Allen Tate value such subtle craftsmanship and careful reading: the best artists are those who not only make details vivid and effectively render a scene but also shape and control the meaning of the story through those same details. The artist, then, presents a picture true to human experience that—because it is a picture—is also a selected, purposefully structured artifact. Along these lines, Tate argues that Poe's stories are inferior to, say, those of Henry James because Poe does not dramatize his details (*HF*, 54). Yet James's "The Beast in the Jungle" is not as great as Joyce's "The Dead"; Tate charges that James's symbolism "tends to allegory because there is not enough detail to support it" (*HF*, 151). These twin dictates of verisimilitude and unity shape the arguments in other commentaries as well, so that Capote and Faulkner, for instance, are praised for their ability to render the dialect of their southern characters convincingly, while Poe is extolled for recognizing the importance of unity in a shor.. story (*HF*, 384, 333, 54).

The term *impressionist*, which was "frequently used by Ford," Gordon's instructor in fictional techniques, "probably has its source," as Ashley Brown explains, "in James's essay, 'The Art of Fiction' [1884]: 'A novel is in its broadest definition a personal, a direct impression of life.'" Ford, summarizing his own principles in terms of the impressionist tradition, agrees with Flaubert that "the intrusion of the author" destroys "the illusion of the reader." Yet the author remains in control of the fictional world. He is compared to an impersonal "creating deity" who, because of the need for verisimilitude, is somewhat limited in his knowledge: "The author . . . must stand neither for nor against any of his characters, must project and never report. . . . He must write his books as if he were rendering the impressions of a person present at a scene; he must remember that a person present at a scene does not see everything and is above all not able to remember immensely long passages of dialogue." So, too, James's image of the house of fiction, which Tate and Gordon quote on the title page of their anthology, implies that the artist's observation and recording of human experience and the demands of fiction as a created, crafted object are not meant to conflict.[22]

Nevertheless, in an impressionist novel, one of the difficulties is preserving a meaningful tension between formal considerations and "the amount of felt life," as Henry James phrases it in his preface to *The Portrait of a Lady*. Calling attention to readers who misunderstand Ford Madox Ford's work, Caroline Gordon quotes a portion of his own defense in the epilogue to *A Call*. Ford professes to use "as few words as I may to get any given effect, to render any given conversation." Yet he finds that his meaning is not always clear to the

---

22. Ashley Brown, "The Achievement of Caroline Gordon," *Southern Humanities Review*, II (1968), 280; Ford Madox Ford, "Techniques," *Southern Review*, I (1935), 23. Tate makes similar statements on the importance of an "objective structure" and the narrator's "inherent authority," in "The Post of Observation in Fiction," *Maryland Quarterly*, I (1944), 63.

reader: one type of reader overlooks the significance of Ford's carefully ordered details and another reads too much into those same words.[23]

Caroline Gordon has had similar problems. To many, her control is too strict. James Rocks feels that "Miss Gordon's technique so rigidly informs her materials that much of the vitality is robbed from the emotions." Even at its best, that mask which enables the artist to narrate "objectively" demands, as Stuckey remarks, "moral and esthetic responses that many readers are unable to make." John Bradbury similarly describes the effect of her technique on readers: "Miss Gordon's instinct is for pattern; she works most effectively, therefore, with the historical movement, the family group, the typical, rather than the individual, character. Not until her later novels does she attempt any deep penetration into her protagonists' minds or psychological processes and seldom then does she enter into them with any strongly participative warmth. . . . Perhaps largely for this reason, she has never achieved great popular success, though her work has stood high in critical esteem." It is no wonder that *Aleck Maury, Sportsman* is one of Gordon's most popular books, for, uncharacteristically, it provides a narrator who is also a character with a personality to express, not purely a medium. Ironically, the quest for what Tate calls "the inherent authority of the action or the scene, a presented validity" is based on a flattering concept of the reader as one who does not wish to be "told how to understand" but would rather find that his knowledge is "demonstrable" in the unified action of the story. As Ashley Brown reminds us, formality is not an end in itself, but necessary discipline; the impressionist writer "assumes that a public reality is accessible to a private vision."[24]

Southern letters may have depicted the region as leading the country in reconciling public reality and private vision, but the demand for so-called morally responsible art has been widespread in the twentieth century. Wayne Booth, in fact, concludes *The Rhetoric of Fiction*

23. Caroline Gordon, "The Elephant," *Sewanee Review*, LXXIV (1966), 865–66; Ford Madox Ford, *A Call: The Tale of Two Passions* (London, 1910; facs.; Ann Arbor, 1967), 300, 303–304.

24. James E. Rocks, "The Mind and Art of Caroline Gordon," *Mississippi Quarterly*, XXI (1968), 13; Stuckey, *Gordon*, 11, 12; John M. Bradbury, *Renaissance in the South: A Critical History of the Literature, 1920–1960* (Chapel Hill, 1963), 58; Tate, "Post of Observation," 63; Ashley Brown, "Achievement," 290.

(1961) with words not so different from T. S. Eliot's 1920 argument for impersonality. In Booth's final chapter "Morality of Narration," he defines the artist's duty in broadly religious terms: "The artist must . . . be willing to be both a seer and a revelator; though he need not attempt to discover new truths in the manner of the prophet-novelists like Mann and Kafka, and though he certainly need not include explicit statement of the norms on which his work is based, he must know how to transform his private vision, made up as it often is of ego-ridden private symbols, into something that is essentially public."[25]

Similarly, the New Critical emphasis on technique is never just an interest in form for its own sake. Rather, form makes the private reality accessible to others. This blend of aesthetic and moral considerations is evident even in the New Critical endorsement of "irony." Conceiving of human nature as dualistic, John Crowe Ransom, in his June, 1925, editorial in the *Fugitive*, depicts irony as the mode for bridging the spirit within and the material world outside. He claims, "Irony is the rarest of the states of mind, because it is the most inclusive; the whole mind has been active in arriving at it, both creation and criticism, both poetry and science."[26]

This definition of irony is based on the assumption that tension is necessary between the polarities of feeling and thought, creation and analysis, poetry and science. Eliseo Vivas' analogy between art and the process by which we establish and nurture civilization develops this conception: art, which disciplines creative impulses and feeling, permits individual experience to be shared and evaluated. Similarly, Mark Schorer credits art with the power to civilize, so to speak, to transform the stuff of life into comprehensible, meaningful form: "Technique is really what T. S. Eliot means by 'convention'—any selection, structure, or distortion, any form or rhythm imposed upon the world of action; by means of which . . . our apprehension of the world of action is enriched or renewed. In this sense, everything is technique which is not the lump of experience itself." Offering society the means for synthesizing and making sense of experience, "technique" performs a function which many modern writers feel

25. Wayne C. Booth, *The Rhetoric of Fiction* (Chicago, 1961), 395.
26. Quoted in Louise Cowan, *Fugitive Group*, 200.

science by itself cannot. Hart Crane, whose comments on the quarrel between science and poetry show the influence of his friendship with the Tates, declares that the function of poetry "in a Machine Age" is the same as in other times and that poetry's "capacities for presenting the most complete synthesis of human values remain essentially immune from any of the so-called inroads of science."[27]

Because science operates on just one level, the scientist as such can only probe, measure, and report on what he observes; he cannot fully explain or evaluate according to human values. Yet, properly understood, science is not antagonistic to art or morality—simply different. Jacques Maritain, a friend of the Tates from their days at Princeton, illustrates that the activities of the scientist are not unlike those of the artist. The morally responsible man may be a scientist or an artist, but what is relevant in defining his moral character is his concern for "being" rather than "doing." In fact, both the scientist and the artist use their intellects in order to perform their respective tasks: "The Scientist is an Intellectual who demonstrates, the Artist is an Intellectual who makes, the Prudent Man is an intelligent Man of Will who acts well." Elsewhere Maritain explains that the significant conflict for the artist is not between art and science but between art, "the creative or producing, work-making activity of the human mind," and what he calls poetry: "By Poetry I mean, not the particular art which consists in writing verses, but a process both more general and more primary: that intercommunication between the inner being of things and the inner being of the human Self which is a kind of divination (as was realized in ancient times; the Latin *vates* was both a poet and a diviner)." A significant work of art communicates this "poetry" through its language and structure. Essentially in agreement, then, with Tate and Gordon, Maritain holds that the individual can perceive "the spiritual in the things of sense." His is another argument for the "symbolic imagination"; technique—or "art," as Maritain uses the word—gives form to the artist's private vision, guarding

27. Mark Schorer, "Technique as Discovery," *Hudson Review*, I (1948), 69; Hart Crane, "Modern Poetry," in Brom Weber (ed.), *The Complete Poems and Selected Letters and Prose of Hart Crane* (New York, 1966), 261, and see Crane to Gorham Munson, 224–29, Crane to Yvor Winters, 241–47. Malcolm Cowley provides an account of the relationship between the Tates and Crane in "Two Winters with Hart Crane," *Sewanee Review*, LXVII (1959), 547–56.

the artist from the tantalizing but destructive solipsism that results when "pure" poetry masquerades as mystical knowledge. Poetry must express itself "in the things of sense" or, vampirelike, it destroys the humanity of the artist, a process Allen Tate ascribes to the "angelic imagination."[28]

Given such emphasis on the special and necessary knowledge that symbolic structures provide, it is not surprising that the twentieth-century novel has increasingly relied on the devices of poetry. Tate and Gordon, who conceived of the contemporary novel as a blending of the tenets and practices of French symbolist poetry with those of American naturalistic fiction, credited the practitioners of impressionism with achieving "something of the self-contained objectivity of certain forms of poetry" (*HF* 1950, vii). Because contemporary writers were striving for a unity and intensity hitherto associated with lyric poetry, New Critics were able to read such fictional works carefully for the pattern and meaning evoked in the details and images. Gordon, sensitive to such ordering, thus finds that Faulkner "has accomplished what Flaubert himself longed to accomplish, the union of concrete historical detail with lyricism" and that Ford Madox Ford has "produced the long work whose tensions are as nicely adjusted, whose tone is as sustained as that of the short tale or lyric poem."[29] This is not to say that Tate and Gordon perceive the novel as another kind of poem; they explain that the fictionist of the past century did not "*discover*" the use of "dramatically active detail," but "he revived and elaborated it in a *genre* in which its greatest exploitation was possible, as it was not in formal poetry" (*HF* 1950, vii).

Whereas Ashley Brown, for example, has examined the poetic influence of T. S. Eliot and Dante on Caroline Gordon's novels and Jane Gibson Brown has thoroughly treated the allusions to historical

28. Jacques Maritain, *Art and Scholasticism and The Frontiers of Poetry*, trans. Joseph W. Evans (New York, 1962), 20; Maritain, *Creative Intuition in Art and Poetry* (New York, 1953), 3; Maritain, *Frontiers*, 128. Maritain develops the vampire image in "Concerning Poetic Knowledge," in Jacques Maritain and Raïssa Maritain, *The Situation of Poetry: Four Essays on the Relations Between Poetry, Mysticism, Magic and Knowledge*, trans. Marshall Suther (New York, 1955), 52–55.

29. Caroline Gordon and Allen Tate (eds.), *The House of Fiction: An Anthology of the Short Story with Commentary* (New York, 1950), vii, hereinafter cited parenthetically in the text as *HF* 1950; Caroline Gordon, "Notes on Faulkner and Flaubert," *Hudson Review*, I (1948), 226 (compare with *HF*, 332); Caroline Gordon, Contribution to "Homage to Ford Madox Ford—A Symposium," in *New Directions in Prose and Poetry*, 475.

and mythological figures, Gordon herself reminds readers to look beyond conventional signs for deeper, more complex meanings in the details of the action. In an interview with Catherine Baum and Floyd Watkins, she complains that she is "impatient with the word *theme*" because "it so often gets in the way of symbol." She adds, "There are three young men writing about it [her fiction] now, and each one of them finds out symbols that never entered my head." The interviewer asks, "Can they be valid if they didn't enter your head?" She replies, "I don't believe they're ever valid if they enter your head." In other words, the artist does not impose his or her preconceptions but strives to perceive the world clearly and openly. Mary McCarthy, in an effort to correct her readers' excessive hunt for symbols in an autobiographical narrative entitled "Artists in Uniform," describes the "natural symbolism" in fiction that comes from the artist's efforts to discern, not impose, a pattern: "Every short story, at least for me, is a little act of discovery. A cluster of details presents itself to my scrutiny, like a mystery that I will understand in the course of writing or sometimes not fully until afterward, when, if I have been honest and listened to these details carefully, I will find that they are connected and that there is a coherent pattern." [30]

Technique is the discovery, then, of pattern and levels of meaning. "It has been through Flaubert that the novel has at last caught up with poetry," Allen Tate writes in "Techniques of Fiction," speaking of Flaubert's success both in unifying his work and in rendering it completely. Although unifying the novel and making the action vivid require a high quality of craftsmanship, Gordon and Tate suggest that the artist is able to render life and show its unity because the world is already ordered; the artist need only present the world concretely, sensitively, and accurately. [31]

According to Tate, Gordon, and others of their contemporaries,

---

30. Ashley Brown, "Achievement," 287; Ashley Brown, "The Novel as Christian Comedy," in William E. Walker and Robert L. Welker (eds.), *Reality and Myth: Essays in American Literature in Honor of Richard Croom Beatty* (Nashville, 1964), 161–78; Jane Gibson Brown, "The Early Novels of Caroline Gordon: The Confluence of Myth and History as a Fictional Technique" (Ph.D. dissertation, University of Dallas, 1975); Catherine B. Baum and Floyd C. Watkins, "Caroline Gordon and 'The Captive': An Interview," *Southern Review*, n.s., VII (1971), 460; Mary McCarthy, "Settling the Colonel's Hash," in her *On the Contrary* (New York, 1961), 240.

31. Tate, "Techniques of Fiction," in his *Essays*, 140, 131.

symbols and metaphors are invaluable in expressing the levels of meaning that operate in this world because these figures appeal to both the rational and the nonrational powers of the intellect. W. K. Wimsatt, in his significantly titled essay "The Concrete Universal," discusses metaphor as "the structure most characteristic of concentrated poetry," asserting that "behind a metaphor lies a resemblance between two classes, and hence a more general third class. This class is unnamed and most likely remains unnamed and is apprehended only through the metaphor. It is a new conception for which there is no other expression." [32] Although Wimsatt speaks specifically of poetry, his ideas can well be applied to the type of fiction that emulates the unity, intensity, and symbolic language of poetry.

Another southern writer, Eudora Welty, offers an interesting image for the way that fiction evokes several planes of reality.

> Some of us grew up with the china night-light. . . . The outside is painted with a scene, which is one thing; then, when the lamp is lighted, through the porcelain sides a new picture comes out through the old, and they are seen as one. A lamp I knew of was a view of London till it was lit; but then it was the Great Fire of London, and you could go beautifully to sleep by it. The lamp alight is the combination of internal and external, glowing at the imagination as one; and so is the good novel. Seeing that these inner and outer surfaces do lie so close together and so implicit in each other, the wonder is that human life so often separates them, or appears to, and it takes a good novel to put them back together.

Welty's emphasis on the interpenetration of "internal" and "external" realities resembles Caroline Gordon's notion that everyday objects and events are infused with a greater order, though Gordon would call that order supernatural and Welty would be more reluctant to name it. Whatever the nature of the hidden reality—whether a supernatural power, as Tate and Gordon believe, or an inexplicable mythical and archetypal pattern or something unnamed—these writers are alike in positing a dimension to the world that only the full resources

32. W. K. Wimsatt, Jr., "The Concrete Universal," in his *The Verbal Icon: Studies in the Meaning of Poetry* ([Louisville, Ky.], 1954), 79.

of the imagination can grasp and make accessible using the technical devices of the artist. Looking at the history of the American novel, Richard Chase observes that a "symbolic or symbolistic literature responds to disagreements about the truth," whereas allegory "flourishes best . . . when everyone agrees on what truth is." "For the purely symbolistic writer 'technique is discovery,' to use Mark Schorer's phrase. Thus a poetic symbol not only *means* something, it *is* something—namely, an autonomous truth which has been discovered in the process by which the symbol emerged in the context of the poem." [33]

In Caroline Gordon's own fiction and critical writings, she strives to discover truth through symbol. Perhaps the neglect and the relative unpopularity of her works may be attributed to her increasing preoccupation after her conversion to Roman Catholicism in 1947 with one notion of the truth—a Christian perspective—that may alienate many readers. In 1963 Gordon wrote to her friend, a Trappist monk, "I have come to believe that there is only [one] plot (the scheme of Redemption) and that any short story, or novel, any fiction (detective story, folk tale, any story anywhere in any time) is a splinter, so to speak, of that plot—if it's good." Ten years earlier in "Some Readings and Misreadings," she had also argued for the pervasiveness and importance of this single plot: "I believe that it could be shown that in the nineteenth century and in our own century as well the fiction writer's imagination often operates within the pattern of Christian symbolism rather than in the patterns of contemporary thought. The peculiarly Christian element of the great nineteenth century novels is their architecture. Many of them are based on the primal plot: the Christian Scheme of Redemption." James Rocks observes how Gordon's interest in theme began, with this 1953 essay, to dominate her evaluations of literature: "To Miss Gordon a work of fiction must deal with the conduct of life; treat the themes of redemption, grace, and charity; and exhibit, through its careful structure, the divine ordering of the universe." Yet, in "Some Readings and Misreadings," Gordon follows Maritain's definition of "Christian," as contrasted with "Church," art. She does not prescribe a certain sub-

33. Eudora Welty, "Place in Fiction," *South Atlantic Quarterly*, LV (1956), 60; Richard Chase, *The American Novel and Its Tradition* (Garden City, N.Y., 1957), 82.

ject for fiction, believing that the writer who is true to his or her art will offer the most complete perspective on life, for as Maritain urges, "If you want to make a Christian work, then *be* Christian, and simply try to make a beautiful work, into which your heart will pass; do not try to 'make Christian.'"[34]

Gordon's intentions are not, then, those of the "myth critics" Richard Chase describes, whose "exclusive interest in myth" leads them to overvalue works that "promise the immanence of grace, of final harmony and reconciliation, in a world whose contradictions it seems no longer possible to bear."[35] For example, in "Some Readings," although Gordon emphasizes religious themes in works by Henry James, James Joyce, Graham Greene, and Evelyn Waugh, she does not restrict her discussion of specific novels to locating the archetypal pattern: she faults François Mauriac for poor craftsmanship and she contrasts a novel by George Bernanos with *As I Lay Dying* to illustrate Faulkner's superior verisimilitude.

Although Gordon's own later novels do promise grace to those who recognize and accept it, she, like Flannery O'Connor, does not ignore the world's mysteries and contradictions. Rather than shirking the heritage of romance in the American novel, as Chase claims the myth critics do, Caroline Gordon is more like Henry James, the writer she so admires, who, as Chase phrases it, "gave up what he considered the claptrap of romance without giving up its mystery and beauty." In fact, the dualism Chase ascribes to James resembles Caroline Gordon's understanding of human experience: "James thinks that the novel does not find its essential being until it discovers what we may call the circuit of life among extremes or opposites, the circuit of life that passes through the real and the ideal, through the directly known and the mysterious or the indirectly known, through doing and feeling."[36]

Nonetheless, despite all her usual close critical reading and techni-

---

34. Caroline Gordon, "Letters to a Monk," *Ramparts*, III (December, 1964), 10, and "Some Readings and Misreadings," *Sewanee Review*, LXI (1953), 385, both hereinafter cited parenthetically in the text; James E. Rocks, "The Christian Myth as Salvation: Caroline Gordon's *The Strange Children*," *Tulane Studies in English*, XVI (1968), 150 n; Maritain, *Art and Scholasticism*, 66. Gordon refers to Maritain's ideas in "Some Readings," 384–85.

35. Chase, *American Novel*, 245.

36. *Ibid.*, 118–19, 27.

cal consideration, Caroline Gordon does try to reconcile specific works with archetypal Christian concepts or, failing that, finds the books flawed. Her analysis of Maupassant in *The House of Fiction* faults his stories for excluding the psychological and moral dimensions of life (*HF*, 114). Similarly, Hemingway's "The Snows of Kilimanjaro" does not adequately integrate the levels of meaning for which Gordon looks (*HF* 1950, 422–23). In "Notes on Hemingway and Kafka" and later in *How to Read a Novel*, she complains that Hemingway's treatment of the supernatural is unsure. Comparing Capote's fiction to Flannery O'Connor's, Gordon finds Capote's work inferior because he does not admit the supernatural reality that O'Connor incorporates.[37]

At times, Gordon detects Christian affinities in authors who do not profess the faith, so that, for instance, she reads Kafka's work as Christian allegory. After showing that Yeats's poem "In Memory of Major Robert Gregory" characterizes the friend "in terms of *objects* he loved," she concludes, "That kind of patient, passionate portrayal of natural objects is a recognition of the natural order which I can only call Christian, 'Christian in hope.'" Especially in her discussion of Henry James's novels, Gordon looks for the archetypal pattern of Christianity. Her reading of *The Golden Bowl* depicts Verver as a hero who must "save his country from a menace," comparing him to Saint Martha subduing the dragon—in this case, Verver's wife Charlotte. She sees Maggie as a heroine living by the principle of Christian charity, or *caritas*. James, Gordon summarizes, "was able through his genius to apprehend the archetypal patterns of Christianity and to use them as no novelist before him had used them. But it took him a lifetime to do it. *The Golden Bowl* is the only one of his major creations that is a comedy in the sense that Dante's great poem is a comedy, the only one in which virtue is wholly triumphant over vice."[38]

Some of Gordon's insistence on the supernatural may seem irrele-

---

37. Caroline Gordon, "Notes on Hemingway and Kafka," *Sewanee Review*, LVII (1949), 226. See also, *HRN*, 100–102. Gordon comments on Truman Capote's fiction in *HF*, 386. She makes similar points in "Flannery O'Connor's *Wise Blood*," *Critique*, II (Fall, 1958), 3–10.

38. Gordon, *HF*, 190–92; Gordon, "Notes on Hemingway and Kafka," 222–26; Gordon, "Some Readings," 403, 384; Gordon, "Mr. Verver, Our National Hero," *Sewanee Review*, LXIII (1955), 46. She makes similar points in other of her essays.

vant, the result of personal conviction and predisposition. Yet, as a writer of a literature and criticism of "protest," Gordon desires to impose critical standards that would correct the more popular secularism of the age. In contrast, for example, to what M. H. Abrams calls the "Natural Supernaturalism" of the romantic poets, Caroline Gordon values the Christian pattern underlying western civilization not as a myth revealing man's most noble image of himself but as testimony to God's active participation in the physical world. Abrams explains that the impulse of the eighteenth and nineteenth centuries was, in varying degrees, "to naturalize the supernatural and to humanize the divine." However, like T. E. Hulme, who deplored the deification of man as a weakening of religion, the Fugitive poets and Caroline Gordon condemned the romantics for promoting such a split between the truly supernatural and the natural. Thus, Tate writes that John Keats needed "an ordered symbolism through which he may *know* the common and the ideal reality in a single imaginative act" and laments that Keats never fully understood the relation between physical and spiritual love, attributing the flaw in Keats's poetry to the romantic attitude—"a decline in insight and in imaginative and moral power." As James Rocks comments, Caroline Gordon's acceptance of "Hulme's classic position of religious orthodoxy and of man's inheritance of original sin" is one step away from her conversion to Roman Catholicism, a religion offering a transcendent view of life and grace to mortals.[39]

In "Letters to a Monk," Caroline Gordon writes, "It is taken for granted by the majority of reviewers of fiction that grace—supernatural grace—is not a proper subject for fiction, when it seems to me, the interworkings, intertwinings of natural grace and supernatural grace (or the lack of it) are the only subjects for fiction, from the Greek tragedians on down" (10). If her insistence on this religious theme may not have provided the most helpful context for some works, Gordon brought important insights to others. Her reading of *A Portrait of the Artist as a Young Man* was one of the first to consider

39. M. H. Abrams, *Natural Supernaturalism: Tradition and Revolution in Romantic Literature* (New York, 1971), 68; Allen Tate, "A Reading of Keats," in his *Essays*, 271, 279, 280; Rocks, "Christian Myth," 152. For Hulme's influence on the Fugitives, see Louise Cowan, *Fugitive Group*, 176, and Radcliffe Squires, *Allen Tate: A Literary Biography* (New York, 1971).

Joyce's criticism of Stephen Dedalus through the myth of Daedalus and Icarus.[40]

Caroline Gordon as Teaching Writer

I am . . . a novelist by profession, and . . . I am *not* a critic.
—CAROLINE GORDON, "Rebels and Revolutionaries"

In her correspondence with Flannery O'Connor and in her dealings with her larger public, Caroline Gordon has portrayed herself as a writer talking about her art. Some of her critics are just as careful not to call her a "formal critic." James Rocks, for one, places Gordon in the tradition of Flaubert, James, Ford, and Conrad, asserting that no writer "in this tradition, including Caroline Gordon, conceived of his criticism except as an adjunct to his fiction."[41] Yet, as one would expect, the creative writing courses that Caroline Gordon taught over the years encouraged her to articulate her views on craft. Furthermore, as teachers in universities and colleges, Gordon and Tate became aware of the need for a textbook that would show students how to read analytically. Their *The House of Fiction* helped spread the ideas of New Criticism throughout the nation. "We wanted," they wrote, "to keep the critical discussion brief and practical. . . . For this practical purpose we assumed that people cannot be taught to write either masterpieces or family letters, but that as young persons (of whatever age) they can learn to read at least as well as the editors of this anthology, and to enjoy it" (*HF* 1950, vii, viii). Although Tate and Gordon shared the skepticism of other New Critics that writing could be taught, they wanted in *The House of Fiction* to provide young fiction writers with appropriate models. The teacher can never supply the vision, motivation, and skill that make a writer good, but as Brooks and Warren explain: "*There is no ideal form, or set of forms, for the short story, but there are certain principles to which one may become more sensitive by studying stories.* These principles involve the functional relationships existing among the elements of a story, the adjusting of means to ends, the organization of material to create an expressive unity."[42]

40. Gordon, "Some Readings," 388–93, *HRN*, 210–15, and "Letters to a Monk," 8.
41. Rocks, "Mind and Art," 3.
42. Cleanth Brooks, Jr., and Robert Penn Warren, *Understanding Fiction* (New

Though Gordon and Tate are modest in their claims for teaching writing, they both believe that established writers are well suited for shepherding new talent. According to Gordon, the artist is better able to recognize successful innovations in literature than the formal critic. With Baudelaire's review of *Madame Bovary* as one example, she comments, "As far as I can gather, there is no instance of a revolutionary talent—or technique—being recognized by any literary critic, who was not himself an artist." Allen Tate offers his observations in "Techniques of Fiction" not as a critic but as one "outside criticism," arguing that because formal criticism is the product of a particular sensibility at a given time, it serves but a passing function. Therefore, it is the knowledge of novelists, which is embodied in the works themselves, that "ought to be our deepest concern." Participants in what Tate calls "the living confraternity of men of letters, who pass on by personal instruction to their successors the 'tricks of the trade,'" both Tate and Gordon emphasize the "'constants' or secrets of technique" in *The House of Fiction* (ix).[43]

For Flannery O'Connor, Caroline Gordon was an indispensable critic. Gordon not only read O'Connor's manuscripts and suggested revisions but, after publication, also reviewed her books and explicated them in numerous essays. O'Connor's letters show how extensive was Gordon's help. After Gordon provided her with many valuable revisions for *Wise Blood*, O'Connor habitually sent all of her work to Caroline Gordon. She told the Robert Lowells, "I'm getting up a collection of stories that I'm going to call *A Good Man Is Hard to Find*. I send them to Caroline and she writes me wherein they do not meet the mark." Nearly four years later, O'Connor was still depending on Gordon for advice: "Whenever I finish a story I send it to Caroline before I consider myself really through with it. She's taught me more than anybody."[44]

York, 1943), 571, and see xiii. Gordon discusses what the teacher can actually teach the young writer in *HRN*, 20–25.

43. Caroline Gordon, "An American Girl," in Melvin J. Friedman and Lewis A. Lawson (eds.), *The Added Dimension: The Art and Mind of Flannery O'Connor* (New York, 1966), 125; Tate, "Techniques of Fiction," in his *Essays*, 129, 124, 129.

44. Flannery O'Connor to the Robert Lowells, January 1, 1954, O'Connor to Cecil Dawkins, December 22, 1957, both in Sally Fitzgerald (ed.), *The Habit of Being: Letters of Flannery O'Connor* (New York, 1979), 65, 260. See also Sally Fitzgerald (ed.), "A Master Class: From the Correspondence of Caroline Gordon and Flannery O'Connor," *Georgia Review*, XXXIII (1979), 827–46.

Caroline Gordon's advice to the young writer was often specific. To improve *Wise Blood*, she urged stronger active verbs, appropriate diction for the omniscient narrator, more details to make a given scene or character vivid, and she recommended interspersing a character's speech with descriptions of the listener's response. Unsurprisingly, her practical advice is consonant with the principles she delineates in *The House of Fiction* and later in *How to Read a Novel*. To evoke the physicality of a scene or a character, Gordon recommended Flaubert's technique of giving the reader at least three sensuous details, advice that Flannery O'Connor later echoes in her own critical writings. For greater unity and clarity, Gordon suggested that O'Connor better prepare the reader for the meaning of the title, that she reinforce the significance of certain actions by repeating them but in a slightly different way, and that she make a scene more vivid by moving outside it, using a description of landscape, for example, to contrast with the action. So valuable were Gordon's letters that Flannery O'Connor eventually mailed them to her friend "A." so that another aspiring writer could benefit from them.[45]

Gordon's reviews and critical essays helped to bring recognition to the merits of Flannery O'Connor's fiction. The book jacket of *Wise Blood* featured Caroline Gordon's words of praise, and when *A Good Man Is Hard to Find* was published, Gordon reviewed it for the *New York Times Book Review*. Flannery O'Connor's correspondence records her delight with Gordon's essay in *Critique* (1958), a quotation from which was later incorporated into the jacket design of *The Violent Bear It Away*. Gordon also helped to promote O'Connor's works in France by writing an introduction to one of the translations. Moreover, the 1960 edition of *The House of Fiction* included "A Good Man Is Hard to Find" and a commentary drawn from the article in *Critique*. After O'Connor's death in 1964, Caroline Gordon continued to write and lecture on her friend's work.[46]

45. Sally Fitzgerald (ed.), "A Master Class," 833–37 (compare *HF*, 456–58); O'Connor to "A.," March 7, 1958, in Sally Fitzgerald (ed.), *Habit of Being*, 271. Gordon also mentions Flaubert's sensuous detail in *HF*, 24. Compare to Flannery O'Connor, "The Nature and Aim of Fiction," in her *Mystery and Manners: Occasional Prose*, ed. Sally Fitzgerald and Robert Fitzgerald (New York, 1969), 69–70.

46. O'Connor to Sally and Robert Fitzgerald, [April, 1952], O'Connor to "A.," October 11, 1958, December 19, 1959, O'Connor to William Sessions, July 22, 1956, and see O'Connor to Robert Giroux, November 15, 1954, all in Sally Fitzgerald (ed.), *Habit of*

Gordon's own fiction provided Flannery O'Connor with worthy models to emulate. Writing to "A.," O'Connor recalls that "Old Red" taught her how to use a symbol, "and I sat down and wrote the first story I published." To *The Malefactors*, O'Connor responds, "I have read Caroline's novel with all my usual admiration for everything she writes. I look at it from the underside, thinking how difficult all this was to do because I know nothing harder than making good people believable. It would be impertinent for me to comment on the book, simply because I have too much to learn from it." O'Connor's admiration is more specifically outlined in her appraisal of "Summer Dust" as "an impressionistic short story." Gordon, she writes, "is a great student of Flaubert and is great on getting things there so concretely that they can't possibly escape—note how that horse goes through that gate, the sun on the neck and then on the girl's leg and then she turns and watches it slide off his rump. That is real masterly doing, and nobody does it any better than Caroline. You walk through her stories like you are walking in a complete real world. And watch how the meaning comes from the things themselves and not from her imposing anything."[47]

Flannery O'Connor well appreciated Gordon's masterly fictional technique and in her letters she often comments interestingly and usefully on Gordon's ideas, but she does not hesitate to disagree on occasion. At one point, O'Connor admits that Gordon "probably exalts James overmuch out of admiration for his technical achievements," and sometimes she feels that her friend is too preoccupied with stylistic matters. Yet, only once does she complain that Gordon's advice was irrelevant: "Caroline gave me a lot of advice about the story ["Parker's Back"] but most of it I'm ignoring. She thinks every story must be built according to the pattern of the Roman arch and

Being, 33, 299, 363, 167, 72. See also Caroline Gordon, "With a Glitter of Evil," *New York Times Book Review*, June 12, 1955, p. 5. In addition to "Flannery O'Connor's *Wise Blood*," Caroline Gordon wrote "Flannery O'Connor: A Tribute," *Esprit*, VIII (Winter, 1964), 28; "An American Girl" (1966); "Heresy in Dixie," *Sewanee Review*, LXXVI (1968), 263–97; the foreword to Kathleen Feeley's *Flannery O'Connor: Voice of the Peacock* (New Brunswick, N.J., 1972); "Rebels and Revolutionaries" (1974); and she also participated in a panel discussion printed in *Flannery O'Connor Bulletin*, III (1974), 57–78.

47. O'Connor to "A.," January 25, 1957, O'Connor to Denver Lindley, January 15, 1956, O'Connor to "A.," December 11, 1956, all in Sally Fitzgerald (ed.), *Habit of Being*, 200, 129, 187.

she would enlarge the beginning and the end, but I'm letting it lay."[48]

If Caroline Gordon's advice occasionally seemed too technical for O'Connor, those times were rare. As a rule, the two writers were perceptive about and appreciative of each other's art; the admiration each felt was no doubt strengthened because they agreed on the essential purpose of fiction. In "The Nature and Aim of Fiction," following a discussion of "Summer Du ⋅," O'Connor describes good fiction as a fusion of mystery and reality, a definition that Caroline Gordon herself could have written: "The type of mind that can understand good fiction . . . is at all times the kind of mind that is willing to have its sense of mystery deepened by contact with reality, and its sense of reality deepened by contact with mystery." Above all, O'Connor and Gordon would agree that the scheme of Redemption is the best plot for fiction. On the subject of contemporary fiction, O'Connor asserts: "As great as much of this fiction is, as much as it reveals a wholehearted effort to find the only true ultimate concern, as much as in many cases it represents religious values of a high order, I do not believe that it can adequately represent in fiction the central religious experience. That, after all, concerns a relationship with a supreme being recognized through faith. It is the experience of an encounter, of a kind of knowledge which affects the believer's every action."[49] When Gordon writes that Flannery O'Connor's characters are "displaced persons," those who are "'off center' . . . because they are victims of a rejection of the Scheme of Redemption," she is sympathizing with and approving of a concern she, too, found pressingly vital (*HF*, 386).

Just as Caroline Gordon's technical heritage from Ford has been handed down to an incalculable number of younger writers, including Robert Penn Warren and Flannery O'Connor, so her other "stu-

48. O'Connor to "A.," December 14, 1957, O'Connor to Catharine Carver, April 18, 1959, O'Connor to "A.," July 25, 1964, and see O'Connor to "A.," March 24, 1956, for an interesting sketch of Gordon, and O'Connor to Ashley Brown, August 13, 1963, for O'Connor's dislike of Gordon's monograph on Ford Madox Ford, all *ibid.*, 258, 328, 594, 149, 534. Flannery O'Connor was very ill when she wrote "Parker's Back," and Gordon later regretted having sent the advice when her friend was so near death. See Gordon, "Heresy in Dixie," 265–66.

49. Flannery O'Connor, "Nature and Aim," in her *Mystery and Manners*, 79. See also "Novelist and Believer" and "The Fiction Writer and His Country," both *ibid.*, 160, 33.

dents"—her readers—have gained from her invaluable perspectives on the "constants" of fiction. *The House of Fiction* was one of a number of textbooks that changed the method of teaching literature in American higher education. As William Van O'Connor remarked in 1962, "English departments nowadays look at literature pretty much as writers do," and that largely as a result of the New Criticism.[50]

Like the criticism in *The House of Fiction*, Gordon's stance in *How to Read a Novel* is essentially practical, as the title indicates, and is best understood as a writer's reflections on her craft. Little of the material is original, which she readily admits; moreover, she makes many of the same points in *The House of Fiction* and in the essays she published in various periodicals. One contemporary reviewer William Bittner complained that the book is much too derivative: "I am not quite sure what Caroline Gordon's 'How to Read a Novel' is good for, but it certainly is not much help in illuminating the complex problem of the novel. 'Gleanings in the Field of Henry James' might be a better title." A more sympathetic reviewer, Gordon's colleague at Columbia University Robert Gorham Davis points out that since Gordon intends to present to a general audience "that view of the novel which has become orthodox in the best American colleges in the last twenty years," the book is not to be faulted for synthesizing the ideas of others.[51]

The discussion of point of view, which ranges over four chapters, draws heavily upon Percy Lubbock's *The Craft of Fiction* and, of course, James's own writings on the subject. The chapter on plot, "Complication and Resolution," applies the terminology of the *Poetics* to the novel, using two very different plots—those from *Oedipus Rex* and Beatrix Potter's *Jemima Puddle-Duck*—to suggest the relevance of Aristotle's concepts to any well-constructed narrative. "The Decline of the Hero," a chapter providing insight into Gordon's fictional themes, deplores the failure in the modern novel to portray heroic action.

50. Stewart mentions the help Gordon gave to Warren in *Burden of Time*, 141, 449. William Van O'Connor, "The Writer and the University," in his *The Grotesque*, 183.

51. William Bittner, "For the Ladies," *Saturday Review*, November 16, 1957, p. 20; Robert Gorham Davis, "It Isn't Life That Counts," *New York Times Book Review*, October 27, 1957, p. 6. Stuckey, in *Gordon*, mentions the unoriginality of Gordon's critical theory, 18.

The first and last chapters, "How Not to Read a Novel" and "Reading for Enjoyment," repeat Gordon's strictures for both reader and writer. The good novel does not argue for a personal moral code (granted that the novelist's background and beliefs cannot help but structure his perceptions, the novel is not primarily an argument). The good novel does not include only pleasant happenings but presents the complexity of life. It does not try to be popular for popularity's sake, and it is not mainly concerned with ideas, except as they are embodied in action. Although Gordon provides some sensible guidelines for reading novels, she also contradicts herself. At times, Gordon seems all too similar to the aunt she describes in Chapter 1, who refuses to consider any book that trespasses against her own moral code. Gordon's disdain for the novels of Gide and Sartre is morally grounded: she disapproves of their views of human life but unconvincingly argues against them for primarily aesthetic reasons.

How to Read a Novel is limited. Those familiar with Gordon's earlier and later criticism will sometimes recognize not only the arguments and formulations but also the examples and even the phrasing. Moreover, the book lacks sophistication. Even Davis complains, "For the kind of reader she has in mind, Miss Gordon does not explain fully enough or originally enough how the nature of an author's concern for life finds expression in and is modified by the nature of his art and how both ultimately are to be judged." Flannery O'Connor's remarks also point to the book's problem with audience and its sometimes jejune content. To Cecil Dawkins, a writer and English teacher, O'Conner comments, "Have you seen Caroline Gordon's latest book out . . . called *How to Read a Novel*? I think it's badly titled because it isn't really for readers but for writers. I think it would be good for your freshmen though."[52]

Many of Gordon's students complained of the dogmatism that also marred some of her criticism. Danforth Ross records his teacher's impatience with students who wished to digress from the issue at hand or who complained that a particular work, by Flaubert for example, was dated. Ross admits that most of the students, to varying degrees, reacted against the dogmatism, but he defends Gordon: "Dogmatism, of course, has very obvious dangers; and yet it may be a

52. Davis, "It Isn't Life," 6; O'Connor to Dawkins, December 22, 1957, and see O'Connor to "A.," November 30, 1957, both in Sally Fitzgerald (ed.), *Habit of Being*, 260, 256.

justifiable reaction against a looseness that has crept into our civilization." To reach an audience whose dogma is, for the most part, so unlike her own, Caroline Gordon may have felt the need for what Ross calls "the shock treatment," a stance with which Flannery O'Connor would readily have sympathized.[53]

Gordon's criticism suffers not only from the dogmatic tone but also from her need to project her own moral and religious viewpoints on the works she examined. At its worst, such criticism supplies an irrelevant context for appraising a work, or it distorts the work's meaning. Noting how exclusive and proscriptive her judgments could become, Wayne Booth condemns Gordon's search for constants. He may be unnecessarily harsh, but Gordon's preoccupations do influence her interpretations, sometimes inordinately. And some of her criticism is too preoccupied with concerns more appropriate to her own work. Just as her Christian outlook conditioned her preference for Kafka over Hemingway and Flannery O'Connor over Capote, so her treatment of Ford Madox Ford's works reflects her interest in archetypal and mythical patterns. When she wrote *A Good Soldier: A Key to the Novels of Ford Madox Ford*, she was conceiving the book later to be entitled *The Glory of Hera*—a novel that examines the relationship between the hero, Heracles, and Hera, a white goddess figure. A review of Gordon's monograph on Ford exposes her occasional tendency to interpolate: "Readers familiar with Ford's work are likely to find that Miss Gordon's key does not in fact open many doors. Nevertheless, she does direct attention to a recurrent treatment of beautiful, cruel women which is an important strain in Ford's novels, even though it is not quite so central or so mythic as she proposes." Here, Gordon's interests, inadequately controlled, have distorted her reading.[54]

Whatever the limitations of a few specific interpretations, Caroline Gordon's criticism is most interesting today for its place in literary history. A synthesis of ideas about fiction adapted from the European

53. Ross, "Golden Ball," 69. See Flannery O'Connor's comments on shocking the reader in "The Fiction Writer and His Country," in her *Mystery and Manners*, 33–34.

54. Booth, *Rhetoric of Fiction*, 26–27, 202, 280 n; Review of *A Good Soldier: A Key to the Novels of Ford Madox Ford, Times Literary Supplement*, October 4, 1963, p. 794. Peden complains of dogmatism in *HF* 1950; see "From Poe to Welty," 18. For a defense of Gordon, see Robert Scott Dupree, "Caroline Gordon's 'Constants' of Fiction," in Thomas H. Landess (ed.), *The Short Fiction of Caroline Gordon: A Critical Symposium* (Irving, Tex., 1972), 33–51.

impressionist tradition and influenced by the principles and concerns of the Southern Renaissance, her instruction helped to raise a generation of readers and writers keenly attuned to the possibilities of technique as a method for discovering aesthetic and moral values. For Gordon, Melville's statement—"genius, all over the world, stands hand in hand, and one shock of recognition runs the whole circle round"—becomes a telling metaphor for her vision of art and artists: "If you observe the members of this band closely enough, passionately enough, you will not only find them stretching out their hands to each other across time and space but you will find that in all ages, in all places, they are *doing the same things.* It is as if artistic creation were a mighty dance, in which, upon appointed signals, the dancers perform certain steps, tread certain measures, with the paradoxical result that the dance, instead of crystallizing into a set form, becomes ever more unpredictable, more various, more glorious" (*HRN*, 24). With this Dantesque image, Caroline Gordon concretely and beautifully expounds her belief in a universal and timeless community of letters and, by implication, modestly takes her place in the "mighty dance" of artistic creation.

"The 'man of letters' has become obsolete," wrote Lewis Simpson in 1973, explaining that technology has produced new modes of communication so that literary expression no longer remains "the verbal center of civilization." "The story of the Agrarians and of the whole history of modern Southern letters," he said, is an attempt to reinstate the writer as a spokesman for his community. William Van O'Connor agrees: "We don't have men of letters nowadays, except for Malcolm Cowley and Edmund Wilson." Instead, he remarks, more and more writers have affiliated themselves with universities and colleges, many of them as full-time teachers in English departments. O'Connor calls these "academic writers," people interested in writing who "teach in order to support themselves," and he wonders "whether the campus helps or hinders" the writing careers of these professionals.[55]

It is a question Donald Davidson addresses in "The Southern Writer and the Modern University," where he maintains that, al-

55. Simpson, *Man of Letters*, 254; William Van O'Connor, "The Hawthorne Museum: A Dialogue," "The Writer and the University," both in his *The Grotesque*, 228, 181–82.

though the contemporary writer often needs the financial support and the freer, more leisurely atmosphere of the university, even there he or she risks succumbing to the standardization that industrialism imposes on our culture. Davidson's agrarianist leanings, evident in his strong distrust of industrialism, resemble those of his friends Tate and Gordon. A professor of English and the author of books of poetry, a writing textbook, as well as numerous essays and reviews, Davidson can well be described as a "teaching writer," whose purpose, as he defines it, is to educate students in the language, whether or not he turns out novelists and poets. Yet Davidson, who earned his livelihood primarily by teaching, persistently conceived of himself as a man of letters. He comments: "Vanderbilt writers have been persons who have chosen to confront the world by composing poems, stories, novels, plays, literary essays rather than by entering the laboratory or its academic equivalent, and resting content with its highly special and partial, though certainly useful, procedures. To confront the world with a poem or a story means that you face it, not in the dissevered pieces, the sections and dissections, which necessarily determine the consideration of science and social science, but in its complex totality." This writer of the Southern Renaissance articulates a traditional belief that the artist has a public responsibility: a responsibility best fulfilled by writing good literature, which presents society with a whole image of human experience.[56]

Caroline Gordon continued throughout her life to believe with the Agrarians that art serves a social function, even though her conversion modified her idea of what its social function should be. She summarizes her developing notions in "Letters to a Monk": "The analogies between the religious life and the working life of the artist are striking—and, I'm sure, dangerous to contemplate because we are tempted to press them too far. I was nearly fifty years old before I discovered that art is the handmaid of the Church. Up to that time it had been the only religion I had and I served it as faithfully as I could" (6).

Caroline Gordon's novels record her lifelong concern with the artist's proper role in society. In her earliest works, she criticizes the

56. Donald Davidson, quoting from a preface he wrote for a volume of verse and prose by Vanderbilt students in "The Southern Writer and the Modern University," in his *Southern Writers in the Modern World*, 75–76.

myths by which civilization lives, evaluating the pioneers' restless conquest of the wilderness, the agrarianism of the Old South, and the modern belief in progress. From her authoritative position as the effaced omniscient narrator, she exposes the weaknesses of these systems—performing, though in retrospect, what the effete and self-absorbed intellectuals of the early novels fail to do. The later fiction, which more closely scrutinizes the growth of the individual psyche, portrays the writer as the figure in modern society who is most sensitive to the deficient spiritual condition of the age and yet who is by nature also most capable of leading the community towards a more complete vision of human life.

Chapter II / The Early Novels

The Narrator As Revelator

> —what
> Is man but his passion?
> —ROBERT PENN WARREN, *Audubon*

> The poet has, not a 'personality' to express, but a particular medium, which is only a medium and not a personality.
> —T. S. ELIOT, "Tradition and the Individual Talent"

The naturalist Audubon in Robert Penn Warren's poem is both artist and adventurer, a man of imagination as well as a heroic explorer seeking to discover nature's secrets as he encounters the wilderness and the often savage inhabitants of the beautiful and brutal natural world. Caroline Gordon, a southern writer of the same generation as Warren, initially shunned any conception of the artist as hero. In her early fiction, men who lead an artist's life—concerned with aesthetic contemplation and the creative ordering of their world—are rarely men of action; however, the struggle of these intellectuals to surmount the difficulties of expression, to move beyond an egocentric contemplation of life and address a community, becomes, especially in the later works, the primary focus.

For Gordon, whose "only one true subject for fiction" is the adventures of a hero or heroine, heroism is not a given quality: "Heroes don't start out as extraordinary men. They become extraordinary men by performing extraordinary deeds" (*HRN*, 171, 191). The men and women in Caroline Gordon's five early novels do live their passions and, in their dedication to whatever values structure their lives, may ultimately prove their valor. Yet the passions of the characters may not always inspire them to make selfless sacrifices like those of the often unqualified heroes of our mythical and historical past. The five early novels—*Green Centuries* (1941), *Penhally* (1931), *None Shall Look Back* (1937), *Aleck Maury, Sportsman* (1934), and *The Garden of Adonis* (1937)—can be ordered to show the decline of southern society and culture from the mid-eighteenth century to the Depression years of the 1930s. But more significantly, each novel criticizes the actions of the protagonists, illustrating that in every age there are few who become heroes and none whose heroism is uncomplicated by some selfish motive or by pride.[1]

The pioneer, the soldier, and the sportsman are roles that still offer men some possibility for heroic action—though admittedly, as several Gordon novels show, the figure of the hunter, from which the pioneer, soldier, and sportsman all descend, is no longer heroic when he debases himself by pursuing ignoble goals. Because she perceives human concerns as universal, Gordon can compare her pioneer hero Orion Outlaw, for example, with the ancient Greek hunter Orion, the soldier Rives Allard with Saint George, and the twentieth-century sportsman Aleck Maury with Aeneas. Although her allusions are sometimes ironic, she does find heroism in every age.

A number of critics have analyzed Caroline Gordon's interest in the "decrescendos of heroism." However, it would be more accurate to say that she deplores the waning public recognition of heroes, a subject she treats specifically in one of her later works, "Cock-Crow" (1963): "For a long time now, these men who stayed at home [because age or a disability kept them from going to war] and more recently, the women, who, whether they like it or not, must be defended and, latterly, the very children, who if *they* are to grow up to be heroes, must be protected, have been markedly slow to render the hero the homage which is his immemorial due."[2] In ages that decreasingly believe in the possibilities of heroism, the traditional responsibility of the artist—to proclaim the values of the community by upholding heroes worthy of emulation—is more difficult. Novels set in the

---

1. Louise Cowan has remarked that Caroline Gordon is concerned with the decline of heroism. By ordering Gordon's novels to emphasize the decline of the hero in the West, Jane Gibson Brown develops that thesis in her dissertation and in a similarly titled later article (which is essentially the introductory chapter of her dissertation). See Louise Cowan, "Aleck Maury, Epic Hero and Pilgrim," in Landess (ed.), *Short Fiction*, 7–31, and Louise Cowan, "Nature and Grace in Caroline Gordon," *Critique*, I (Winter, 1956), 11–27; Jane Gibson Brown, "Early Novels" (dissertation), and "The Early Novels of Caroline Gordon: Myth and History as a Fictional Technique," *Southern Review*, n.s., XIII (1977), 289–98. Hereinafter, references to Jane Gibson Brown, "Early Novels," are to the dissertation, unless otherwise noted.

2. Caroline Gordon, "Cock-Crow," *Southern Review*, n.s., I (1965), 559. Radcliffe Squires uses the phrase "decrescendos of heroism" in summarizing Frederick P. W. McDowell's argument. See Squires, "The Underground Stream: A Note on Caroline Gordon's Fiction," *Southern Review*, n.s., VII (1971), 468, and McDowell, *Gordon*.

twentieth century deal extensively with this problem, but earlier societies also suffer when their men of thought fail to contribute to and direct their communities.

Although Gordon bluntly declares in *How to Read a Novel* that the artistic sensibility is not a heroic subject and that the individual whose aim is self-expression is not a real hero (191), she does believe that the artist is indispensable to the community for preserving and criticizing its religious and secular traditions. In the early novels, the omniscient narrator fulfills those roles. The action in these novels, except for *Aleck Maury, Sportsman*, is reported by an effaced omniscient narrator who conforms to an Aristotelian ideal of disinterested observation by speaking "as little as possible in his own person."[3]

Louise Cowan cites the exchange between the two men of letters Heyward and Pleyol in "Emmanuele! Emmanuele!" to show Gordon's distinction between an artist who perceives that his first duty is "to confront himself" and one who feels that "an artist's first duty is the same as any other man's—to serve, praise, and worship God." Using James Joyce and William Faulkner as her examples, Cowan identifies these same opposing atittudes towards art among Gordon's contemporaries, holding that "most Southern writers in general have regarded their task as the discovery of an already existent pattern in actual experience rather than as the imposition of an ideal pattern upon experience."[4]

Having inherited this southern predisposition to what Cowan calls the "sacramental" view of the world, Gordon easily subscribed to T. S. Eliot's description of the artist as a medium, not as someone with a "'personality' to express." Eliot's "Tradition and the Individual Talent" emphasizes the essentially receptive, in some ways passive, role of the writer whose task is to continue to trace the meanings of western civilization through its inherited structures of belief and learning: "The poet must develop or procure the consciousness of the past. . . . The progress of an artist is a continual self-sacrifice, a continual extinction of personality."[5]

As an impersonal voice revealing meaning, the artist takes on some

3. Samuel Henry Butcher (ed.), *Aristotle's Theory of Poetry and Fine Art, with a Critical Text and Translation of the "Poetics"* (4th ed.; London, 1923), 93.

4. Louise Cowan, "Nature and Grace," 11, 12.

5. *Ibid.*, 12; Eliot, "Tradition and the Individual Talent," in his *Sacred Wood*, 56, 52–53.

of the sanctity and power of the priest or prophet. Without necessarily calling the role heroic, Caroline Gordon and others do, in fact, assign a formidable task to the artist. Louise Cowan thus summarizes Gordon's position: "The artist is not, in Miss Gordon's view, the hero. The artist—the poet—is a seer, whose consciousness gives form to the total history of man. True, he observes the hero and appreciates him, understanding his courage and his mission because both have an inner voice to guide them, both are aware of dragons, both stand solitary over the abyss. Nevertheless, the artist has a different kind of toil: to construct an image of that essentially epic struggle." Reacting against writers who assume the artist's role as a means of glorifying the self, Gordon endorses a formal stance that permits the reader, like the viewer of a drama, to participate more actively in the ordering and interpreting of reality. In the broadest sense, then, the artist's duty is a religious one, and the novelist specifically, whose work was once considered to be among the lowest forms of art, fulfills, to borrow James's phrase, a "sacred office."[6]

Given the extensive influence of Percy Lubbock, Henry James, and Gustave Flaubert on Caroline Gordon, it is no surprise that the point of view used in her fiction evolves towards the "viewpoint of the central intelligence." Andrew Lytle praises Gordon's early novels for their authoritative narration and successful self-effacement, claiming that if Gordon "did not sign her name, it would at first be hard to know her sex. This is a way of pointing out the strictness of her objectivity, and I suppose it to be the last refinement of it." Lytle's insistence on objectivity calls attention to an important tenet of New Criticism. As he explains, creating the work of art is a balancing process in which the artist's sense of form and the complexities of human experience are synthesized and held in judicious tension. The artist, then, is a seer, and formality, his discipline.[7]

The influence of T. S. Eliot's *The Waste Land* on Gordon's early novels is evident in her themes and her frequent allusions to myth

6. Louise Cowan, "Aleck Maury," in Landess (ed.), *Short Fiction*, 12–13; Henry James, "The Art of Fiction," in his *The Art of Fiction and Other Essays*, ed. Morris Roberts (New York, 1948), 6. Ian Watt comments on the inferior status of the novel since its beginnings, in *The Rise of the Novel: Studies in Defoe, Richardson, and Fielding* (Berkeley, 1957), 258.

7. For Gordon's emphasis on point of view, see *HRN*, 72–95, and 120–44. Andrew Lytle, "Caroline Gordon and the Historic Image," *Sewanee Review*, LVII (1949), 562, and 561.

and history, but it is her adaptation of Eliot's oracular narrator—who identifies himself at one point as Tiresias and, like the Sibyl of the epigraph, presents fragments of religious and literary traditions for the reader to interpret—that is most interesting. In Caroline Gordon's novels, the reader's involvement not only increases his pleasure through participation, it reinforces one of her themes—that the past is accessible to the present age and teaches us the constants in the human condition. So Lytle analyzes Gordon's fictional use of history to show the affinity of the drama she creates with religious vision: "This historic image of the whole allows for a critical awareness of a long range of vision, by equating the given period to the past and future, sometimes explicitly, always implicitly. . . . Such a restriction upon the imagination adds another range of objectivity to the post of observation, another level of intensity to the action (as if the actors while performing expose to the contemporary witness, the reader, the essential meaning of their time). This is literary irony at a high level. It is the nearest substitute for the religious image."[8] Following Henry James's example, Caroline Gordon consciously positions herself before the windows of the House of Fiction to present reality authoritatively to her audience.

Among her five early novels, *Aleck Maury, Sportsman* is the only one in which a first-person narrator tells the story. Yet, even here, Gordon follows Lubbock's and James's tenets by making her narrator's limited knowledge an integral part of the novel's meaning. An omniscient narrator, however, controls *Green Centuries*, *Penhally*, *None Shall Look Back*, and *The Garden of Adonis*. This narrator is able to suggest a multiplicity of points of view by filtering the action through the consciousnesses of the important characters. When the omniscient narrator does focus on a scene through the eyes of one of the characters, the account is psychologically richer, colored as it is by the personality and preconceptions of the character. A novel that provides several such views not only explores the psychology of the characters as the story unfolds, but also suggests a complex concept of reality. The narrator who chooses and integrates these various singular views evaluates through her selection and becomes, in one sense, an important character in the process of understanding the world.

Although Caroline Gordon initially foreswore autobiography, she

8. Lytle, "Historic Image," 569.

made us conscious and appreciative of the novelist's "impersonal" task. "Vigorously 'dramatic' books that require of readers almost as much talent in the art of reading as their author has lavished on the art of their writing,"[9] Gordon's novels resemble the stories in Joyce's *Dubliners*, whose difficulty challenges the intelligent and dedicated reader: "To take hold of them the reader must make an effort which is proportionate to the almost superhuman effort which was required for the writing of them. The result is that one looks back on the stories with somewhat the same feeling that one might have after a hard day's mountain climbing. One never forgets the magnificent view one had from the summit, but the steep climb lingers in the memory, too" (*HF* 1950, 441–42). For most of her career, Gordon did not attempt what Robert Penn Warren has successfully accomplished, for example, in *Brother to Dragons*. There, Warren makes himself a character, though the poet identified with the initials "R. P. W." is not so much an autobiographical depiction as a figure responsible for collecting and organizing the truths of this "tale in verse and voices." If in *Brother to Dragons* the reader is to follow R. P. W.'s literal and metaphoric journey in search of human glory, in Gordon's earlier fiction the reader is expected, so to speak, to climb the mountain himself.[10]

Gordon remarks on the consistency of her purpose as a writer: "I suspect that my knowledge and my lack of knowledge will come to the same thing, in the end. Two branches of a lifelong study: the life and times of the hero. A hero—any hero—spends his life in combat with the common, the only enemy, Death." Examining individual conflicts and human communities across time, Caroline Gordon's fiction requires the reader's concentration and his participation in recognizing the patterns of human experience. Although she makes no explicit comparisons, Gordon as artist is like the Tiresias she describes in "Cock-Crow": "preeminent among the Greek seers for the reason that he saw further and more clearly than any of his priestly *confrères*. His vision extended into both the past and the future."[11] It is up to the reader to interpret that vision carefully and perceptively.

9. Stuckey, *Gordon*, 12.

10. Robert Penn Warren, *Brother to Dragons: A Tale in Verse and Voices: A New Version* (rev. ed.; New York, 1979).

11. Gordon, "Cock-Crow," 558, 563.

Green Centuries

I see all things apart, the towers that men
Contrive I too contrived long, long ago.
Now I demand little. The singular passion
Abides its object and consumes desire
In the circling shadow of its appetite.

—ALLEN TATE, "Aeneas at Washington"

The American pioneer in his "singular passion" asserted himself not only against the wilderness but also against laws and codes that chafed individual freedom. Orion Outlaw, the protagonist of *Green Centuries*, has inherited the curious surname his father took when he fled Scotland after an unsuccessful rebellion against the king. Yet the name is equally suited to the son, for Rion escapes from the Yadkin settlement after ambushing the king's men in protest against taxation laws. Living outside the community, Rion is both "outlaw" and romantic hero. Although we admire his courageous pursuit of his ideals, the selfishness of Rion's quest destroys the freedom he has won. Ultimately, the unquestioned individualism of the frontiersman causes spiritual isolation, what the characters in the novel call melancholy.[12]

Rion, like other pioneers, mistakenly identifies his enemies as social codes and the natural world. His true antagonist is time, which eventually forces him to admit the hollowness of his values and to face his own mortality. In pointed contrast to Rion's qualified heroism is the omniscient narrator's understanding and control of time. Unlike the main character of the novel, the narrator does not live in that "ignorance of time" the epigraph describes but enlarges the scope of the linearly moving plot with historical and mythological allusions. Gordon further criticizes the pioneers' limited perspective by ascribing to the Indians in the novel a more expansive concept of time and history—a romanticized depiction that, for all its hortatory uses, may ultimately strike the contemporary reader as naïve.

The criticism of the pioneer is every bit as rigorous in *Green Centuries* as in the John Peale Bishop poem that lends the novel its name.

12. For the explanation of Orion's surname, see Caroline Gordon, *Green Centuries* (1941; rpr. New York, 1971), 410, hereinafter cited parenthetically in the text. See also Thomas H. Landess, "The Function of Ritual in Caroline Gordon's *Green Centuries*," *Southern Review*, n.s., VII (1971), 502.

Caroline Gordon selects four lines from "Green Centuries," the second in a series of four poems called "Experience in the West," to state her theme succinctly:

> The long man strode apart
> In green no soul was found,
> In that green savage clime
> Such ignorance of time.

Like Bishop and like her husband, who uses a similar metaphor in "Aeneas at Washington," Gordon depicts the pioneers as brave people with magnificent dreams of conquering a new Eden, an idyllic place and time "When every day dawned Now?" Yet, as Bishop also phrases it, this blind dream is destructive: "A continent they had / To ravage, and raving romped from sea to sea." Jane Gibson Brown identifies as a major theme in *Green Centuries* this judgment against the principles of frontier expansion: "Heroes such as Orion Outlaw are fated to destroy themselves because, in Miss Gordon's view, the irreconcilable claims of freedom and equality become destructive in democracy. This conflict is finally inevitable because order in the American experience is not based on a hierarchy of principles derived from a sense of the divine but based rather on a set of idealized rights impossible to actualize at any given time."[13]

Viewing themselves as new Adams, the frontiersmen have, in fact, almost no regard for the natural world and little appreciation for any supernatural order. When Rion does find his Eden, he does not realize that it exists in time. Before he fled the Yadkin, Rion was a farmer, accustomed to measuring the year by the seasons; but now as hunter and explorer, he feels nearly freed from time. Gazing at the new land he later settles, Rion thinks what a "queer thing" it is "to go through a whole season without raising anything. He remembered once he'd asked Daniel Boone about that, how he felt on those long hunts of his when spring came. Didn't he ever want to break up some ground? Boone said no; said when he was off in the woods away from everybody the seasons weren't the same as in the settlements. He could go off and stay a year, ten years, if it warn't for his family, and be content

---

13. John Peale Bishop, "Green Centuries," ll. 3–6, 12, "O Pioneers," ll. 15–16, both in Allen Tate (ed.), *The Collected Poems of John Peale Bishop* (New York, 1948, 1976), 79, 81; Jane Gibson Brown, "Early Novels," 49. See also Lytle, "Historic Image," 572; Louise Cowan, "Nature and Grace," 22.

not to put his hand to a plough" (188). In this passage Rion identifies himself with Boone as a hunter who would free himself from the restraints of community, including the responsibilities of caring for a family. Seemingly self-sufficient, the hunter may begin to think that he dominates the natural order, and surely one of the pleasures in exploring, as Rion discovers, is the control that naming seems to give (188). Yet the Rion who names the creeks and the mountains in the new land is unlike the Adam of Genesis 2 who, in giving names to the animals of God's creation, has a greater sense of the trust bestowed on him. Rion feels that he has a right to the land and seizes it, although he is practical enough to placate the Indians who have lived there before with hatchets and cloth (203). The attitude of the older Indians is much different from Rion's; they remember that the site harbors a sacred grove and hesitate to surrender it. But the young braves—greedy for more goods—persuade their elders to capitulate (202–203).

Rion's irreligious attitudes, which are beginning to infect the Indians too, signify the major flaw in the pioneers' ethic. The much quoted comparison between Rion and the constellation Orion does more than comment on the irony of Rion's name; the passage implicates all pioneers in the destruction caused by their ruthless idealism. Leaving his wife's deathbed and going outside to look at the sky, Rion thinks, "Did Orion will any longer the westward chase? No more than himself. Like the mighty hunter he had lost himself in the turning. Before him lay the empty west, behind him the loved things of which he was made. Those old tales of Frank's! Were not men raised into the westward turning stars only after they had destroyed themselves?" (469). Here, Gordon echoes another poem in Bishop's series "Experience in the West" to reinforce her criticism of Rion and all pioneers who blazed a destructive trail in their westward trek:

> Yet gaunt—bone, guts, sinews—
> Something like man pursued
> And still pursues
>
> What? Wheel of the sun
> In heaven? The west wind? Or only a will
> To his own destruction? [14]

14. Bishop, "Loss in the West," ll. 16–21, in Tate (ed.), *Collected Poems of Bishop*, 80–81.

The concluding sentences of the novel ominously reconfirm the final emptiness of Rion's pursuit of freedom. Having discovered that Cassy is dead, he stays a moment beside her body, while the candle goes out: "Standing alone beside the bed until the walls closed in, he stumbled out of the room to where the others sat under the dark trees" (469). The coffinlike walls that seem to close in on Rion warn of his destruction. He joins others sitting in the dark, who like himself have sought freedom at a high cost. Isolation and death—a dark communion—await them.

But as the "old tales" remind us, the blind search for license has exacted its price again and again. Rion Outlaw's naïve concept of time is all the more apparent for the larger contexts the omniscient narrator provides. Jane Gibson Brown outlines Gordon's use of myth "to define the archetypal nature of the central and enveloping actions" in the novels. These myths often serve as ironic measures of the protagonists, so that, for example, "Orion Outlaw's escape from society" is contrasted with "the inherent order and ritual of the timeless Orion"; for although the constellation represents the plight of a hunter who must track his prey forever, it is part of the seasonal order. Rion, however, is a hunter unwittingly caught by time's advance.[15]

Parallels between Rion and Oedipus and Rion and Cain not only qualify the protagonist's actions but, by linking the American pioneer with other heroic figures in the past, suggest the archetypal nature of human conflicts. Jane Gibson Brown details the points of comparison: like Oedipus, Rion Outlaw does not know who his parents really are; he is the common-law husband of Cassy (Jocasta) who commits a kind of suicide by allowing grief to destroy her. Like Cain, Rion is responsible for the death of his brother.[16]

Rion's self-identification with the historical figure Daniel Boone is similarly damning, for Boone is not the exalted hero of legend. As Brown observes, this "symbol of the frontier expansion" is shiftless; he is in debt; and he destroys the natural world. To a lesser degree, Rion shares these flaws, although, like Orion, Oedipus, and Boone, Rion is courageously daring in his striving after an impossible goal.

15. Jane Gibson Brown, "Early Novels," 17, 41.
16. *Ibid.*, 44–47.

His efforts to find freedom would place him, like the hunter Orion in the sky, somewhere between man and the gods. Yet as his affinity with Cain reminds us, his pursuit, however valorous, is destructive.[17]

The novel corrects the myth of the American frontier expounded by such historians as Frederick J. Turner, but Caroline Gordon does not fault the pioneers alone. Through allusion, the epigraphs to the four sections of the novel criticize all those who sacrifice community in their quest for freedom. The second part of the novel, for example, begins with a quotation from the first chapter of Thucydides' *History of the Peloponnesian War*: "And as they thought that they might anywhere obtain their necessary daily sustenance, they made little difficulty of removing: and for this cause they were not strong, either in greatness of cities or other resources." The nomadic life of the early Hellenes weakened the communities, leading, in Thucydides' opinion, to political turmoil and war. Their restlessness is analogous to that expressed by Daniel Boone at the beginning of Part I: "I think it time to remove when I can no longer fall a tree for fuel so that its top will lie within a few yards of my cabin."[18]

Gordon holds that spiritual alienation afflicts all wanderers: ancient Greeks, American pioneers, and modern individuals as well. Those "first inhabitants of Kentucky and Tennessee," as the botanist and explorer François André Michaux describes them, have developed a "long habit of a wandering and idle life" that has "prevented their enjoying the fruits of their labours." As this epigraph to the third part of the novel suggests, without community the individual suffers from a despair that makes his free life unfulfilling. In the text this "melancholy" is a psychological problem associated predominantly with the white society. The Ghigau, the one Indian who reportedly is melancholic, is well beloved and even speaks in council as a warrior (239), but because of her love for white men she has become emotionally distanced from her tribe. The Cherokees believe that "the Ghigau was one of those who live on without the soul" (330). Frank Dawson supplies a similar definition from Lucretius' *De Re-*

17. *Ibid.*, 34, 35.
18. Jane Gibson Brown discusses Gordon's critique of Frederick J. Turner's views *ibid.*, 33. Gordon appears to be quoting from Sir Richard Livingstone's translation and edition of Thucydides' *The History of the Peloponnesian War* (London, 1943; rpr. New York, 1972), 34.

rum Natura when Daniel Boone, the representative of the pioneer spirit, complains about his spells of "profound melancholy":

> "The spirit weakened by some cause or other often appears to wish to depart and to be released from the whole body. . . ."
> "Lucretius argues that the spirit is mortal," Frank said. . . .
> Boone shook his head. A wise look came on his face. "You mean the spirit rots same as the body? When I was a boy and used to go to meeting I heard 'em talk about man's soul being immortal. . . ." (325–26)

Despair is an emotional disease dating back at least to the ancient Greeks. And Flaubert's words beginning Part IV confirm that the melancholy felt by the pioneers is also a modern malady. He writes to Louise Colet, "Je porte en moi la mélancholie des races barbares, avec ses instincts de migrations et ses dégoûts innés de la vie qui leur faisaient quitter leur pays comme pour se quitter eux-mêmes."[19]

As the flight for freedom undermines the whole identity of the individual, the consequent despair of these would-be Adams suggests a condition that, in Christian theology, is attributed to original sin. Thus, the immortality of the soul and the concept of sin become increasingly important issues for the characters of *Green Centuries*. Fallen from grace, with no God or system of beliefs for guidance, the human soul is "lost" in specifically Christian terms but also in the literary language of the early twentieth century. Individuals without the possibility of community or communion are homeless *Waste Land* caricatures like the "nymphs" who have departed and "their friends, the loitering heirs of city directors," who have "left no addresses."[20]

The scholar and the clergyman—figures in the pioneer settlements who ought to have less egocentric notions of time because of their interests in the literature, history, and beliefs of western civilization— are no less isolated than their less contemplative fellows. In *Green*

---

19. William Stuckey offers this translation: "I have in me the melancholy of the barbaric races with their migratory instincts and inborn tastes for a life that makes them leave their country rather than change themselves." See *Gordon*, 66.

20. T. S. Eliot, *The Waste Land: A Facsimile and Transcript of the Original Drafts Including the Annotations of Ezra Pound*, ed. Valerie Eliot (London, 1922; facs. and rpr. New York, 1971), 139, lines 179–81.

Centuries the scholar Frank Dawson and the Reverend Murrow are not men of action but only selfish and contained men of contemplation who cannot make their knowledge a source of meaning for others.

Francis Dawson, the son of an Anglican minister and Rion's brother-in-law, is, in fact, a much more independent and admirable person while he is living in the Yadkin settlement. There, he joins the Regulators to oppose the unfair taxes of the king. Although he does not participate in the ambush Rion leads, Frank does ensure the success of the attack by organizing the men and bribing the king's officials.

Frank has a great deal of knowledge, as his job as schoolmaster would suggest. Yet even in the Yadkin, his knowledge is not necessarily superior to Rion's. In contrast to Frank, who learns about plants through reading, Rion, with his woodsman's experience, knows the common names and the uses of plants and scornfully remarks that Frank could learn more about the pharmacopoeia of the Indians by leaving his books and going to "live with them a while" (82–83). Frank's knowledge in itself is not remarkable; moreover, he has the unfortunate tendency to withdraw into his studies. On the journey westward when Rion's brother Archy disappears, Jacob and Rion search hard and long for the lost boy while Frank waits behind, telling the women who are preparing the evening meal, "when I am distraught it is a relief to read a few minutes in a book" (162).

Given Frank's selfishly contemplative nature, it is no wonder that the competent woodsman Rion comes to resent him. Responsible for the safety and health of his party, Rion complains at one point that Frank cannot shoot and "couldn't even dress game after somebody else had brought it down" (185). He believes that Frank, a "born schoolmaster," has "no business in the woods." Only reflecting on his own superiority quiets Rion. "He wondered what would become of Frank if you turned him out in the woods by himself. Most likely he would starve to death and somebody some day would find a few buttons or those books he carried in his pack scattered at the foot of a tree and that would be the end of Master Francis Dawson, son of the Church of England minister. He was pleased by the picture and his anger died" (186). Ultimately, Frank becomes little more than a parasite. Especially after the bullet that lodged in his spine during an

Indian fight confines him to bed, Frank totally depends on Rion. Occasionally he reads a letter for Rion, but in all, he can take care of himself no better than a child and appropriately he is killed with the children when the Indians ambush the house during Rion's absence.

Frank's good traits—his curiosity and his appreciation of nature and the Indian culture—are not enough to make him a useful member of his society. With the visitor John Adair, he can discuss Adair's book on the Indians, and with Daniel Boone, he displays his knowledge of Greek and Latin. Nonetheless, this knowledge is ineffectual because Frank does not genuinely care how ideas are related to moral or spiritual values. He does nothing, as Thomas Landess observes, to see that his sister is married to Rion; he only watches disinterestedly that first night on the trail when Rion motions to Cassy to spread her blanket beside his (154). Frank does not practice his father's faith and restricts spiritual questions to intellectual debates such as the one with Boone. Significantly, in that discussion of melancholy, it is Boone—not Frank—who remembers his religious training and speaks of the immortality of the soul.[21]

For all of his learning Frank is as godless as the majority of frontier people. In the talks with John Adair and the Reverend Murrow, Frank again is more interested in books than in speculating about the soul. Even such a noncontemplative person as Rion reflects more on religious matters as he listens to the exchange. Earlier, in the Yadkin settlement, Rion was still conscious of guilt, blaming himself, for instance, for the accident that scarred and crippled his sister Jane (26). Yet he realizes that he has thought little of religion since he moved west: "Well, sin was something he had never understood very well and hadn't worried about much, of late years anyhow. When a man battled the wilderness he had enough on his hands without pondering the future life. Was that what made the people here on the Holston so godless, for godless they certainly were, with the exception of a man here and there like James or Charles Robertson" (409).

Fittingly, the Reverend Murrow enters the action of the novel just before Frank dies and takes his place, so to speak, as the intellectual and contemplative man. Like Frank, Murrow is inept as a woodsman, needing Rion's help to survive in the wilderness (430). Perhaps Mur-

21. Landess, "Function of Ritual," 505.

row's inadequacies as a frontiersman would be understandable and excusable if he served a worthy and necessary role as a clergyman. Yet, though he teaches Cassy that she has neglected her spiritual life, he does not help her deal with her despair and sense of worthlessness. Confronting the inexplicable loss of her brother and two children, she blames herself for their deaths. Since the minister does not provide her, as Thomas Landess expresses it, with a "sacramental means of expiating" her guilt, Cassy becomes a victim of her own intense depression.[22] At one point she complains to Rion that she has asked the minister for help in overcoming her guilt but cannot get a "straight answer" from him: "He was like Frank, couldn't express himself without using big words. . . . *Cast away from ye all your transgressions whereby ye have transgressed and make you a new heart and a new spirit. . . .*" (431).

Rion's practicality and intelligence, in contrast, do protect him from Murrow's misguided teachings. Rion tells the minister that Cassy refuses to have sex with him, then abruptly voices his dissatisfaction with Murrow's "solution":

> The Reverend had thrown his head back and thundered out quite a piece, standing there on the path. "The disposition to regard the body as intrinsically evil and all natural impulses as worthy only to be trampled on, is a Manichaean heresy . . ."
> "That may well be," Rion said, "but it don't help me none."
> (432)

Although Murrow may talk about the need to create a new heart and spirit, he offers no real spiritual guidance, with the unfortunate result that Rion finds a practical solution to his unfulfilled sexual drives: he takes Anne Mulroon as his lover. This betrayal only drives Cassy further from him.

Thus, godless and soulless, the pioneer, who is alienated from any natural and supernatural orders, finds that his personal relationships are analogously flawed. Rion's affair with Anne exemplifies love fallen to lust; Cassy's grief festers unnaturally until it deadens her to love and life. The spiritual condition of these protagonists finally resem-

22. *Ibid.*, 506.

bles the postlapsarian Adam and Eve before they are granted any hope of redemption.

Unlike the hopeless existence of the pioneers, the Indians' life—as Gordon conceives it—secures the individual in meaningful relationships with others. Examining this contrast between the disorienting individualism of the frontier society and the rituals of the Cherokees, Thomas Landess observes that the Indian way of life is so greatly preferable that Archy Outlaw chooses to remain with the tribe rather than return to the white settlement with his brother Rion. "In that green savage clime," it is not the Indian but the pioneer who is innocent of time; the Indian, who perceives the supernatural in the natural and human realms, feels part of an order governing all life—past, present, and future.[23]

In the novel, even the Indians' art ritualistically satisfies the individual's need to be integrated in time. Preparing to paint a carpet that will honor her husband, the Dark Lanthorn includes in her sketches images that link her husband's past with the entire history of the tribe. Because the Indians believe they are descendants of animals and therefore part of the supernaturally governed physical world, the Dark Lanthorn can also suggest the interrelationship of the human, natural, and divine in the series of pictures she draws: "In one corner a wolf, for her husband's clan. In the opposite corner her own ancestor, the deer. . . . in the lower right-hand corner a great dogwood blossom because the carpet had been woven in the time that the dogwood was in bloom. In the middle she would depict some event in the life of her husband, the great peace chief, Atta Kulla Kulla. As always when she thought of that small, wrinkled old man, her heart grew warm. She wondered how she should show him, whether on the hunt, on the warpath, or in council" (234–35). In her design she has already linked specific memories with the far past by showing the peace chief's ancestry and her own; and by depicting the dogwood blossoms, she connects the past with the present spring. Her confidence in life's order enables the Dark Lanthorn to contemplate without anguish her own inevitable death. Even as she works she calcu-

23. *Ibid.*, 501. In depicting the Indians as such noble moral examples, Gordon may well be following the early nineteenth-century Indian captivity narratives. See, for example, James Arthur Levernier, "Indian Captivity Narratives: Their Functions and Forms" (Ph.D. dissertation, University of Pennsylvania, 1975), 256–71.

lates that this carpet may well be her last (235). Conscious of her husband's place in time, the squaw also thinks of her role in the community, finally deciding to draw a picture of the time her husband crossed the ocean to speak to the English king (241). The other events that she considers painting in the center of the carpet are also important and memorable because they mark Atta Kulla Kulla's triumphs for his people.

Artist and historian, the Dark Lanthorn is also a loving wife. Their sense of community makes the Indians seem generally more loving towards each other than the pioneers are, and the special bonds between Indian husband and wife, sanctified by tribal rituals, appear to foster deeper ties of love. In contrast to Rion and Cassy whose common-law marriage is never legitimized by either church or state, the relationship between Archy and his Indian wife Monon continues to deepen in affection and respect. Archy and Monon's happiness seems almost paradisal. The description of this married couple, like Milton's account of Adam and Eve before the Fall, is of two people so attuned to each other's needs and so agreed on their responsibilities that they know no division between work and love.[24]

Gordon underscores the Indians' still-preserved links to Eden with her references to John Adair, whose book establishes the similarities between the Cherokee language and ancient Hebrew. The Cherokee name for wife is "A-wah" or "Eve," instructs Adair, exclaiming, "They give woman the name of our first mother!" (409). Ironically, the pioneers fail to realize this shared heritage with the Indians and in their self-righteous conception of themselves as new Adams, they destroy the very essence of Edenic life. Rion's gleeful counting of Indians killed in battle is but one example of the white men's refusal to recognize their common humanity with the Indians (368–69). Through the dispassionate eyes of the white men out to surprise Dragging Canoe's war party, we see the murder of Archy and Monon: "A young man had come out of the end cabin. He yawned and stretched himself, then going over to where the woman stood put his arms about her and catching hold of the mall began to work it up and down. The yellow feather in his hair jerked to and fro as his arms

24. Landess also contrasts Rion and Cassy's relationship with that of Archy and Monon, in "Function and Ritual," 505, 507.

moved. The woman struggled a little in his embrace, then stood still. Their laughter floated thinly across the meadow. From the cane behind them came a shot" (462–63).

As Dragging Canoe reminds his people in his war speech, whole nations of Indians have "Melted away before the white man like snowballs before the sun" (311). In the pioneers' savage trek westward, they have ravaged the continent, as Bishop would phrase it, and in so doing have inevitably destroyed themselves. Cassy's despair and the emptiness that Rion feels at the end of the novel are examples of that same melancholy afflicting all those without allegiance to a social and religious community. This lawlessness of the pioneers represents a worse kind of sin: the alienation of the self from its soul or, in Eliot's popular phrase, "the dissociation of sensibility."

The ancient Greeks, the American pioneers, modern society have all produced wanderers whose homelessness is, on the deepest level, a spiritual condition. Caroline Gordon regards this conflict between the individual's desire for freedom and his need to feel communion as a universal predicament—one that cannot be resolved by any self-made order. Her technical devices, however, do imply a solution: a sounder understanding of the individual's place in time. Like the Dark Lanthorn, the narrator of *Green Centuries* seeks to locate the individual in a meaningful design, one that makes the context of all cultures and all times the proper abode for the human spirit.

Penhally and *None Shall Look Back*

Pluck fast, dreamers, prove as you amble slowly
Not less than men, not wholly.
—JOHN CROWE RANSOM, "Antique Harvesters"

In the story of the Old South told in both *Penhally* and *None Shall Look Back*, southern society began its denouement after the climactic Civil War, as the self-serving supplanted the dignified but decrepit adherents of the old order. These loyal idealists, made stubborn dreamers by the war, are analogous to John Crowe Ransom's "antique harvesters" who, slowly garnering treasure for the Lady they serve, are urged to pluck fast before the harvest spoils. Now "full bronze," the legend of the Old South is already menaced by the gray that "will quench it shortly." That gray—the color of the Confederate troops—is also the ominous sign of age and decay.[25]

Time, the enemy of a declining social order, is the antagonist of Caroline Gordon's *Penhally*, a novel spanning nearly a hundred years of southern history. Like an album of photographs, the novel pictures the Llewellyn family over the years, magnifying those moments that most clearly frame the changes in their community. The method, however, has its disadvantages as a number of critics have remarked. Frederick Hoffman, for example, faults *Penhally*, along with *Green Centuries* and *None Shall Look Back*, for having "a clutter of personalities instead of a wealth of characters." Even Ford Madox Ford in his contemporary review of *Penhally* admits that the characters are a little vague but insists that they are alive. Moreover, he lauds the episodic nature of Caroline Gordon's first novel, a quality that has since been criticized. Ford finds *Penhally* remarkably organized and praises its interwoven themes, holding that the story "progresses forward in action and back in memory so that the sort of shimmer that attaches to life attaches also to the life of the book." [26]

Indeed, the episodic structure, by creating an interplay of time, makes history ever present. Gordon juxtaposes moments in the past to reveal the essential conflicts in southern history and finally to suggest a method for recovering meaning in the present age. But the Old South provides but one example of a society brought to ruin because of its faulty values. Allusions to the myths of the house of Atreus and of Cain and Abel, as Jane Gibson Brown explicates in great detail, reinforce the identification of the South with other familial and social orders.[27]

Those who uphold the legend of the Old South after the war has exposed its weaknesses are heroic though their ideals are imperfect. In the advent of industrialism, even a flawed agrarian society seems preferable, and consequently, those who sacrifice themselves to cere-

25. John Crowe Ransom, "Antique Harvesters," *Selected Poems* (3rd ed.; New York, 1969), 83–84. Caroline Gordon, *Penhally* (1931; rpr. New York, 1971), and *None Shall Look Back* (1937; rpr. New York, 1971), hereinafter cited parenthetically in the text.

26. Hoffman, *Art of Southern Fiction*, 38; Ford Madox Ford, "A Stage in American Literature," *Bookman*, LXXIV (1931), 375. See also McDowell, *Gordon*, 17.

27. Jane Gibson Brown, "Early Novels," 50–86.

mony and order are admirable. The fault of these protagonists, however, is their inability to imagine new courses of action or new systems of belief that could revitalize the failing culture. Men of action, prepared to die for their cause, have literally nothing to live for, and men of learning escape into their contemplations, constructing a narcissistic world apart from their chaotic society.

So many years are covered in *Penhally* that the novel, in effect, outlines Caroline Gordon's view of southern American history, while focusing in particular on the disintegration of one family.[28] Beginning in 1826 when Nicholas Llewellyn quarrels with his brother Ralph over primogeniture, the action shifts quickly to the Civil War when the menace to society comes from both within and without. The second section of the book is predominantly the flashback of Nicholas' nephew John. Through memory, John reconstructs the events of the years following the war until the suicide of his son Frank some twenty years later. Paralleling the quarrel between their forebears Nicholas and Ralph, in the final part of the novel John's grown grandsons fight over the land.

During these approximately one hundred years, admirable men of action become rare. Broken men who wander without purpose, merchants who prey on their fellow human beings, caricatured versions of the gentleman and sportsman—none of these truly preserves the ideals of the landowners of the Old South. Men's roles weaken so much that by the twentieth century women are usurping masculine duties and activities.

Although the antebellum South imagined itself as following the model of the traditional hierarchical society of Europe, the agrarian way of life did not necessarily unite the landowners as a cultured and civilizing class. Old Nicholas' obstinate stand against changes in the agrarian system helps to destroy the very life-style he would defend. Because Nicholas despises his brother so much for wanting to divide the family property, Ralph refuses to remain on the family estate, Penhally, and moves to Mayfield.

Just as Nicholas' beliefs permanently separate him from his brother, so, when the Civil War breaks out, he alienates himself from his community by refusing to support the Confederate cause. Although he

28. *Ibid.*, 50.

does supply horses to individual members of the family and hides Charles while he recuperates from a wound, Nicholas will not endorse the war because it endangers the land. Believing that the war is not being fought for self-defense but for economic gain, he finally blames the whole conflict on "new-fangled politicians, landless men, with nothing to lose and everything to win" (94). In some respects Nicholas is right: there are many like old Mr. Atkins who are "ready to go to war now to get the steamboat trade back" (93). Nicholas protects his economic interests from such mercenaries, and he does endure the war. Ralph, in contrast, is ruined because of his altruism; he is able to maintain a hospital for wounded Confederate soldiers only by selling off his land and finally he goes bankrupt refusing to exchange his Confederate money for gold (172).

Despite the selfishness of his efforts to protect himself and his land, Nicholas is capable of heroism. When he shoots the Yankee soldier who taunts Mrs. Brady (151–52), his brave defense of the woman's honor upholds a code recognized both by southerners and by the Union men who do not harm Nicholas for shooting their comrade. In this incident Nicholas again acts not as a Confederate patriot but as the protector of his property and defender of the women who have put themselves in his trust.

Nicholas fails to perceive the limitations of agrarianism. The omniscient narrator, however, makes us aware from the first page of the novel of the inevitable decline of the system. Walking about his grounds, Nicholas recalls his family, some of whom have long been dead, and, significantly, passes beneath a large sugar tree that suggests the broad spread of his family tree. Besides linking Nicholas with the novel's future generations, this image implicates Nicholas in the decaying order that underlies the family history: "1826. The shadows that laced the gravelled walk shifted and broke and flowed away beneath his boot soles like water. . . . Passing the big sugar tree he tapped it smartly with his cane. It must be rotten at the heart by this time, though it did not sound hollow. It had been an old tree when little Sister Georgina—dead twenty years ago in August, 1807—no, 1808—made her doll's playhouse between its roots, out of bits of broken china and the white pebbles that lay at the bottom of the spring" (1). The "rotten" heart of the sugar tree, like the flawed social order resting on slavery, may not sound hollow in 1826, but with time its fall is certain. By the Civil War the depravity shows itself in monetary greed and in the desire to serve self above all else—motives Nicholas detects among his secessionist friends.

Nevertheless, the war does offer real opportunities for heroism. Both of Nicholas' nephews, Charles and John, learn how serious are their responsibilities as men of action. Charles, who formerly spent his time in the stables or gaming in town (39), becomes a fine officer (120); and John, who once regarded himself as Lucy's cavalier (183), regains some of the original meaning of that term when he joins the cavalry.

Yet war inevitably destroys the soldiers, whether literally or figuratively. Charles dies in battle, and John, though he physically survives, is dominated after the war by his wife, Lucy. As his grandson Chance notices, John seems to be too tired to be fully the man: "There was some sort of compulsion on him that made him do her least bidding . . . without argument" (230). John's guilt in marrying Lucy for convenience has given her power over him.

John's impotence in personal relationships is only part of a larger pattern for the Confederate veterans. The Reconstruction government attempts to keep the war-enervated men weak by denying them social responsibilities. Chance remembers that his grandfather was deprived of the franchise because he had fought on the Confederate side: "It had pretty near killed the old fellow not to be allowed to vote" (239). Two generations later, Chance himself is much less political, but by volition: "He wondered if his grandfather would care so much about voting if he were alive to-day. . . . He himself would not give a damn if they took his vote away from him for the rest of his enduring life" (240).

Since the Civil War the men have become increasingly cut off from a real community. Frank, John's son and the father of Chance and Nick, is a transitional figure who, having left his home and family, tries to make his love for a woman the meaning of his life. When his parents find Frank with his cousin Fanueil in her bedroom at the Allards' house, the two lovers are forced to run away and marry. Although Frank has had a university education and eventually does find a job in a law practice, he drifts without any real sense of vocation or belonging. Love is the primary value for Frank, and when his wife is unfaithful he kills himself.[29] Appropriately, when John broods over his son's suicide, he recalls the image he always had of him, "wandering over the face of the earth." John "seemed to see him on dark, interminable slopes, or walking down street after street of some city, rain falling . . ." (203).

Frank's sons, Chance and Nick, suffer no less from confusion over their roles as men, although, of the two, Chance is more conscious of his loss of vocation and community. Nick, a banker, regards the family property as no more than a commodity. Chance inherits a love for the land, but he cannot make it productive because legally the estate is not his; moreover, the land is no longer fertile. Desperate, Chance turns to violence, his idealistic belief in the land's importance to the family leading him to murder Nick.

By the 1930s then, the image of the Lady of the Old South is defiled by her own devotees. Those "dreamers" who used to serve her well were "Not less than men, not wholly," but her twentieth-century worshippers have a less ambiguous status: they are certainly less than men. As the men in the society become weaker, the women wield their power destructively. The increased power of the women does not equalize relations between the sexes; it only shifts the locus of authority without redefining the terms of the relationship.

Not all of the women intentionally supplant masculine authority in order to gain power. But even Emily Kinloe's romanticizing of the Confederate soldiers undercuts their true heroism. At least Emily examines her views and recognizes that her chauvinism is, in part, a defensive reaction to people like the Parrishes who thrive on the defeat of the old southern order. Escorting the despised Parrishes around Penhally, she probes her feelings:

> Very old people—people who had been living while the war was going on—did not feel as she did. They said that the war was over and we were all one country now! But she had always been fiercely Confederate. They had left her too much in the library when she was a little girl, with her grandfather. . . . There was a

29. Both Jane Gibson Brown and Lytle attribute the cause of Frank's suicide to Faneuil's infidelity though the text is not explicit. See Brown, "Early Novels," 55, and Lytle, "Historic Image," 577.

steel engraving on the wall just above his arm chair: "The fall of the Gallant Pelham." . . . And on the street just back of the house Father Ryan had written "The Conquered Banner." "The gall*ant* hosts," her grandfather said when he read it to her, "the gall*ant* hosts are shattered, over *whom* it floated high. . . ." His voice would break when he came to that and she would cry, too, sitting on an ottoman beside him. (253)

As Emily observes, "you cannot let a little girl spend all her time reciting Father Ryan with Confederate veterans without having her turn out a little queer" (253).[30]

Emily's fiancé, Chance, holds a more complex view of the Confederate soldiers because of his grandfather John. Although he admires his grandfather's bravery and free thinking, he also realizes that Lucy dominated him (230). Certainly Chance's analysis is closer to John's own perspective just after the war. John realizes that his weariness prevents him from meeting Lucy's emotional needs and compares himself to "The tired horses of the Second Kentucky," who "in their last charge had been able only to breast the fences, not to clear them" (196). John had to live "by the consequences of that fatigue" for the rest of his life (196). Emily, however, overlooks the failure of the war heroes to revitalize personal relationships and the South after the war. She dwells instead on her grandfather's tales. Admittedly her sentimentality is a fault. She seems quite silly, for example, to have cried over the miserably written poems about the South that she found in a book collector's apartment in Paris (253–54).

If Emily remembers the Confederate soldiers only as "gall*ants*," others do not cherish the past for even those naïve but moving memories. The "time of debauchery and carnival" (196) that characterized the Reconstruction continues into the twentieth century as both southern and northern people turn the traditions of the old order into rules for a pretentious social game. Unlike Emily, Nick's wife Phyllis does not resent the northerner Joan Parrish but emulates her. Thus, bored and rich Joan Parrish finds that she can persuade

30. Father Ryan was the poet laureate of the Confederacy. His verses were set to music in the popular song "The Conquered Banner," which was written near the end of the war. See Louis D. Rubin, Jr., "The Image of an Army: The Civil War in Southern Fiction," in R. C. Simonini, Jr. (ed.), *Southern Writers: Appraisals in Our Time* (Charlottesville, 1964), 50.

southern women into any scheme. As Emily realizes, "If she stayed here long enough she would have to do something about Gloversville at large . . . organize a hunt club, perhaps. . . . Well, no matter what she did, they would all follow her like sheep" (249). When Joan persuades Nick to sell Penhally to her, she does, in fact, transform the estate into a hunt club, ironically mocking the legend of the South as the last sanctuary of European genteel traditions.

The scene in which Chance tours the hunt club—formerly his family home—and comes upon the portrait of Nicholas Allard Llewellyn is the context for a recapitulation of the South's fall. Standing before the painting of his forebear, Chance thinks, "If he had not been so hell bent on entailing property and all that business, this red-faced woman would not be walking around in here now. He wished he could remember her name. Something with a hyphen. That meant she was divorced—or English" (270). By refusing to modify his beliefs, Nicholas Llewellyn perpetuated a flawed system, and his heirs—who have inherited the system along with the land—fail when the old order finally proves false. In the twentieth century, anglophiles reduce social traditions to fashion. The distorted past is useless except as ornament, and Penhally is now a hunt club for Joan Parrish and her cronies.

That sport has been debased is obvious from the pun Chance makes when Mrs. Sabin, at the club, asks him to identify a woman:

> "I didn't catch her name," he said, "some sporting woman from up north."
>
> He had said "spo'ting." When negroes said "a spo'ting woman" they meant a whore or keeper of a whore house. But this would be a woman who had her picture in the rotogravures. The Nashville *Tennesseean* rotogravure . . . that was where he had seen this woman's face, the broad, good-humored face, framed by a horse's forward pricked ears, shot at you like the projectile from a cannon: Lady Somebody on Play Boy. (271–72)

The puns on "Play Boy" and "sporting" highlight the improper roles of these twentieth-century women; yet the men, in allowing their authority to diminish, have encouraged the women to debase themselves.

Before the war, men who shirked their responsibilities as men of action, though tolerated, were considered mad—as the lives of John's father, Jeems, and Cousin Cave both exemplify. Jeems Allard, a scientist whose experiments are potentially beneficial to society, is, as his own son admits, "mad as a hatter" (197). In Part I of *Penhally*, where we see Jeems's eccentric behavior for ourselves, we realize that his temperament and pursuits make him a failure as a father and husband. On the morning of his wife's funeral, the family cannot find him because he has gone on his customary morning walk (37). Although Jeems has had a university education and is even a friend of the learned Thomas Jefferson (36–37), most of his projects are unwelcomed by the family. His efforts to poison tobacco worms seem worthy, but the community ridicules most of his projects, including eating mussels from the Mississippi River and drinking a coffee substitute made from soybeans (32–33). Jeems's behavior in company, always a real embarrassment to his grown sons (197), illustrates the scientist's main flaw—his inability to interact with and respond to others. Even his physical appearance sets him apart: "A tall, stooped, preternaturally thin old man, [who] wore a coat that was bottlegreen in some places, in others merely frayed. His long, white hair floated to his shoulders. He turned a blue, childlike stare on the company" (60).

Living some years after Jeems, the classical scholar Cousin Cave is also mad; his learning, as Chance realizes, "would never be any good to anybody" (234). The family attributes Cousin Cave's derangement to an "over-application to his studies when he was a very young man" (234). Now he is content as long as he has his books, and so Chance pictures the old scholar: "Probably concocting some of the verses now [to his blank verse translation of "The Bride of Lammermoor"]. Sitting there staring at vacancy; exactly like a dog in a dead set. His 'beautiful detachment' Emily called it. The old fellow had never had anything to detach himself from. Life had just gone on past him, without his knowing it was there" (234). Once Cousin Cave was thought harmless enough to instruct the young men in the neighborhood, yet in the changing society there is no place for a crazy classical scholar. When Penhally is sold and Cousin Cave is sent to live with the Kinloes, he disturbs the family next door with his nightly pacing and reciting of poetry. Emily has to remove him to her house so the neighbors will stop complaining to her parents (278).

Cousin Cave's insane dependency on his books is markedly different from the value once placed on a classical education. Old Nicholas Llewellyn could remember his father reading Plato under a tree while a slave boy fanned him (20–21). Education then was the privilege of a leisured class; however, Nicholas, a practical man conscious of his responsibilities to the land and to family, could find little use for the classics even in his day. In contrast to old Nicholas is the twentieth-century intellectual Douglas Parrish whose studies occupy all his time.

Although his parents are southerners, Parrish was raised in France, and thus he knows the South mainly through reading and second-hand accounts. Despite his wish to recover the South's history, he keeps it as past, as artifacts that he can catalogue in his collection. Slightly different from Emily's romanticizing, Douglas Parrish's view of the South is equally distorted. His collection does not impress Chance, a native southerner, who can see no reason for saving "a set of gourd dippers and a set of gourd dishes, carved and stained with pokeberry juice; old smoke-house keys; the flat rock, even, from some South Carolina smoke house" (243).

When Chance gives the Parrishes a tour of Penhally, Douglas searches through the house, borrows old books, and records dates from tombstones in the family graveyard—with Emily all the while telling her patriotic stories. Nonetheless, Parrish's intellectualism is worse than Emily's sentimentality because he uses it to retreat from personal relationships. Douglas is such a poor husband to Joan that even Emily has sympathy for her (251). Left to herself, Joan Parrish becomes a real menace to what is valuable in the southern past, a threat that is suggestively foreshadowed as the two couples leave the graveyard at Penhally. As Douglas is busy pocketing his notebook full of dates and facts, Joan walks beside Chance, "flicking with her crop at the grass that grew beside the path. An extraordinarily beautiful woman, longer legged in riding breeches than you would have thought, but graceful in every movement. . . . The sun, declining, sent their shadows monstrously before them over the grass. The gigantic woman's hand might have been swinging out to uproot the big sugar tree, or demolish that whole row of ragged cedars. . . ." (256). The sugar tree, the image that began the novel, is endangered by seemingly innocuous people, and certainly Joan's huge shadow can suggest strength only because she threatens a structure already "rotten at the heart," a structure that a shadow could topple now. The violent conclusion of that internal deterioration finally erupts when, to avenge Nick's selling the family estate, Chance shoots his brother at the hunt club.

Caroline Gordon's fiction, as William Stuckey aptly phrases it, reveals a quest "for heroes who would not only embody qualities of courage and bravery but would also display a sense of responsibility for the welfare of other human beings."[31] Not just a hero's actions but the quality of his ideals determine his worth. After the Civil War, the southern men do not seem successful in finding ideals large enough to live for; instead they end up dying, or even killing, for mere frustrated dreams. Men of action thus become men of violent reaction. And those with the imagination and intellect to correct the values of society only participate in a more passive kind of destruction. Creating dream worlds, men like Douglas Parrish or Cousin Cave withdraw and allow women, who in Gordon's traditional view lack the necessary experience or wisdom, to determine the direction of society. Thus, in tracing the fall of southern culture through the history of one family, the effaced omniscient narrator not only reveals the pattern of decline but suggests some reasons for such deterioration.

*

Since in the emergency of war all men with the physical strength to fight are called into action, few are then granted the leisure and calm for scholarly or scientific work. The Civil War, demanding the commitment and energy of every able-bodied man, is the setting and focus for *None Shall Look Back*. Though *Penhally*, with its wider scope, necessarily treats the war in less detail, in both novels the cavalier young gentlemen come to realize the seriousness of their soldierly roles. Both Rives Allard and his cousin George Rowan learn that serving a woman and fighting for her protection are part of a larger cause—defending their country. In that larger service the self is destroyed, and the loved ones whom the soldier protects must relinquish him to his own immolation. Providing panoramic scenes as well as closer views through the consciousness of individuals, the omniscient narrator again discloses the paradoxes of heroism and the complexity of response such noble self-sacrifice elicits.

31. Stuckey, *Gordon*, 31.

The demands that love and war make on a man cannot be equally fulfilled, although in his naïveté George Rowan assumes that both are romantic conquests. Gradually George understands that he can serve but one mistress, war. Unsuccessful one night at soliciting Lucy's affection, George cheers himself as he rides away by singing a hunting song (58). He feels that love and war share a similar passion and that both are hunts, with different quarries. But in Part III, as the armies are preparing for the battle later known as Chickamauga, George perceives that conquests in love are small in comparison to those of war: "'I am willing to give my life for my country,' he said proudly. The words spoken in the quiet woods rang a little theatrically on his ear yet evoked a sudden, immediate sense of beauty. He recalled fox-hunting nights when still fresh at dawn he had ridden home through wet woods, recalled other softer nights. That peculiar, excited feeling that came when he was on the verge of making a conquest that most people would have said even he couldn't make. Love itself never had a moment to match that feeling" (242). Remembering the night that Lucy Churchill refused him, George realizes that he never suffered because of it: "It was as if he knew that he was soon to be caught up into greater affairs" (242). The lady that the soldier ultimately serves is his ideal of country and honor, a dark lady—as Lytle writes—exacting death.[32]

The women, too, have to be educated to the deeper implications of the soldier's service. Early in the novel Lucy thinks of both George and Rives as her "cavaliers" (46). However, once she has imagined her husband dying in action, she understands that being a soldier has none of the romance and lightheartedness that "cavalier" connotes. Recalling that night she rode with George, Lucy remembers, as he later does, his self-dramatization and his naïveté. He had recited to her, implicitly comparing himself to Troilus, Cressida's lover and a great Greek warrior,

> *On such a night as this . . .*
> *. . . . .*
> *. . . . When the sweet wind did gently woo the trees*
> *And they did make no noise*
> *Troilus, methinks, mounted the Trojan wall*

---

32. Lytle, "Historic Image," 576.

> And sighed his soul toward the Grecian tents
> Where Cressid lay . . . (219)

For all of George's theatricality that night, he does, in fact, die a hero at Chickamauga. Like Troilus, George ultimately finds that the duties and glories of war are more significant to him than the pleasures of love-making.

Similarly, George's cousin Rives has depended on his hunting experiences to anticipate the reality of war. Still waiting for his first battle, Rives thinks about the war and "with these thoughts came the same excitement he had known months ago on a fox hunt when, riding home through the wet woods, he had seen the sun rising over the Brackets woods and had asked himself whether going to war would be like the chase or would have in it perhaps some excitement sterner, more terrible than any he had ever imagined" (78). Rives and his comrades are now defending their invaded land (23, 25). Like the fox hunt, where the social distinctions between "'gentleman' and common soldier" are dropped (78), war unites its participants in the more serious comradery and more rigorous discipline of combat. Before the war, men such as Rives's Cousin Edmond at Music Hall could regard fox hunting and fishing as serious pursuits that served to bind together a community of men in a ritualistic test of skill and fortitude. Now, however, the war becomes the test of manhood, a proving ground for heroes, demanding the greater sacrifice of life.

Both George and Rives die in battle. Ned Allard, who manages to survive his imprisonment and return home, is nearly a walking corpse so thoroughly has the war broken him. All three men are destroyed because of their commitment, and paradoxically, they leave defenseless the family they have striven to protect. When Rives realizes that should the Confederate States fall, he will find no happiness except in death (286), he has already consented to sacrifice himself and abandon his wife and mother to their own devices. Thus, for soldiers, the loss of individuality necessitated by the war is at one extreme a selfless death wish and at the other a failure in human feeling. The narrator who shows us the grandeur of individual acts of heroism also reveals men reduced to animals by war, exploring the metaphor of the hunt to suggest how man can be at once hunter and prey.

We would expect that the commanding officers—who, like omniscient narrators, position themselves to watch the movements of many thousands of soldiers—would come to regard their men not as individuals but as part of a group. Leading his Union troops towards Chattanooga, General Granger thus perceives his exhausted men "still in line but flat on the ground, panting, most of them, like dogs" (258); and again he remembers the morning's fighting as a confrontation between animallike forces, where the Rebels "swarmed like hornets" (259). Through gradual shifts to the omniscient narrator alone, we see the near absurdity of the soldiers' movements. When a Confederate general views the action below Fort Donelson, the description of the battle as a fatal game between children could either be the narrator's or the general's: "When it [the smoke from the cannon] cleared away the two armies were revealed blazing away at each other like boys swinging gigantic firecrackers" (96). Here, the general's detachment and the fantastic and ridiculous action are equally emphasized.

In a similar passage, a Federal commander, who is eating his sandwich and watching from the top of a hill, regards the combat "like a man at a circus who finds himself unable to concentrate on one ring for fear of missing what is going on in the others" (97). The narrator, whose position is now clearly established, portrays the war as deadly amusement. "Then the General shifts his gaze to the next regiment which seems, seen through his glasses, engaged in a game of checkers with the regiment adjacent. Men are falling fast and the action of their comrades in stepping over them is absurdly like 'taking' a man at draughts. But no such frivolous thought enters the General's mind. He is absorbed in noting that these two regiments with soldier-like precision close up each gap, always toward the colors. 'Pretty work,' he murmurs once and strikes his hand on his broad knee" (98).

Whereas the officers perceive how combat changes men into animallike hordes or into well-functioning units, the individual soldiers, who are not often granted a larger perspective, tend to see at close range the savagery of war. Watching the Yankee soldiers charging Fort Donelson, Rives thinks of "a horde of shining ants" (85). Later, as part of the conscript guard, Rives, even more detached, compares the squealing of the "recruited" boys to the "shrill squeaking" of rats (308). Especially in prison, the soldiers tend to view their fellow men as animals. Because the Union men treat them so inhumanely, the

Confederate prisoners are forced, as animals would be, to concentrate on survival. Starving, they catch and eat rats or dogs (292, 335); when they try to escape, they are mercilessly butchered—their bodies left to rot in the open (291).

If man's need to survive does not reduce him to an animal, the soldiers' shared purpose, at the very least, makes them subservient to their grim hunt. A Federal general's aide appraising Birge's sharp-shooters realizes that these men, now hunters of men, take almost an aesthetic pleasure in a good day's shooting. Having lost their individuality, the marksmen move alike and even look alike, so much has their common pursuit marked them (81). The Confederate cavalrymen also become hunters who have surrendered themselves to the discipline and esprit of the company. Before the battle of Chicka-mauga, the boy Henry Dunbar sees the men ride past: "these men, moving secretly through the woods, were not soldiers. They were hunters, hunters who had chased the same quarry so long that they had come, all of them, to look alike" (234).

Moving smoothly and quickly from one perspective to another, the omniscient narrator renders the complexity of war. Ashley Brown admires the way that this shifting point of view fuses two levels of action, "public and private." Praising especially the climactic battle scene in which the narrator shifts from Rives's eyes to those of General Bedford Forrest as he seizes the colors from the dying Rives, Brown observes, "Rives' tragedy is caught up in the larger action of which Forrest is the representative, and for this to be credible Forrest must participate in the pathos himself. This Miss Gordon accomplishes through her adroit shift in the point of view, the technical feature peculiar to the novel."[33]

Another fusion of public and private worlds, which has not been examined adequately, is the juxtaposition and merging of war scenes with domestic ones. Those who stay at home—Mrs. Allard, Cally, Jim Allard, and especially Lucy—comment on the changes war brings and measure the heroism of their soldiers. Because of the war, people can be classified as "those that'll fight for what they think

33. Ashley Brown, *"None Shall Look Back*: The Novel as History," *Southern Review*, n.s., VII (1971), 493.

right," as Cally says, or "those that don't think anything is worth fighting for" (340). And the omniscient narrator allows us to examine the psychology of even those who will fight for nothing except their own self-interest.

Appropriately, then, Jim Allard describes for us the home scene in fall, 1864, when it is becoming increasingly apparent that the South is losing. Unlike his brother Ned, who has been fighting for the Confederacy, Jim favors business interests and economic competition and has married into the family of the town merchant. Jim's physical handicap and selfishness have preserved him during the war so that now he represents the ascending power. He still has the energy to take over the society that the returning veterans can no longer preserve. Cally accuses Jim of being "no better than a spy or a deserter" for refusing to sell coffee to a customer who has only Confederate money (330), but Jim replies angrily: "You think so much of being an Allard, but let me tell you something, Madam. You'll see Allards doing lots of things you never thought to see before you're through with it. You better be glad one of us has got enough sense to keep a roof over your head" (331).

Through Cally's eyes we also see the same period. Her outrage is an index of her brother's betrayal and the ruthlessness of his practical-mindedness. Moreover, it is Cally who reprimands Love for flirting with Arthur Bradley, Jim's brother-in-law, while she is still wearing mourning for her dead fiancé George Rowan. Later when she learns that Love is planning to marry Arthur, Cally wearily admits, "They say we're losing the war. I reckon if we do people like him'll rule this country. You may be glad, Miss, that you married a Bradley. . . ." (340–41).

Although Cally realizes that Jim and the Bradleys will prosper, she despises anyone like Arthur who has not fought in the war and is willing now to take advantage of the fall of the old order. Despite the kindness of Arthur's father, Joe Bradley, in allowing the Allards to stay in one of his cottages at no expense, Cally resents the debt of gratitude he exacts and loathes him as a reminder of the family's dependency: "I hate him . . . I wish he was dead. Dead and rotten" (327). Yet Cally's curses on Bradley's "spry old back" (327) are useless. As Stuckey notes, in Caroline Gordon's fiction "the superior man is destroyed because of his superiority. The cautious or self-seeking man always survives."[34] Whereas Bradley still has vitality, Cally's father has become senile and paralyzed by the stroke brought on when the Yankees set fire to the family home. The ascendancy of those like her brother Jim and Joe Bradley only reminds Cally all the more of the loss of the South's best men.

The close examination of domestic life permitted by these various points of view discloses a society threatened from without and within. Walter Allen overlooks the importance of these scenes when he writes: "This is a heroic novel in the strict sense. It contains no consideration of the causes of the War, no criticism of the warring parties, no analysis of the motives of those engaged in the action. It is haunted by images and premonitions of death; its theme is duty and the heroic attitude in the face of death and defeat." Allen claims that Caroline Gordon does not evaluate the Old South and isolates slavery as one moral issue which is never examined. Focusing on Lucy's complaint that the slaves have all deserted the Allards since the Yankee troops entered the area (128), Allen reveals the character's limited attitude to prove that Gordon only "unwittingly" reveals "the moral corruption that was fundamental to Southern society, the negation of human rights on which it was based."[35] True, the novel is concerned with analyzing the dynamics of heroism, but approximately half of the chapters are reported through the points of view of family members at home; the novel's scope is larger than Allen admits. If the southern characters do not regard slavery as a moral question, it is because they are too preoccupied with their own survival to question the values upon which their society is founded. This is a profound failing, but it is psychologically appropriate. The Confederates say they are defending their homeland; they do not claim to fight for some abstract system of values. In fact, before Rives goes to war he realizes, "it was not a question of slavery" (25). On the other side, the Union officer who righteously informs Mrs. Allard, "I don't hold with slavery" (156), is, ironically, the same man who supervises the

34. Stuckey, *Gordon*, 31.
35. Walter Allen, *The Modern Novel in Britain and the United States* (New York, 1964), 113, 114. For a similar judgment against northern abstractionism, see Gordon's short story "The Forest of the South" and Melvin E. Bradford's "The High Cost of 'Union': Caroline Gordon's Civil War Stories," in Landess (ed.), *Short Fiction*, 113–29.

demolition of the Allards' home. Thus, Gordon very "wittingly" shows the failure of both sides to examine the discrepancy between their ideals and their actions.

Lucy, whose point of view predominates in the domestic scenes, gives us the best understanding of the complexity of heroism. That war dehumanizes is not denied. Tending the wounded, she realizes the sacrifice required. As she holds a hemorrhaging captain, she is surrounded by men agonizing in death; in another room a doctor is amputating a man's leg: "The terrible loud groaning kept on. Once a man's high voice cut across it. 'Shut up, Joe! They got to do it.' There was a cry after that more bestial than any of the others and then that too died away into a faint whimpering that might have been made by an injured dog trying to go to sleep" (216). And when the captain dies, Lucy cries not so much for him as for her husband whose death she now knows is inevitable (219–20).

Lucy sees how war can reduce men to animals but also appreciates the sacrifice her husband will make. Intuitively, she knows the absurdity and nobility of his action. As Susan Allard reads aloud the letter describing Rives's death, Lucy looks out at the landscape and her imagination reconstructs the paradox of heroism:

> "He was killed instantly while carrying the colors forward against the enemy."
>
> "Instantly," Lucy said.
>
> She had been staring at the dark woods that rimmed the horizon. They took strange shapes, a boy in a peaked cap fleeing a giant along a forest road, a man on horseback contending with a dragon. She turned around. The letter had slid from Susan's lap to the floor. She was bent forward, sobbing.
>
> "She has never seen him die before," Lucy thought. (377)

William Stuckey has noted a similar element of fantasy earlier in the novel—a "sinister fairy tale quality" in Rives and Lucy's trip to Georgia. Pointing out such conventions as the dark forest, the arrival at dusk, the barking hounds, and the hooded woman in the cottage that is to be Lucy's home, Stuckey compares Rives to "an innocent robber-bridegroom leading Lucy to death." At the conclusion, that fairy-tale quality enters again in the images of the giant and the dragon that Lucy perceives. The comment Stuckey has made in the earlier context has bearing here: "In the fairy tale, the bridegroom turns out to be sinister; in Miss Gordon's novel, it is life itself." Like David against Goliath, like Saint George against the dragon, or like any of their mythical archetypes, the soldiers have participated in a primal conflict and proven themselves the stuff legends are made of. Although is is impossible, ridiculous even, for a man to fight a dragon or a boy to take on a giant, the hero braves the insurmountable, for as Caroline Gordon herself writes, "that has always been the task of the hero, the confrontation of the supernatural in one or other of those forms which men of every age have labelled 'monstrous.'"[36]

Identifying the source of the title, Jane Gibson Brown explains its significance in terms of this definition of heroism: "In Nahum [2] : 8, the war is depicted as lost because the men flee from the battle and only the heroes stand." But this biblical description of the fall of Nineveh is also important for the implicit parallel between the fall of the Assyrian empire and the fall of the Old South. The war not only tests the men who fight on both sides, it assesses a society grown comfortable in affluence and power. Furthermore, the biblical allusion is significant for its prophetic tone: like Nahum who foretells the end of an empire that has subjected other nations, the narrator of *None Shall Look Back* describes the ruin of a region whose economic system is based on slavery. The South—blind to its internal weakness—becomes easy prey for the increasingly powerful, self-serving capitalists. In *Penhally*, old Nicholas Allard refuses to endorse a war that he feels was fought for economic gain, and his intuitions are to some extent correct. Indeed, as Walter Allen comments, at the end of the war, "the only survivors . . . are the commercially minded."[37]

The narrator's "prophecy" of the South's fall comes from the hindsight of history; her tone, though less declamatory than a religious prophet's, is equally authoritative. In a contemporary review Mark Van Doren praises this nonintrusive method: "*None Shall Look Back*, as I have said, is all detail. This may be why certain persons of my acquaintance have found it difficult to read. I do not see why it should be, but they say it is; and I fancy it is because Miss Gordon has not stepped out of her story from time to time and led them by

36. Stuckey, *Gordon*, 50–51; Gordon, "Cock-Crow," 562.
37. Jane Gibson Brown, "Early Novels," 111; Allen, *Modern Novel*, 113.

the nose, or by the foretop."[38] However, as we have seen, Caroline Gordon's seeming objectivity always implies a judgment.

That the title of the novel comes from one of the biblical books of prophecy suggests again the serious duty of the author. Examining without sentimentality the nature of heroism and criticizing those who fail to live up to heroic standards, the author as omniscient narrator manipulates time and point of view to provide a complex and significant comment on the historical action, recreating, as Jane Gibson Brown phrases it, "an heroic past for a generation in need of heroes."[39]

Aleck Maury, Sportsman

Here come the hunters, keepers of a rite.
—JOHN CROWE RANSOM, "Antique Harvesters"

Aleck Maury, like the sportsman Cousin Edmund in *None Shall Look Back*, has no time except for hunting and fishing. Though Cousin Edmund does not regard himself as "a solitary" (52), Aleck Maury realizes that his life of sport cuts him off from society. Obsessed by "the old, desperate desire for time, more time," Maury decides not to waste his treasured hours on people and chooses continually to pursue what for him is nearly a religious experience—the "peculiar" and "almost transfiguring excitement" of the chase.[40]

Identifying *Aleck Maury, Sportsman* "as almost the prototype of the novel-of-experience," William Van O'Connor places Caroline Gordon in a line of twentieth-century writers, beginning with Henry James, who treat extensively the innocent's confrontation with the reality of experience. Caroline Gordon, O'Connor writes, "is able to cast a cold eye on excesses, to compare expectation with event, theory with experience, and especially to show us Time as antagonist."[41] Although critics have not developed the role of time in the other early novels, many have analyzed Aleck Maury's obsession with time. The

38. Mark Van Doren, "Fiction of the Quarter," *Southern Review*, III (1937), 168.

39. Jane Gibson Brown, "Early Novels," 111–12.

40. Caroline Gordon, *Aleck Maury, Sportsman* (1934; rpr. New York, 1971), 226, 223, hereinafter cited parenthetically in the text.

41. William Van O'Connor, "The Novel of Experience," *Critique*, I (Winter, 1956), 42.

relationship of his roles as sportsman and as narrator have not, however, been adequately discussed.

Caroline Gordon has noted that her original, preferred title for the
novel was "The Life and Passion of Aleck Maury," and surely—as
Lucy in *None Shall Look Back* realizes of Cousin Edmund—Maury's
commitment to sport is anything but frivolous. For Maury, deeply
concerned with the passage of time, knows he cannot delay or stop
his movement towards death. Nonetheless, he is determined to make
the most of his life, devoting himself to a *carpe diem* philosophy with
all the seriousness of an epic hero. However, Maury's persistent defiance of time does take him outside the community: he is an irre-
sponsible husband and father; and he is a scholar not because of any
strong ideals of education but because reading the classics gives him
pleasure and teaching allows him to make an adequate living. Maury,
finally, is faulted for his selfishness and his unfeeling detachment from
the people around him.[42]

Yet Aleck Maury is also, as Frederick McDowell recognizes, "a
man of imagination." And Gordon seems to have a special affection
for this character based as he is on her own father, for of all the
protagonists in her early novels, only Aleck Maury is allowed to tell
his own story and in that telling to dramatize the major conflicts in
his life. Although Maury reveals his own limitations when, to borrow
William Stuckey's example, he forgets details about his family life or
reports them in a "half-abstracted, bemused way," he is on the whole
a reliable and entertaining narrator. Despite his failings, he does distinguish himself by his efforts to be a man both of action and of
imagination. And so, he differs significantly and admirably from the
Harry Morrows who would turn education into an industry or the
Stephens who make learning a dry intellectual exercise.[43]

Perceived by many critics as a modern Ulysses or Aeneas, Aleck
Maury strives to follow a code of honor in spite of the society disin-
tegrating about him. He has special knowledge that enables him to
make his life meaningful. Jane Gibson Brown, for instance, who calls
Maury a "twentieth-century hunter, a contemporary counterpart of

42. Caroline Gordon, Afterword to *Aleck Maury, Sportsman* (New York, 1934; rpr.
Carbondale, Ill., 1980), 289. Louise Cowan develops the concept of Maury as epic hero
in "Aleck Maury," in Landess (ed.), *Short Fiction*.
43. McDowell, *Gordon*, 18; Stuckey, *Gordon*, 35.

Orion Outlaw," remarks that Maury "is saved from Orion's aimlessness by a classical education which reminds him all too painfully of what has been lost." Aleck, then, is like "other heroes of twentieth-century fiction in that he finds a private code to give his life meaning in a society dominated by industrial 'robber-barons.'"[44] While the professor does not depend on his classical education to give meaning to his life, his foundation in the history and literature of another age does provide him with a perspective that an uneducated, often uncontemplating man like Rion Outlaw cannot have. Through imagination Maury appreciates the mysteries of the natural world and the magnificence of human history, that tradition of ideas and values preserved in what Rion might disdainfully term "book-learning." In addition to his imaginative capacity, Maury differs from Rion and from his twentieth-century contemporaries in his knowledge of time. Instead of ignoring the fact of human mortality, he defines his life in a noble stance against death.

Comparing *Aleck Maury, Sportsman* to *Penhally*, William Van O'Connor recognizes that both novels "deal with trying to stay the hand of time."[45] The stature of the man of action in *Penhally* declines as the ideals for which the hero fights become increasingly untenable. Yet, unlike the sentimental Emily Kinloe or Chance Llewellyn who violently protests his disinheritance, Aleck Maury does not fight against the decay of southern culture. He has never been content with the values society thrusts on him: his quarrel with time is a more personal one.

The structure of the novel, which calls attention to the theme of time, also focuses on Aleck's artistic and imaginative powers. As William Stuckey observes, the "loose, episodic" quality of the book is "deceptive, for the events of Maury's life have been carefully arranged to emphasize certain qualities in Maury and to give his story a dramatic structure." Though *Aleck Maury, Sportsman* is a first-person narrative, it is not mere character study, which Caroline Gordon disdains. In a letter to William Stuckey, she explains Ford Madox Ford's response to one of her early stories: "When he read it . . . he said

44. Jane Gibson Brown, "Early Novels," 15. Among others who have portrayed Maury as a modern Ulysses or Aeneas are McDowell, in *Gordon*, 17–19; and Louise Cowan, "Aleck Maury," in Landess (ed.), *Short Fiction*.

45. William Van O'Connor, "Art and Miss Gordon," in his *The Grotesque*, 174.

merely, 'Humph, that's ver' nice.' 'I realized later,' she says, 'what was the matter with it. It was not a story. Nothing happened. Like many first efforts it was simply *about* a character.'"[46] Certainly Maury's reminiscences are more than nostalgic description. The drama of *Aleck Maury, Sportsman* is in his gradual realization that his ideals of the hunt are too limited.

Except for those few occasions when his wife's health worries him, Maury does not think of others but spends as much time as possible either hunting or fishing or at least planning an excursion. During his youth, hunting initiated Aleck into the world of men, but as he grows older and especially after his leg begins to fail him, Maury turns increasingly to fishing, a pursuit that usually takes him out alone.

By himself he enjoys the natural world and his sport more. Indeed, the pleasure of contemplating nature and the ability to hunt down and lure game are related, since both pastimes demand disinterested observation and creative thinking, skills that Maury developed in his classical training. Early in his life when Aleck moves in with his uncle's family at Grassdale, he discovers that "Life at Grassdale— masculine life—was centred about sport" (56). So keen are the young boys on sport that they go ratting when there is nothing else to do. Yet concomitant with the growing sense of male identity is Maury's appreciation of the secret pleasures available through hunting. In Maury's account of his first hunt, the private spiritual aspects of the experience are more important than the initiatory purposes: "I think that life, the life of adventure that is compacted equally of peril and deep, secret excitement, began for me in that cabin [the cabin of Rafe who first took Aleck hunting] when I was about eight years old" (7).

As Aleck Maury ages, he prefers to hunt alone: "I used to love fox hunting but looking back on it I see that it was for me at any rate a boy's callow love, founded on excitement and the sense of rivalry. The hullaballoo, the shouting, the looking back to see if So and So is following you over that fence—that is all very well when the blood runs freely through the veins and excitement is the breath of the nostrils. But as I have grown older I have learned to take my pleasure more subtly. I like better now to hunt alone" (149). Maury's age makes him slow down, of course, but his motives for hunting and

---

46. Stuckey, *Gordon*, 34. Gordon's letter, May 5, 1968, is quoted *ibid.*, 13.

fishing alone are more complicated. When Burn Lorenz accuses Aleck of fishing by himself so that nobody can steal his methods, Aleck admits that Burn is right in part. Because he has spent years experimenting, Maury wants to keep his knowledge to himself (203). That pursuit of knowledge, finally, is a private avocation that compels him to shun company.

Maury's efforts to learn the habits of his prey approach a contemplative, even aesthetic enjoyment. When, for example, the young Aleck discovers a recipe for sucker bait, his excitement resembles the thrill he felt in translating a passage from the *Aeneid* that his father could not decipher (15). Appropriately he copies the recipe on the flyleaf of his first copy of the *Aeneid* (23–24).

From his uncle James, Maury learns early that sport is the pursuit of secret knowledge. After his uncle discovers that quail cannot be raised in a confined place (because the cocks will fight each other to death), he remarks to the boy that "a man—a sporting man he meant, of course—might observe every day of his life and still have something to learn." Strongly affected by his uncle's words, Maury tells how he "was fired with a sudden, fierce desire" to know the "secret life" of the animals around him: "To this day that desire has never left me. I never walk through the woods or stand beside a body of water without experiencing something of that old excitement" (57). Truly, that joy in contemplating the secret life never leaves Maury, and throughout the course of the novel, he is continually observing nature—describing the spawning of bass, for example, or explaining the habits of quail (85, 149).

His imaginative impulses lead Maury outside of the self to seek an experience that Stuckey compares to both religious devotion and art: "Maury, however, is more than an ordinary fishing enthusiast: he is an artist, not a romantic artist, to be sure, but the kind of artist Miss Gordon herself might be expected to admire. He is passionately devoted to discovering the techniques of fishing and hunting that will make him a master of these arts. Indeed, for him, the pleasure of a sport comes as much from the mastering as from the exercise of the craft, though ideally the two are joined."[47] His curiosity and close observation bring Maury close to understanding the natural world,

47. *Ibid.*, 38–39.

but nature's secrets seem part of a larger inscrutable reality so that, ultimately, Maury's disinterested sportsmanship allows him to participate in greater mysteries. Properly humble, Maury admits that his skill in hunting depends, to a large extent, on luck; he prides himself only on his perseverance, not on superior knowledge or ability. "I had known from the first that it [finding the transfiguring excitement in the chase] was all luck; I had gone about seeking it, with, as it were, the averted eyes of a savage praying to his god. But I had brought all my resources to bear on the chase. I had used skill and caution—nobody but myself knew what patience I had always expended on my careful preparations for my sport—and I had succeeded as few men, I told myself now with some arrogance, had ever succeeded" (224).

Maury's appreciation of the sacred quality of knowledge is close to the Thomist views summarized by the philosopher Jacques Maritain, later a friend of the Tates and an influence on Caroline Gordon's work. Even at this early date, her affinity with Maritain's Thomism is evident. Maury seeks a "transfiguring" knowledge and effaces himself in the search as would any sincere catechumen. "To know is to *become*; to become the non-I," writes Maritain.[48] Maury's curiosity and his desire to master seemingly insoluble problems are lifelong traits, remaining with him even when he appears to have given up fishing. After he retires from teaching and temporarily quits fishing, he turns his energies to fish breeding and invents ingenious devices for feeding and controlling the stock.

His need and urge for sport return and motivate him to quest again for the choicest fishing spots. Maury, however, does not sustain a similar enthusiasm for and commitment to classical study. Certainly he enjoys reading the classics and seems to turn to them, at least obliquely, for comfort—the class is reading the final chorus of *Oedipus Tyrannus* the day after Molly's funeral—but his attitude towards classical studies is a practical one: "Poor Molly had always wished that I would take more interest in my work but I could not do it even for her. My feelings were, perhaps, reprehensible but they were practical. Very soon in my career I realized that Latin and Greek were dead languages in more ways than one. I myself had loved them

48. Jacques Maritain, "On Human Knowledge," in his *The Range of Reason* (New York, 1952), 12.

in my youth and I would instruct young men in them as long as any young men could be found who desired instruction but it was becoming more apparent all the time that fewer and fewer young men desired instruction" (198).

Compared to Harry Morrow, the assistant at the seminary in Oakland, Aleck is much less ambitious (144). Years later, it is Morrow who offers Maury a job at his school, Rodman, in Popular Bluff, Missouri. Yet Aleck Maury does not look on Harry's position as a significant advance. In fact, when Molly begins to speculate how Harry has changed over the years, Aleck compares the development of Harry's character to that of a pollywog—completely predictable (188). Harry's ambition is his most consistent characteristic. He is a friend to Aleck as long as it is convenient. After Lawson Selby, the railroad tycoon, endows the school with money for a new classics department and "an up and coming" classics scholar, Harry—always the businessman—asks the professor to retire (222).

Maury also exercises more imagination and independent thinking than his son-in-law Stephen, Sally's "scholar," as he patronizingly terms him (242). This conflict between the sportsman and the intellectual, which Frederick Hoffman calls one of Caroline Gordon's most interesting concerns, reveals itself in this early novel in the sharp contrast between the vital Aleck Maury and his somewhat stuffy son-in-law. Steve is like *Penhally*'s Douglas Parrish in that, as he categorizes and intellectualizes, he robs the life from the objects and phenomena he perceives. When, for instance, Steve comments on the dogrun in the Potter place, which he and his wife are considering renovating, Maury recalls a dogrun he knew as a child, and his memory is much more vivid than Steve's book-knowledge:

> Queen and Rattler and Old Muse lay snoring there through the longest day and anybody who wanted to go through this open hall had to step over them. But Uncle Sam would have got after them pretty quick with his blacksnake whip if they had intruded into his and Aunt Mahaly's bedroom. I thought of Uncle Sam and wished that Steve might have seen him in his prime and then I reflected that after all it was a good thing that Uncle Sam was dead or he and Old Rattler and Old Muse—and Aunt Mahaly to boot—might have been clapped into a museum. (276)

Both daughter and son-in-law are stereotyped intellectuals (good-humored caricatures of Gordon herself and Tate), but at least Steve appreciates the stream at Caney Fork that Maury sees as promising. Although he wishes that they could take off a few days to fish, Steve will not, however, make the time for sport. He feels "pressed for time" because they need to find a house (281). In contrast, Maury advises that they leave the stream because "You can't do any good, fishing, unless your mind's settled" (281). Steve's is the response of a dilettante.[49]

"I'm seventy years old . . . this November I was seventy years old" (286): these words mark the professor's unhappy awareness of another important difference between himself and his son-in-law—Steve is only twenty-eight. Immediately following this exclamation, Maury slips away from Sally and Steve, who are so busy planning to restore the old Potter place that they forget Maury's needs. Calculating how long repairs would take, Sally has said to her father, "It wouldn't kill you to go without fishing three months, would it?" (285). Yet three months away from his sport could kill him, and so Maury feels he must escape from his unsympathetic daughter and son-in-law.

Since Maury tells his own story, his consciousness of time becomes all the more striking, for he decides what times in his life have been most significant and creates out of these events an artist's pattern. Ironically, Maury's narrative more strongly defies time than his actual efforts. Art preserves the past, making it immediate to its readers; moreover, Maury's story will last as long as there are people willing to hear the tale. A criticism of his own efforts to outrun time, the narrative records the impossibility of defeating the natural movement towards death and suggests the need for more enduring structures.

Although the creative process does not supply final answers, it provides the matrix and method for the quest. A distinction Maritain makes between the speculative reason of the philosopher or scientist and "poetic knowledge" is useful here in explaining Maury's eventual

49. Frederick Hoffman comments on the conflict between the sportsman and the intellectual in both "Caroline Gordon: The Special Yield," *Critique*, I (Winter, 1956), 33, and *Art of Southern Fiction*, 38. William Stuckey analyzes Sally's insensitivity to her father's needs, in *Gordon*, 37; he also mentions that Sally and Steve—the prototypes of Sara and Steve in *Strange Children*—are caricatures of Gordon and Tate, p. 41.

failure as an artist. Most often Maury knows through observation and conceptualizing, not through poetic intuition, which Maritain defines as the knowledge of the artist "who, in order to reveal to himself his most secret being in a work that he produces, is given in his creative intuition or emotion, through the impact he receives from reality in the unconscious life of the spirit and the depths of subjectivity, a non-conceptual knowledge of the things of the world and their secrets."[50] Only on a few occasions does Maury experience a timelessness that reveals the inadequacy of his ideals of sport. The fall that Molly is expecting their first child and, many years later, after Molly's death, Maury's anxiety and grief force him to question the feasibility and worthiness of his race against time.

While he and Molly are waiting for the baby, he is unable to fish or hunt; in fact, he seems to lose his identity so overwhelming are his emotions: "There are times in every man's life when he does not seem to be living, when every faculty is held in suspension while he waits for events to shape themselves. It was like that with me, those last few weeks. I could not follow any of my usual pursuits. I could not even think with my own mind. I could only wait and wish it were over" (117). Much later in his life, after Molly has told him that she must have an operation, he feels again that "it was as if time had stopped" (216). Waiting at the train station for Sally and his mother-in-law Mrs. Fayerlee, Maury experiences that "feeling of timelessness," in which the present seems to exist apart from time's continuum (217). He recalls how the doctor's voice, asking him to bring Molly to the hospital, had reiterated "now": "Not the following day as had been planned, or even this evening . . . But now . . . *Now*, I said to myself and tried to think what this present that I was living through was . . ." (217).

The same day that Sally and Mrs. Fayerlee arrive, Molly dies. Instead of speaking of his emotions, Maury records without elaboration how the time passed, giving the date of Molly's burial and telling when the family departed for their separate homes. The following Monday, he returns to school to teach the chorus from *Oedipus Tyrannus*. Even as the students translate, the professor seems unaware of the significance of death (219). The student who mistakes θήνητον

---

50. Maritain, "On Human Knowledge," in his *Range of Reason*, 17.

(death) for θνητόν (mortal) should make Maury realize that his wife's death is a reminder of his own. The timelessness that he feels in these anxious waiting times prefigures the eternity of death.

Too numb to feel his loss when Molly dies and incapable of contemplating his own death, Maury seems paralyzed and abstains for several months from his greatest pleasures, hunting and fishing. Even two years after his wife's death, he can only force himself to go down to the river (220–21). The "transfiguring excitement" that the hunt had always guaranteed him is no longer enough: "These last few weeks out on that blue river when I had found myself over and over wondering dully why I was there, why I should be doing this particular thing had been the first time in all my life it [sport] had ever failed me" (224).

Eventually he conquers his despair and comes to enjoy sport again, but Maury never finds values to provide meaning where sport has failed him. The "real grandeur of soul" that Aleck ascribes to his aunt Vic is not his own (55). He has discipline and commitment—qualities that were hers as well—but not her religious belief or her unselfish love for others: "She was a truly religious woman and spent a great deal of time in prayer. She must have got up early in the morning to attend to her private devotions for she kept busy all morning with household affairs and our lessons were sandwiched in between the giving out of provisions, the doctoring of sick negroes and a thousand and one duties" (55). In contrast, masculine life at Grassdale was, by definition, a life of sport, not of service to others and to God. As a boy Aleck learned to regard the spiritual life as the woman's concern and to view the man's role as the assertion of self against whatever forces bind the human spirit, including the strictures of religious training. Aleck and his cousin, therefore, are constantly devising ways to circumvent the studies and religious devotions Aunt Vic sets for them. In certain of the short stories, Caroline Gordon develops this theme more particularly: Maury is repeatedly withstanding women who try to keep him from his sport and to bind him with social conventions and obligations.[51] In the novel itself, the society that teaches its young boys to aspire to be men of action does

---

51. "To Thy Chamber Window, Sweet—" and "Old Red" are two examples of stories in which Maury resists the demands that women make on him.

not really encourage any allegiance to a spiritual reality. Maury is unusual in coming as close as he does to perceiving forces greater than the self, but the near religious devotion he exercises in sport does not meet all his spiritual needs. Like Rion Outlaw, Maury faces the death of his wife and recognizes that his ideals as a man of action are inadequate. He cannot, however, honestly comfort himself with religion as could his aunt Vic.

The short story "The Presence," written many years after *Aleck Maury, Sportsman*, dramatizes his final appreciation of his aunt's faith. William Stuckey discusses the addition of this later story to the Maury narratives in light of Caroline Gordon's conversion to Roman Catholicism and views "The Presence" as a "rewriting of Aleck Maury's old dilemma": "In the earlier stories, Aleck Maury was frequently depressed by the prospect of death, but he always managed to find some way to cheer himself up, usually through sport. In 'The Presence,' Maury is made to face the issue and is not permitted any earthly consolation. Indeed, he is faced with a meaningful death but is denied the power to unlock the meaning."[52] Even without Caroline Gordon's later clarification of his spiritual condition, it is evident that, for all his imagination, Aleck Maury finally does not have the resources to remove himself out of time, though the story he tells more successfully controls time than his own efforts as sportsman. Poetic knowledge is akin to the perception of religious insights, according to Maritain, and for Caroline Gordon, too, Maury's inability to intuit spiritual truths becomes an artistic failure as well.

"Art and poetry cannot do without one another," writes Jacques Maritain: "By Art I mean the creative or producing, work-making activity of the human mind. By Poetry I mean . . . that intercommunication between the inner being of things and the inner being of the human Self which is a kind of divination."[53] In Maury's striving to communicate that "transfiguring excitement" of the hunt, he directs the reader towards an experience larger than the single self and becomes—more fully than even Stuckey delineates—the kind of artist Caroline Gordon would admire. But Maury is not a poet, too. He

52. Stuckey, *Gordon*, 132.
53. Maritain, *Creative Intuition*, 3. I have used this definition for its conciseness, but Maritain distinguishes between art and poetry in much earlier works, such as "On Artistic Judgment," in *Range of Reason*, 19–21.

is a good storyteller who, in reviewing his life, perceptively confronts the inadequacies of his role as sportsman. If he does not perform the role Gordon later assigns the poet—"to serve, praise, and worship God"—Maury courageously faces the insurmountable forces in life and pushes the human frame to its limits.

Although his commitment to sport provides a flawed ideal, Maury's escape to Caney Fork at the conclusion of the novel is still a triumph. He asserts his vitality and pursues his fishing in spite of the unthinking efforts of others to make him an old man. The stance is, as Louise Cowan rightly observes, epical: "epical heroes endeavor to maintain manliness and courage in a communal and cosmic realm."

> Let every man in mankind's frailty
> Consider his last day; and let none
> Presume on his good fortune until he find
> Life, at his death, a memory without pain.

The final chorus of *Oedipus Tyrannus* is a fitting epitaph for the man who has measured life in terms of his resilient defiance of time and death.[54]

The Garden of Adonis

> God's mercy rest on Captain Carpenter now
> I thought him Sirs an honest gentleman
> Citizen husband soldier and scholar enow
> Let jangling kites eat of him if they can.
>
> —JOHN CROWE RANSOM, "Captain Carpenter"

"It occurred to me that everybody in the world except me seemed to have more time on his hands than he needed" (266): so Aleck Maury complains of his twentieth-century contemporaries who, like the pioneers in *Green Centuries*, live in "ignorance of time." To compare the inhabitants of the industrializing community depicted in *The Garden of Adonis* to pioneers emphasizes the similar criticisms Caroline Gordon makes of both societies and identifies her

---

54. Louise Cowan, "Aleck Maury," in Landess (ed.), *Short Fiction*, 7–8. The final chorus of Sophocles' *Oedipus Tyrannus* is given in Greek on p. 219 of *Aleck Maury*. The translation I have cited comes from Dudley Fitts and Robert Fitzgerald's *Oedipus Rex*, in their collaborative translation *The Oedipus Cycle: An English Version* (New York, 1949), 78.

all the more strongly with the Agrarians whose tenets infuse this novel especially. As in *I'll Take My Stand*, where John Crowe Ransom defines industrialism as "the contemporary form of pioneering," in *The Garden of Adonis* Gordon's characters who endorse such "pioneering on principle, and with an accelerating speed" find themselves as unsatisfied as the pioneers in their abandonment of social and religious codes. One of the main protagonists, Jim Carter rejects the sportsman's role and the agrarian society of his youth to become, in notable contrast to a hunter like Aleck Maury, one who hunts only women and seeks his own physical pleasure above all else. Although Caroline Gordon prefers agrarian values to the narcissism of a man like Jim Carter, agrarianism does not go uncriticized in the novel: Ben Allard, the proponent of that older economic and social structure, is nearly as responsible for his downfall as those who cause it directly.[55]

Remarkable in *The Garden of Adonis* are the ironic effects that the omniscient narrator achieves with her manipulation of time. Arranging the past and present to highlight the inconsistencies and duplicities of human behavior, the narrator, as in *The Waste Land*, allows the reader to articulate the appropriate indictments. The epigraph and title of *The Garden of Adonis*, drawn from Frazer's *The Golden Bough*, attest to Gordon's affinity with T. S. Eliot and the "mythical method" he endorsed. Certainly, the image patterns of the novel are familiar to the reader of *The Waste Land*. Industrialism—represented by the machine and the capitalist—is perceived as a menace to the human spirit; the drought suggests the spiritual wasteland of modern life; and sex becomes an expression only of physical appetites.[56]

As in *Penhally*, agrarianism in *The Garden of Adonis* is an imperfect ideological and social system, but as metaphor it teaches the individual to perceive his needs in relation to other people and thus infuses

55. John Crowe Ransom, "Reconstructed but Unregenerate," in Twelve Southerners, *I'll Take My Stand: The South and the Agrarian Tradition* (New York, 1930; rpr. Baton Rouge, 1977), 15; Caroline Gordon, *The Garden of Adonis* (1937; rpr. New York, 1971), hereinafter cited parenthetically in the text.

56. For a useful summary of the title's significance, see Stuckey, *Gordon*, 55–56. T. S. Eliot's review "Ulysses, Order and Myth" was published in *Dial*, LXXV (1923), 480–83. Donald E. Stanford mentions Gordon's use of the "mythic method" in his note "Caroline Gordon: From *Penhally* to 'A Narrow Heart,'" *Southern Review*, n.s., VII (1971), xvi.

private lives with public meaning. For Gordon, the Old South is, in Richard Gray's words, "at once an example and an emblem of a common human impulse, which is the longing to inform experience with a sense of meaning, arrangement, and nobility." Those characters who defend a failing system distinguish themselves by resolutely standing against the battering of time and social change, and because the focus is not on the characters' development but on their steadfastness, the five early novels repeatedly depict the adherents of new values destroying those who believe in an established order. *The Garden of Adonis*, then, portrays an archetypal conflict between discipline and license, order and anarchy: as William Stuckey explains, "man, or the destructive element in him, is responsible for the killing of heroes like Ben Allard." [57]

Applied ironically to the twentieth-century inhabitants of this industrializing region of Kentucky, the Adonis myth helps to interweave the various subplots in the novel. Andrew Lytle complains that the characters are not developed adequately and that the book is structurally flawed, giving the effect of two novels developing "side by side with two sets of characters." Notwithstanding, the characters' lives are paralleled thematically and the episodes do illustrate a single idea—the need for regeneration in a society that supplants enduring values of love and religious faith with fashionable hedonism. So emphatic is this *Waste Land* theme that a character like Ed Trivers appears to have been introduced merely to represent the unpopular spiritual view of life. Once he delivers his sermon, he disappears from the novel. [58]

If character development is sometimes sacrificed, Caroline Gordon is intent on criticizing southern society in the 1930s by contrasting Ben Allard with such selfish, ineffectual males as Jim Carter and the Camps. Thriving businessmen, the Camps are stereotypes of industrialized life and, as such, are not examined with much sympathy or

---

57. Gray, "Acts of Darkness," 151–52, and see 157, 158, for his observations on the difficulties of treating such static characters; Stuckey, *Gordon*, 61. Gordon's 1930–1931 letters to Sally Wood record how the Tates' relationship with the tenants on their farm Benfolly and the concurrent discussions by the Agrarians (who met occasionally in the Tates' home) helped to mold her conception of *Garden of Adonis*; see "Life at Benfolly, 1930–1931: Letters of Caroline Gordon to a Northern Friend, Sally Wood," *Southern Review*, n.s., XVI (1980), 301–36.

58. Lytle, "Historic Image," 581.

given many complexities of personality. Jim Carter and Ben Allard, however, are more intriguing characters, who ironically have both contributed to the decline of the southern community.

Unlike Aleck Maury, Jim Carter feels no real devotion to sport. The hunt in the 1930s is a debased, romanticized pastime. As in *Penhally* where Joan Parrish turns the family estate into a hunt club, the women in *The Garden of Adonis* threaten to take over sport entirely: "Those rich Yankees had a way of turning sport over to their women" (129). Formerly a sportsman, Jim becomes a lady's man, then little more than a rake. Jane Gibson Brown describes him very appropriately as "a married man whose numerous sexual adventures reveal him to be an amoral predator, the human equivalent of the economic system that has destroyed Allard and Ote."[59]

Jim thinks that he can exercise his power over women, but in fact, he is controlled by them. Once he considered being a professional trainer of hunting dogs, only to give up his work with Uncle Joe Burden when his mother asked him to accept an office job in St. Louis so that he could support his sisters in style. "Don't you want to *help?*" his mother had complained to him, "Do you realize that Helen is thirteen this month and Cissy has to have a new evening coat for that dance? Transparent velvet. It's six dollars a yard" (125). Jim never questioned whether buying transparent velvet for his sister's evening coat was worth abandoning his profession as a trainer. Nor has Jim even realized what he has given up by starting to work at such an early age. Some years later, in fact, his mother warns him against sacrificing too much to his sisters: "You gave up your education for them. . . . You may not realize what that meant but I do. I wish I could make it up to you in some way but I never can . . ." (166).

Now thirty-five years old, Jim perceives that he is in danger of being emasculated by the women around him. When he begins to play tennis with Sara Camp and to linger with her and her guests around the pool, he warns himself that he could well turn into a Seely Latham: "a eunuch," a man who "didn't want to have anything to do with women, really, but . . . liked all the flutteration" (160, 158). Jim accurately diagnoses his problem—he knows that he can never "see a woman in distress without wanting to comfort her" (159)—yet he

59. Jane Gibson Brown, "Early Novels," 115.

cannot resist flattering Sara when she elicits his pity for her continual troubles with fortune hunters. He tells her, "There's nothing wrong with you. . . . And if it's any comfort to you you can take it from me: you've got a hell of a lot of sex appeal" (160).

Jim enjoys his role as comforter, though he knows he should not encourage the women to tell him "their hearts' secrets" (160). He does not want intimacy without sex, but as it turns out, he is incapable of being truly intimate with a sexual partner. Eventually, he understands that in saying goodbye to Babe Worsham, he was inordinately cruel to suggest that she had been having sex with him only because she was hoping for money. In retrospect he accurately labels his speech to her as "the basest action of his life" (179).

Forsaking a true sportsman's vocation of training dogs, Jim now participates in competitive games such as tennis or recreational pastimes such as swimming—activities that do not unify the male community, that do not demand a rigorous discipline of the self, only sound technique and the desire to win. Even in his personal relationships Jim seems a debased kind of hunter. Comparing his final scene with Babe to a hunting incident, he recalls the day he was fishing in a boat and saw a rabbit, desperate to escape a pack of hounds, dive into the river and swim "straight for the boat."

> As it got near it raised its head a little. Jim saw the thing's eye, glazed from its exertions but with a light in it. When it was near enough he picked it up and laid it in the bottom of the boat. It lay there, panting but perfectly still. The hounds came on, six or seven of them, crowding into the water. . . . He picked the rabbit up and threw it out. They had it torn in pieces before it hit the water. . . . It was the look in the rabbit's eye as it neared the boat. That girl had had just such a look in her eye that morning. (183)

It is during his honeymoon with Sara that Jim remembers Babe Worsham and how he treated her. Even here his future estrangement from his wife is anticipated. When he tries to hide his thoughts about Babe from Sara, she becomes suspicious and angry, but he does not try to make amends.

That Jim and Sara eloped one night when they were both drunk has already called into question the seriousness of their commitment.

The day after the runaway marriage, Sara's brother Joe Camp embarrassedly assures Jim that he regards his new brother-in-law as "a gentleman . . . a Southern gentleman" (182). Yet, for Jim, the role of gentleman has deteriorated until it means only preserving an appearance of civility.

The night before Jim commits adultery with Bess Watkins, he finds himself once again in the comfortable role of assuring Bess of her own attractiveness. As with Sara, his speech is a prelude to lovemaking:

> He put his hand up and ran it over her shining hair. "You have pretty hair," he said.
>
> She was crying softly. "I went back to Henry Watkins when he was in New Orleans," she said. . . . "And that last morning he said I was nothing but a clothes horse, that there was nothing to me but a mop of hair. I said, 'Well, I haven't had to blondine it yet.' That little tart he was running around with had one of these long yellow bobs. . . ."
>
> "Henry wasn't good enough for you," he said.
>
> She was crying louder. "I wouldn't care," she sobbed; "I could have stood it if he'd only behaved like a gentleman."
>
> "Henry always had a dirty tongue," he said. (190)

It is ironic that Jim, who is about to break his own marriage vow, condemns the ungentlemanly behavior of Bess's husband. When Cally in *None Shall Look Back* divided people into "those that'll fight for what they think right and those that don't think anything is worth fighting for," she provided categories still applicable in the 1930s. For Jim Carter, there is nothing worth fighting for, except perhaps for his own pleasure. In fact, when he later learns that Sara has been having an affair with Rice Bolling, he arranges to meet Rice at the club at ten o'clock. He ponders over the curiously familiar sound of their exchange, then remembers: "In the old days such remarks were preliminaries to a duel. . . . But he was only going over to the club to talk things over" (204).

Worried that he may become "a eunuch," Jim Carter is never unsexed, but he is not fully the man he could be, precisely because he is more preoccupied with sex than with honor. In the economic realm, men fear losing power by going to work for another. Ben Allard's son

Frank, who chooses to work in town, knows that his father thinks "of him as only half a man" since he left the farm (234). Frank at least is realistic in admitting that a man cannot earn a living through agriculture anymore. Ben, however, thinks that even a tenant who does not own the land he farms leads a better life than those who go into business or industry.

Although Ben virtually accuses his son of losing his values by "living in town" (232), the older man himself has unintentionally encouraged the decline of agrarianism. Like the brave but foolhardy Captain Carpenter of Ransom's poem, Ben Allard is the type of man much admired by his southern generation. "An honest gentleman / Citizen husband," Ben leads his society against the forces of disorder. Despite his heroic stance, he is nonetheless innocent, lacking in judgment, and as inadequately armed as Captain Carpenter. By treating his tenant, Ote Mortimer, as a partner, as a surrogate for the son he cannot coax to work the farm, Ben begins to lose some of the authority and respect he has commanded as landowner. When he tries to reassert his power, instructing Ote not to cut the crop of clover they have grown together, Ote kills him.

Whereas the sacrifice of a scapegoat traditionally ensures the fertility of a people and their land, Ote Mortimer's murder of Ben, the Adonis figure in the novel, foreshadows only more destruction. Significantly, Ote kills his boss because he needs money to marry his pregnant girlfriend, a motive which, as Jane Gibson Brown points out, further connects the downfall of the landowner Ben Allard with the plights of the pairs of lovers in the novel.[60] Initially, Ote returned from working in a Detroit automobile factory to find the farm a relief from the drudgery of the assembly line. The dream Ote had repeatedly while he was working up North signifies how industrialized labor tortures the human spirit: "Dead he was and lying in his coffin, only the coffin was the same board that he lay on during his working hours. But even though he was dead the chassis kept moving on over him just the same and as each chassis arrived his living hands reached up out of his dead body to screw on the bolt. The same bolt he had screwed on for eight hours a day for nearly a year. He would be

60. *Ibid.*, 133–34.

screwing it on now if they hadn't laid him off" (3). The farm, however, promises no real rejuvenation, though Ote appears at first to be moving towards a better life as he and Idelle Sheeler fall in love and plan to marry. Eventually Idelle betrays him; she runs off with Buck Chester because she is pregnant and cannot endure the disgrace of waiting for Ote to earn money for the license and a home.

Ote's potentially meaningful life has not been destroyed simply because the values of industrialism—represented by the Camps' business—have invaded the South and caused a decline in morals. As Ed Trivers declaims, men and women fail in their love for each other and individuals fail to live up to worthy ideals because humans are selfish and fallible by nature. The various subplots reveal that failures in love, like the failures in values, represent a universal condition, or as Louise Cowan states the theme of the novel, "nature itself is the inadequate garden, since it cannot sustain and nourish man, the essentially rootless plant."[61]

This lesson is underscored by Ed Trivers' sermon. Urging his congregation to consider their spiritual lives, Ed tells the farmers that the satisfaction of growing a crop of rye, for instance, "ain't nothin'" (105). The congregation sings a hymn with a similar message: "Oh, ye young, ye gay, ye proud, / Ye must die and wear the shroud" (108). Ote and Idelle, young people to whom the message is directed, are too preoccupied with themselves to attend to the verses. Throughout the sermon, as Ed describes the sexual temptation he and Mrs. Taylor had to overcome, and during the singing, Ote so eagerly anticipates another rendezvous with Idelle that he can concentrate only on her promise for "tonight"—ironic in the context of a hymn that speaks of eternity (109).

The secular world portrayed in *The Garden of Adonis* is too much concerned with temporal things, and the manipulation of time in the novel makes us conscious of its passing. Although Lytle finds the structure of the book disjointed, the flashbacks are meant to develop the theme of infidelity in love. Ben Allard's memories of Maggie Carew show that illicit love and betrayal are not new "sins." Ben does

---

61. Louise Cowan, "Nature and Grace," 21. Stuckey examines the parallels between Jim's marriage to Sara and other unsatisfactory relationships in the novel, in *Gordon*, 59.

differ from Jim, however, in his reaction to the unfaithful woman. Whereas Ben was deeply in love with Maggie and still dreams of her, once he learned of her affair he refused to see her again, insisting, "It's no use, Maggie. It's like you were dead. You are—to me" (271).

Notably, Ben remembers Maggie at the point that he suspects his daughter Letty is infatuated with the married Jim Carter: "But then the times, he had told himself on the few occasions he had permitted himself to speculate about his daughter's emotions—the times had changed. Young girls had different manners these days. Perhaps even their emotions were different" (270). Because Ben no longer applies his former standards, he encourages a change in values. The younger generation, indeed, seems to countenance infidelity or at least treat it more casually, so that Jim, for instance, seems much less morally outraged over Sara's affair than was Ben over Maggie's (213). Jim's hurt pride is stronger than any moral consideration.

Not only does Ben's flashback to Maggie permit this contrast between the men's moral outlooks, but the parallels between Maggie and Letty are telling. Ben realizes that his daughter Letty physically resembles Maggie Carew, Rose's first cousin, more than her own mother, and Letty has Maggie's temperament, too. Lacking her mother's "winsomeness" (21), Letty is a flirt, never faithful to any of the many men who care for her. Yet her father suppresses any suspicions of Letty's involvement with Jim until the two have already run away together (269–70, 289–91). Again, the pattern of the past has prepared us for this event. Like a Maggie Carew who takes her own pleasure without considering what is moral, Letty cuckolds her fiancé.

Through the point of view of Letty herself we see how strongly she desires Jim. She dwells on her memories of him. His words, which she remembers when she is alone in her room at Hanging Tree, echo again in her mind when she is with her fiancé (40, 90). Similarly Jim's memories prepare us for his promiscuity. His flight with Letty is no more auspicious than his drunken elopement with Sara. Responsible for one failed relationship after another, Jim has not even asked himself if he is at fault. We learn his history in the long flashback that takes place one morning at Letty's home, before he rises from bed and goes downstairs for breakfast. Since it is Jim's mind selecting the memories, the patterns become all the more revealing, for they reflect his repeated selfishness and insincerity in love.

There is no reason to believe that Jim Carter has learned from his failed relationships how to be intimate with and love a woman. Nor does Letty seem to have changed. The first night she met Jim, after returning from a dance with a man she did not even like, Letty entered the dark, supposedly empty house, and Jim—a stranger to her then—startled her by speaking from the dark living room. Scared at first, she let him comfort her (34). Much later in the novel when this same incident is recounted through Jim's viewpoint, we have learned of his past and identify his role as comforter with his role as seducer. By then we also appreciate the irony of the first meeting between Letty and Jim: that same day Jim had received his wife's letter requesting a divorce.

Repeatedly, love between man and woman is imperfect, and as Ed Trivers' sermon makes clear, human selfishness accounts for the failures. The only person in the novel to try to correct the spiritual depravity of his contemporaries, Ed is too undeveloped a character to be presenting a solution for all members of the society. In fact, there seems to be no character in *The Garden of Adonis* who can evaluate society, no one who invests his imagination in worthy pursuits. The energy that once might have been channeled into making the land productive is now expended in mere landscaping, as the Camps spend their money to transform their property into a prospect. Consequently, Jim finds himself admiring the beauty of their artificial lake, all the while "calculating the cost of the operations" (137). This artificial garden of Adonis is indeed a decadent one, the scene for Jim's flirtation with Sara and for the sexual teasing that eventually leads to their unhappy marriage.

The energy misdirected in creating this bower of bliss parallels the ingenuity and drive behind the Camps' successful business. Joe Camp possesses that facility for "improving" on the present and develops, with the help of a designer from the East, the "Improved Fascinex"— apparently a contraceptive, as earlier descriptions of the Camps' products would suggest (201, 132). Just as nature is remodeled according to the Camps' tastes, even the natural sexual urge—traditionally controlled by social customs and mores—is exploited by them. The billboard advertisement for their products pictures "a young girl smiling vivaciously and leaping high into the air," the captions reading, "Be as gay as the rest" and "Use Fascinex. In three sizes" (132). A sign of that mentality which makes sexual relations a question of fashion rather than of morals, the billboard suggests metaphorically the Camps' selfish hedonism.

When Jim Carter marries the Camps' daughter and joins the family business, he has most certainly betrayed the ideals of his heritage. Especially in comparison to a man like Jim, Ben Allard is a hero. He is one of the few people in the novel who can view the action through the perspective of history—meaning that has been ordered and defined by a community. But Ben's blind adherence to the agrarian system is flawed: he does not see whatever he does not want to deal with—whether it be his daughter's promiscuity or the unhappiness of his tenants. Ultimately, because he refuses to acknowledge these problems, he is destroyed.

Only the narrator offers us a large enough perspective from which to evaluate society. Especially through the manipulation of time and through multiple points of view, the ironies of the characters' searches for self-fulfillment are dramatized. Again and again the characters close to the land discover that the satisfactions the natural world can supply are only temporary, as the drought reminds them. For those who measure days by the cars passing on the assembly lines or—as Eliot remarks—by figures of "profit and loss," the pace of life and its meaning seem to be under human control.[62] In reality, the characters are trapped in chronological time with no conception of a spiritual eternity; their only comfort is to try to live in a perpetual present where satisfying immediate physical and material wants becomes the purpose of human life.

In revealing these faulty conceptions of time, the concealed narrator implies a more embracing view. William Stuckey observes that Caroline Gordon's vocation of writing "has over the years taken on the aspect of something approaching religious devotion." Not only does she strive "to efface herself as a person as completely as she can" so that the story appears to tell itself, but she carefully chooses imper-

---

62. Eliot, *Waste Land*, p. 143, l. 314.

sonal techniques that enable her as an artist to "recognize," as James Rocks explains, "some coherent pattern out of the shifting planes of a seemingly disjointed reality."[63] *Aleck Maury, Sportsman* has dramatized that being a good storyteller is not enough: the true artist allows the reader to share in an expansive vision of experience, which has been shaped by intuited order.

63. Stuckey, *Gordon*, 15; Rocks, "Mind and Art," 8.

Chapter III / The Later Novels

The Violence of Revelation

We become what we look on longest and most passionately.
—CAROLINE GORDON, *The Malefactors*

Interviewed by David Ragan in 1947, Caroline Gordon complained that her contemporaries were unable to read a historical novel: "The majority of novel readers are not capable of the effort it takes to translate yourself into another age." As public reaction to her novels, for the most part, continued to be naïve, indifferent, or dismissive, Gordon increasingly realized the difficulty of educating her readers to her methods and meaning. One of her reasons for preferring more contemporary settings and characters in *The Women on the Porch* (1944), *The Strange Children* (1951), and *The Malefactors* (1956) is evident in her remarks to moderator Louis Rubin during a panel discussion at Wesleyan College in 1960. "The word [historical] has become so debased. I wrote two novels, one in Civil War time and one in pioneer times, but people didn't know how to read them. I wouldn't like to be accused of writing what is known as an historical novel." Perhaps not only the historical but the regional material in her fiction may have restricted her appreciative readers to a small number, as Ashley Brown has suggested: "About the time that she published *The Women on the Porch* Miss Gordon was beginning to doubt whether a 'regional' literature in the South would continue much longer. . . . Probably with some such feeling about her subject she has steadily widened its reference." [1]

Prompted at least in part by her desire to reach a larger audience, Gordon drew increasingly in the three novels written after *Green Centuries* (1941) on the materials of her own life, even modeling certain characters after herself, her husband, or their friends. This

1. David Ragan, "Portrait of a Lady Novelist: Caroline Gordon," *Mark Twain Quarterly*, VIII (1947), 19; Norman Charles (ed.), "Recent Southern Fiction: A Panel Discussion," *Bulletin of Wesleyan College*, XLI (1961), 13; Ashley Brown, "Achievement," 287.

quality of the *roman à clef* marks *The Women on the Porch* and, more notably, *The Strange Children* and *The Malefactors*. In some instances, when the books were published, they were read as a kind of highly crafted gossip. That these years were difficult ones for the Tates may well have invited such speculation: in January, 1946, Gordon and Tate divorced, to remarry a few months later, in April. Whatever personal exigencies shaped her subject matter, the effect of Gordon's change in style and material was to expand her analysis of heroism. In the novels, she focuses on modern individuals who marshal the resources of the intellect and the psyche in order to overcome the monsters within the self, then, having triumphed, seek to love and guide others. These modern protagonists—most of whom resemble Allen Tate or Hart Crane—are artist figures whose fictive lives dramatize on the broadest scale an entire society's spiritual stagnation and its possible recovery.[2]

In each of the three novels, the central male character is an artist who can no longer write: in *The Women on the Porch*, he is Jim Chapman, now a history professor. In *The Strange Children*, he is Stephen Lewis, a poet and intellectual with a great knowledge of southern history. And in *The Malefactors*, poet Tom Claiborne is protagonist. The narration is restricted entirely to Tom's eyes, so that first his inability to write, then his return to creativity become the overriding concerns.[3]

Critical emphasis on point of view in the novels is appropriate; for one of the main purposes of these works is to make the reader perceive reality as these major characters do, to disclose the limitations of their views as well as to show the recovery of spiritual meaning

2. Brainard Cheney provides a useful summary of contemporary reaction to *The Malefactors* and a correction in "Caroline Gordon's *The Malefactors*," *Sewanee Review*, LXXIX (1971), 360–64. Mary Sullivan's annotated bibliography is also a convenient guide to contemporary reviews, in Robert E. Golden and Mary C. Sullivan, *Flannery O'Connor and Caroline Gordon: A Reference Guide* (Boston, 1977), 191–308. Squires mentions the Tates' marital difficulties in *Allen Tate*, 178; he also mentions their separation in the summer of 1955 and their divorce in the summer of 1959, shortly before Tate's marriage to Isabella Gardner, 190–92.

3. The Stephen in *Strange Children* is essentially the same character as Stephen Lewis of *Aleck Maury*. See Stuckey, *Gordon*, 41. For parallels between Stephen and Allen Tate, see Squires, *Allen Tate*, 67–68, 97, 127–29. According to Squires, Tate was quite knowledgeable about southern history. He wrote biographies of Stonewall Jackson (1928) and Jefferson Davis (1929), and began a biography of Robert E. Lee, some of which later inspired *The Fathers*, Tate's novel about the Civil War.

through corrected vision. For the reader, then, and for the main characters, each novel climaxes in revelation. In *The Women on the Porch*,
Jim Chapman's vision of his wife's pioneer forebear attests to his waking from a deluding system of values. Stephen Lewis' vision of spiritual pilgrimage at the end of *The Strange Children* marks his development from the cold intellectual towards the whole man, whose reason
and faith work together. So, too, in *The Malefactors*, imaginative projection concludes Tom's psychological crisis. Driving back from an
unsuccessful attempt to persuade his estranged wife to return and live
with him, Claiborne nearly collides with a gasoline truck. Conjuring
up the fire that could have ensued, he confronts his own death in a
revelatory hallucination; the flames he imagines signal his reintegration, becoming through Gordon's powerful and allusive prose, a pur-
gatorial fire.[4]

For all three male protagonists, the difficulty in producing sound
art is paralleled by difficulties in their marriages. A matrix for regeneration, symbolically uniting the male and female principles of reason
and intuition, marriage—like art—is a life's work, but one conse-
crated by a vow. The climactic reunion of husband and wife, as plot
and as metaphor, discloses the protagonists' new wisdom. Growing
out of egocentricity and an unhealthy, though fashionable, schism
between feeling and thought, the central female and male characters
mature when they realize that the bond between them promises love
and a purpose to life, not dreary duty or entrapment. Thus, these
couples recognize the beauty and significance of the mundane and
transcend this world, not by ignoring it or seeking escape, but by
seeing in the objects and the experiences of this physical existence the
possibilities of spiritual order. Ultimately, each individual is able to
appreciate a larger mystery, to feel love for others, and to participate
in a community.[5]

Among those who have influenced Caroline Gordon's thought
and work, Dante, Carl Jung, James Joyce, and T. S. Eliot all hold that
the phenomenal world reveals subjective truths—a notion related to
Gordon and Tate's concepts of fiction. Their endorsement of symbolic naturalism is based on the philosophical tenet that one does not

4. Ashley Brown explains the parallels between Tom's experience and Canto 27 of
The Purgatorio, in "Novel as Christian Comedy," 173–74.
5. Brainard Cheney, in "Caroline Gordon's Ontological Quest," *Renascence*, XVI
(1963), 6, explains that Gordon uses sexual relationships to indicate spiritual development.

understand reality by merely projecting one's feelings and ideas onto the natural world; rather, one perceives that a higher order, which is "super-natural" in the broadest sense, interpenetrates the physical. In other words, the individual sees *through* nature and society to larger patterns; and this complex reality, which subsumes the physical and the psychic worlds, is timeless, though—for human minds—inextricable from immediate, concrete experience. Here, Gordon's affinity with Jung is evident. Commenting on the archetypal nature of an incident in her short story "The Captive," she has deemed Jung "much more interesting than Freud because . . . he believes that the archetype is operating right now." By her own admission, Jungian archetypes also help to form the pattern in *The Glory of Hera.*[6]

Through her preoccupation with vision in the later novels, Caroline Gordon investigates these archetypal structures and shows how inextricably linked are subjective and objective experience. Because perception is not merely eyesight but a larger awareness of the physical world, compounded by intuitions of an eternal order governing both nature and human society, in *The Women on the Porch, The Strange Children*, and *The Malefactors* Gordon often relies on exaggerated and distorted perception to suggest the importance of these intuited realities: flashbacks are sometimes hallucinatory; dreams are treated as facts, given much the same stature that Jung would bestow on them; and the imaginations of the protagonists often grant them fanciful or grotesque, but nonetheless true, images of reality. While the distortion of time and the symbolic content of these subjective experiences at first suggest dissociation, even mental collapse or immaturity, they indicate finally an enduring and universal reality that the subconscious can discover.[7]

Frequently, the protagonists who see this complex reality are artis-

6. James Joyce's term *epiphany* and T. S. Eliot's *objective correlative* have meanings compatible with Gordon and Tate's symbolic naturalism. Baum and Watkins, "'The Captive': An Interview," 453. Gordon comments on the Jungian influences in *The Glory of Hera*, in Stanford, "From *Penhally* to 'A Narrow Heart,'" xvi. The impact of psychoanalytic theory on Gordon's conception of human development is also evident in Gordon, "A Narrow Heart: The Portrait of a Woman," *Transatlantic Review*, n.s., III (1960), 7–19. *House of Fiction*, especially the second edition, provides additional, earlier examples; see the commentary on Andersen's "The Shadow" (64–66), as well as 430, 382, 384, in *HF*.

7. Jung remarks, "I have . . . made it a rule to put dreams on a plane with physiological fact," in "Dream-Analysis in Its Practical Application," in his *Modern Man in Search of a Soul*, trans. W. S. Dell and Cary F. Baynes (New York, 1933), 6.

tic, in keeping with Jung's observation that the poet "knows that a purposiveness out-reaching human ends is the life-giving secret for man; he has a presentiment of incomprehensible happenings in the pleroma. In short, he sees something of that psychic world that strikes terror into the savage and the barbarian." There is nothing reductive in Jung's choice of words: "the savage" and "the barbarian" are examples of original or primal man—one who is not protected by "the shield of science and the armour of reason" and consequently is closer to subjective truths. Similarly, Gordon stresses the universality of experience between more "primitive" peoples and moderns, even implying in *Green Centuries*, for example, that there is more beauty and directness in the rituals and faith of the Indians than in those of the pioneers.[8]

Analyzing the grotesque, William Van O'Connor has described this "American genre" as "seeking, seemingly in perverse ways, the sublime." Although his list of American writers manifesting this concern does not include Caroline Gordon, her preoccupation with the visionary affiliates her with other contemporary southern writers who employ the grotesque to correct the prevailing dissociation of feeling and thought. Gordon's characters may not be actual freaks as are, say, Cousin Lymon in *The Ballad of the Sad Café*, Hazel Motes in *Wise Blood*, or Popeye in *Sanctuary*. Yet she does share with these writers what William Van O'Connor defines as a belief "that man carries in his unconscious mind not merely wilfulness or the need to indulge himself, but a deep bestiality and dark irrationality."[9]

Jim Chapman's anger and jealousy turn him into a kind of monster in *The Women on the Porch*, so that he nearly strangles his wife. But the grotesque quality in Caroline Gordon's fiction is less often expressed in such outwardly violent behavior. More frequently there is a violence of revelation—a psychic explosion as an old way of seeing the world is destroyed and a more comprehensive meaning is perceived. As in Eudora Welty's fiction, for example, where subjective and objective worlds seem to collide whenever a character tries to control reality, to limit it by reason or by rationalizing the inexplica-

8. Jung, "Psychology and Literature" in his *Modern Man*, 188, 187. For Jung's definition of primal man, see "Archaic Man," in his *Modern Man*, 143–74.
9. William Van O'Connor, "The Grotesque: An American Genre," in his *The Grotesque*, 3, 17.

ble away (*e.g.*, "The Green Curtain," "A Memory")—dreams, memories, and intuitions in Gordon's novels attest to a psychic reality that cannot be permanently repressed without irreparably damaging the individual.

The strength with which the repressed subconscious erupts not only indicates how much violence the individual has done to his psyche in damming up such powerful forces but also serves as a measure of the true awfulness and awesomeness of those forces. Carl Jung describes the terrible encounters that the visionary work of art seeks to record: "The primordial experiences rend from top to bottom the curtain upon which is painted the picture of an ordered world, and allow a glimpse into the unfathomed abyss of what has not yet become." A confrontation with and an appreciation of mystery is the final result. Paradoxically, that recognition of human limitation is also the realization of human possibility—"the life-giving secret for man." [10]

A novelist who strives to convey this "presentiment of incomprehensible happenings in the pleroma"—moreover, a Christian novelist whose faith urges the individual to recognize human limitations and accept a greater ineffable order—has the difficult task of revealing in everyday life a transcendent reality. In attempting to share revelation, the novelist's aims are akin to those of the prophet. So, Flannery O'Connor defines "the prophetic vision" of the novelist as "a matter of seeing near things with their extensions of meaning and thus of seeing far things close up. The prophet is a realist of distances, and it is this kind of realism that you find in the best modern instances of the grotesque." [11]

Since the novelist perceives a reality that others do not acknowledge, her efforts to portray that vision often necessitate shocking the reader—through exposure to the freakish, the violent, the crazy, the terrible. Flannery O'Connor thus justifies her use of the grotesque: "The novelist with Christian concerns will find in modern life distortions which are repugnant to him, and his problem will be to make these appear as distortions to an audience which is used to seeing them as natural; and he may well be forced to take ever more violent

10. Jung, "Psychology and Literature," in his *Modern Man*, 181.
11. Flannery O'Connor, "The Grotesque in Southern Fiction," in her *Mystery and Manners*, 44.

means to get his vision across to this hostile audience. . . . then you have to make your vision apparent by shock—to the hard of hearing you shout, and for the almost-blind you draw large and startling figures." In a letter to Flannery O'Connor, written in November, 1951, Caroline Gordon remarks similarly on the younger novelist's freakish characters: "But homosexuality, childishness, freakishness—in the end, I think it comes to *fatherlessness*—is rampant in the world today. And you are giving us a terrifying picture of the modern world, so your book is full of freaks."[12]

There is an important distinction in Gordon's thinking between a keen-sighted writer like O'Connor who exposes the freakishness in the world and a freakish writer who projects his distorted vision as the true picture of reality. For example, Gordon insists that homosexuality be depicted as an aberration and cites Proust as an author who does just that.[13] In other words, the novelist is responsible for portraying a moral universe and for revealing as abnormalities what she regards as moral and spiritual failures. *The Strange Children* as well as *The Women on the Porch* and *The Malefactors* fulfill these aims by labeling "homosexuality," "childishness," and "freakishness" as misguided, compensatory behavior for fatherlessness; and for Gordon, whether this fatherlessness means, on the literal level, the want of a rational and just human father or the want of an internalized faculty to direct the individual, it is ultimately the absence of divine guidance and spiritual purpose. While Flannery O'Connor's characters and plots may appear more grotesque than do Caroline Gordon's, both novelists strive to show moral "distortions which are repugnant" and to write the "kind of fiction [that] will always be pushing its own limits outward toward the limits of mystery."[14] In *The Women on the Porch*, that mystery must be perceived by both husband and wife before they can be reunited with a fuller understanding of the significance of their marriage.

12. Flannery O'Connor, "The Fiction Writer and His Country," *ibid.*, 33–34. Gordon's letter to O'Connor is quoted in Sally Fitzgerald's "A Master Class," 832.
13. See Sally Fitzgerald's "A Master Class," 831; Gordon makes a similar point in *HRN*, 208.
14. Flannery O'Connor, "The Grotesque in Southern Fiction," in her *Mystery and Manners*, 41.

The Women on the Porch

Tomorrow may loveless, may lover tomorrow make love.
—ALLEN TATE, "The Vigil of Venus"

The Women on the Porch begins with Catherine Chapman's flight to Swan Quarter, her ancestral home in Tennessee, after finding a note written by her husband Jim to his mistress. Jim's betrayal so hurts and shocks Catherine that, in effect, she flees back in time, physically and psychically retreating to the place where her husband is an alien and where perhaps he will not search for her. Returning to the home where the women—without men—sit on the porch, peculiar and estranged in their barren self-sufficiency, Catherine realizes the cost of life without true relationship between the sexes, realizes also the impossibility of escaping into the past, and eventually chooses to return to her husband.

Just as Catherine comes to understand her role in her marriage, so Jim learns his responsibilities as husband. The subplots illuminate the choices each must make: Catherine does not wish to be like her aunt Willy, whose personality is so stunted that she cannot give herself in love to a man; nor like her cousin Daphne, a grotesque character who spends her days collecting mushrooms and savoring the hurt inflicted upon her by the man who abandoned her on their wedding night; nor like the grandmother old Catherine, whose senility has trapped her in the past. Finally, Catherine must realize that her tryst with Tom Manigault, who becomes her lover while she is at Swan Quarter, contains no real possibility for fulfillment.

So, too, Jim eventually perceives that his relationship with Edith Ross is an adulterous, false one and that his marriage is a bond to be honored. In an analogous search for meaning in his work, Jim finds that the literature he teaches requires more than intelligence; it demands a felt response to the archetypal truths it embodies. By the conclusion, Jim, as an intellectual who also perceives a spiritual reality, is able to evaluate past institutions and traditions—unlike Tom, a farmer and a man chained to an inadequate tradition of agrarian values in much the same way that he is bound by his mother's wishes.

Caroline Gordon herself has called attention to the influence of Christoph Gluck's opera *Orfeo ed Euridice* on the structure of the novel. To Frederick McDowell she writes, "I was haunted by Gluck's opera . . . Both by the music and by his version of the Orpheus story . . . it was chiefly the form of the opera which impressed me. At any rate, I was conscious of parallels between the form of the opera and that of my novel." As Willard Thorp notes, the Gluck version of the myth allows Eurydice "to return to the land of the living." With this conscious use of the Orpheus and Eurydice myth, joined by the deliberate allusions to Dante, *The Women on the Porch* is structured as a descent into and a return from hell. While Jim rescues his wife from the grotesque climate of Swan Quarter, she rescues him from the intellectual hell in which he has trapped himself.[15]

Since the characters have created their own hells, they must recognize their predicaments before they can mutually resolve to cherish relationship and return to an active life. Throughout the novel, subconscious forces urge each character to confront the hell he or she has mistakenly chosen. These glimpses of chaos—through Gothic "presences," as well as dreams and exaggerated perceptions—guide the characters in choosing the proper way back.[16]

Catherine's journey to Swan Quarter is, from the first, ominously similar to a descent into a hellish world, where grotesque characters obsessed by their failures in love move and speak, and where ghastly presences of the past stir memories of unsatisfied longings. At the news of her husband's death in battle, intuitive Lucy Allard in *None Shall Look Back* perceives, as she views the natural world, the inexplicable powers that motivate men's action. Her "vision" indicates her sure grasp of deeper truths, placing one human death in perspective with some mysterious larger plan. Catherine Chapman, however, is prone to suppress such insights; and perhaps because of her efforts to ignore what her intuitions are telling her, the landscape at Swan Quarter nearly always seems haunted. Her occasional glimpse of another reality is strongly perturbing. Yet when she arrives at the old house, she does not heed the warnings given her. It is not until weeks later that she realizes how stubbornly she has persisted in losing her

15. Gordon's letter is quoted in McDowell, *Gordon*, 31; Thorp, "Southern Renaissance," 251; McDowell comments on the mutual rescue of husband and wife in the novel, in *Gordon*, 33. Caroline Gordon, *The Women on the Porch* (New York, 1944), hereinafter cited parenthetically in the text.

16. Radcliffe Squires notes the Gothic mode and the "presences" in "Underground Stream," 471.

way. She struggles towards the home, through a dark wood—a macabre, threatening place where even her own dog brought with her from New York becomes a strange, menacing creature as he moves his "snake-like body" through the bushes (9).

Suggesting her disturbed state of mind, this experience in the wood also indicates the danger of her flight. She plunges through a thicket, and "some vine that trailed from all the bushes kept curling about her ankles. It was barbed; she felt her stockings ripping; finally blood oozed from her torn legs" (10). Without a guide, Catherine is moving into some kind of inferno, but she does not comprehend where she is. Her first sight of her cousin, aunt, and grandmother is a hallucinatory omen of death: "The faces, the immobile bodies swam in western light. For a moment it seemed to her that she had never seen these women before" (11).

Radcliffe Squires has observed that in this sixth novel Caroline Gordon's "concern shifts from objective realism toward subjective hallucination. The method shifts from linear narrative toward orbicular scenes folded within scenes."[17] This quality of hallucination marks many of Catherine's ruminations and observations because she does not willingly confront her situation. Beginning in the first chapter as she travels to Swan Quarter, the repressed memories of her husband's note to his mistress thrust themselves into her conscious thoughts. However, so intense is her desire to stifle these recollections that only fragments rise into her consciousness. Not until Chapter 3, when she is settled in at Swan Quarter, does the reader learn in detail what has prompted her flight.

Although the betrayal that Catherine feels prevents her from dealing with her emotions towards her husband, in her dreams there are premonitions of her eventual reconciliation with him. Stopped overnight at a hotel on the road to Tennessee, she dreamed of being buried alive (9)—a sign, as yet unrecognized by her, of her mistake in leaving Jim. Later, at Swan Quarter during the time she is deliberating whether to return to Jim, Catherine has a "grisly dream":

> She had descended, with another woman, into a long, dark tunnel. A man, whose relationship to her was not defined, had walked between them, resting a hand on the shoulder of each.

17. Squires, "Underground Stream," 469.

> The hand was cold. That was because the man was dead, or had
> been dead and now, called back from the grave, hovered between
> life and death. . . . he walked beside her and kept his frail, intol-
> erable hand on her shoulder. She was about to shake it off when
> somebody on ahead called back to her that she must be vigilant,
> that the man's safety depended on her alone. (183)

In this inversion of the Eurydice myth, Catherine is responsible for
her husband's salvation. She tries to repress such thoughts, though
she admits to herself that she is running a risk: "If a great fissure came
in the center of your being, you might turn your vision inward" so
that "people in the outer world would become ghostly" (184). On
this night, she telephones Tom, then sneaks out of the house to meet
him. Waiting for her lover, alone out in the foggy night, she hears a
car coming and panics, expecting to be raped by a carload of drunken
men (187–88). To her relief, the driver is Tom.

Not long after that frightening episode, however, she senses that a
force has been trying to warn her of some evil. Outside in the yard,
she muses that the house has always been haunted, recalling how as a
child she had often felt presences who disturbed her play: "The presences had been then only companions whom one could not conve-
niently address. After she became a woman they had seemed at times
to menace or at least to prophesy evil. Four nights ago their voices
had driven her out of the house, into the fog, into the arms, she
recalled, with a secret smile, of her lover" (191). Despite these warnings against her liaison with Tom, Catherine continues to resist her
duty to her husband, even refusing to act on the revelation that she
can never truly love Tom. Again out in the woods with her lover,
Catherine tells him she is planning to go to Reno for a divorce. Yet by
the end of the chapter, it is clear that her relationship with Tom can
never be a mature one. Filled with images of death—the mushroom
Trompète du Mort, for example (215)—and references to Catherine's
new-felt detachment from Tom—such as her daydream of being
alone on a beach (216)—the chapter ends with an insight into Tom's
obsession with his mother: "The land is not enough for him, Catherine
thought, or his beasts or his friends or the women he will love. There
was something went before. And it is no use to tell him that his
mother is not one to awaken either love or hate. The enchantment fell
too early" (220).

The climax comes after Tom has left her there in the woods. Listening, she notices that "the hush was oppressive, as if some power somewhere had abruptly stilled all sounds. I have made a mistake, she thought, I have taken the wrong road and it is too late to turn back. Am I lost? She trembled. It seemed to her that she was alone in the woods and the glittering light had a voice . . . and the air all around was quivering with the wild, high-pitched, despairing cry that brought her to her feet and sent her racing towards the house" (220–21). What the careful reader understood early in the novel Catherine grasps incompletely even now. She, like Dante, has lost her way in a dark wood in her middle years (she is thirty-five, we learn), but unlike the poet, she has not fully realized that she is in an inferno—one of her own making.

Similarly, her husband Jim perceives only gradually how to correct his error. A man without faith or fidelity, he betrays commitments to his wife and his work. Living in a false community with those who share his condition, Jim Chapman first must see the decadence and death-in-life that surrounds him before he can regain his integrity.

Appropriately, Jim's literal movement in the book is from the city to the country and, then by implication, back to the city. Man's physical structure and social construction, the city is the image of a rational, egocentric system, now the locus of meaninglessness. Jim's present companions include members of his department at the university, among whom is his mistress Edith Ross, and several writers, most of them friends from years ago when they were all making their way in the literary world. Paradoxically, this is a community where words are cheap: "They have grown light and anybody can pick them up" (278). Only late in the novel does Jim realize that a man's *word* means nothing when his *words* have lost their potency. Recalling an anecdote about a message to the eighteenth-century governor Blount, which arrived "much stained" with the blood of the carrier, Jim asserts that language should be as valuable as life itself (278).[18]

In modern American fiction, William Van O'Connor remarks, the city is not "a symbol of civilization, and civilization is no longer an

---

18. Marie Fletcher's argument examines Catherine's choice between the sterile past, represented by Tom, and the "rootless" intellectual world to which Jim belongs. See "The Fate of Women in a Changing South: A Persistent Theme in the Fiction of Caroline Gordon," *Mississippi Quarterly*, XXI (1968), 25.

expression of natural law." In *The Women on the Porch* that certainly is the case: the city is a hell. Unsurprisingly enough, Jim's awakening to that horrible insight is due in part to a new understanding of Dante, whose works he teaches. An encounter in a restaurant with a student who is studying Dante with Jim is the context for several warnings that the scholar has lost his way. The eager student reads aloud to Jim lines from Canto 8, which John Ciardi has translated as,

> And as we ran on that dead swamp, the slime
> rose before me, and from it a voice cried:
> "Who are you that come here before your time?"

Filippo Argenti, one of the Wrathful, asks the question in *The Inferno*, and Dante responds, "If I come, I do not remain"; then he righteously curses the damned one.[19] Chapman, however, is leading the morbid and damned existence. The manner in which the first lines of the poem haunt him after a cursory reading is a sign that he is just beginning to understand his plight.

There is, moreover, some indication of Jim's major error in the allusion to the fifteenth canto, which the student says he would like to hear Chapman read. Set in circle seven, round three of *The Inferno*, Canto 15 describes Dante's sorrowful meeting with Ser Brunetto Latino, a respected writer who influenced Dante. Ser Brunetto is committed to this circle of hell for his crimes against Nature, and although Jim cannot literally be accused of sodomy, as Dante uses the term, he is among those writers who prostitute their God-given gifts and idly spend their powers in illicit and debasing pursuits.[20]

Thinking that he can escape the student and his own uncomfortable thoughts, Jim leaves the restaurant, where the noise rises "as suddenly as shrieks from Dante's damned," and hails a cab (83). However, in traveling towards Chapman's destination, the cab passes the destroyer *Normandie*, anchored in the river. We are hereby reminded that the world is as chaotic and as menaced by self-serving, greedy

---

19. William Van O'Connor, "The Grotesque: An American Genre," in his *The Grotesque*, 18; Dante Alighieri, *The Inferno*, trans. John Ciardi (New Brunswick, N.J., 1954), Canto 8, lines 31–34.

20. Robert Scott Dupree discusses the parallel between Brunetto Latino and the artist in Gordon's short story "Emmanuele! Emmanuele!" See "Caroline Gordon's 'Constants' of Fiction," in Landess (ed.), *Short Fiction*, 37.

and aggressive powers as in Dante's day. Jim's mind turns to Europe: it is September, 1940; France has already fallen, and "The Germans are dropping bombs on Buckingham Palace" (84). All too aware of this hellish world, Jim can only focus on his own impotence to alter it. Yet his ruminations subconsciously affect his behavior: he decides not to visit Edith and orders the cab driver to his apartment.

A man who has compared himself to Count Dracula—with a box full of keepsakes from his family home, which was long since sold (108)—Jim has "never felt at home but once" when, before his marriage, he lived on Eighth Avenue and was busy writing, truly creating (110–11). One night as he wanders about the city, we see some of the causes of his present restlessness and estrangement. The city constrains its inhabitants, deforming human growth. Occasionally, Jim sees through these deformities to the uglier values of the men who have created this condition. Thus, his mind leaps from the bizarre sights in his environment to memories of his affair with Edith: "An odd COFFEE POT sign, that, with the red and green dwarfs leaping over the letters. The one that leaped from T to E had less work to do than the one that leaped from E to C. . . . I don't want anything to eat, but I could do with a drink. *Seduce*. That was the word, all right. She never made any play for me" (113).

Seduce, meaning literally "to lead aside," well describes the courses Jim and others in his world have taken, for they have turned away from significant relationships and work. The extent of Jim's misdirection is illuminated by his encounter with the bum who interrupts his introspection. In spite of the repellent smell of the disinfectant on the bum's clothes, Jim invites the man to accompany him to a bar, where he buys him a drink and dinner. While the man is eating, Chapman continues to ponder what he should do about Edith and Catherine. In an internal debate between two imagined voices, one of which articulates his wife's position, Jim is surprised to realize that he does not intend to marry Edith.

Feeling some responsibility to make conversation, Chapman abruptly turns to the bum, who, in the course of their talk, recites a Latin passage on the snares of Venus to show his learning (118). In response, Jim quotes the refrain from the *Pervigilium Veneris*: "Cras amet qui nunquam amavit quique amavit cras amet." Jim has now become very aware, as he tells the bum who cannot decipher Jim's words, that he has never adequately understood the Latin himself (119).[21]

"Tomorrow may loveless, may lover tomorrow make love"—the refrain of the *Pervigilium Veneris*—gives us hope that Jim will return to his wife and to truly worthwhile work. What began as disturbed and erratic thought processes and a chance meeting with a grotesque character have led to insight. But Jim's problems are still unsolved. Leaving the bum, he takes a cab for home. Depressed, however, by morose thoughts about marriage, he sends the cab driver back uptown (120).

In a bar, Jim encounters Bob Upchurch, a former poet who is currently lecturing at universities and working on literary magazines, and Ed Ware, a newspaperman who would "have been better off if he'd stayed a leg-man" (123). Jim has already had a few drinks, so that when he meets his friends, "He had the impression that he was standing at a little distance from the table and yet his senses registered with unusual precision all that went on" (122).

This "new, critical self" (122), in a detachment exaggerated by drunkenness, notices how his friends have aged and how they have compromised their skills as writers for money. Memories of Hart Crane's death suggest from what ailment these writers suffer: "Crane, a stubble-haired, pop-eyed fellow, who seemed to live only for poetry and had ended his life when it failed him, had had a jerky, nervous voice and was an insufferable egotist" (126; see also 125). Jim has similar thoughts about Bob, whose poetry was influenced by Crane (126).

The blasphemous belief in poetry, as well as an egotism that precluded love of others, would place such poets in one of the circles of hell. Jim complains that he has been unable to write but he fails to extend his criticism to himself. "Perdidi Musam tacendo, nec me Apollo respicit," he says, which Ed Ware translates as "He has lost his Muse by being silent . . . Apollo no longer regards him" (128). This

---

21. Tate's translation of *Pervigilium Veneris* was completed in 1943. The citation in *The Waste Land* of lines from this medieval Latin poem may have brought it to the attention of the literary world. Caroline Gordon's allusion to the poem recalls the voice of *The Waste Land* poet and links Jim Chapman as a man of letters with Tate who was working on his translation while she was writing *The Women on the Porch*. Both associations call attention to the poem's relevance for modern poets. For Tate and Gordon's mutual influence during these years, see Squires, "Underground Stream."

further echo of the *Pervigilium Veneris* links Jim's writing troubles with his failure to love and nurture his wife. Though he now perceives how deep his love for Catherine is, he does not know how to get her back.

Gradually Jim persuades himself that he is on the brink of an abyss. Leaving his friends, he stands alone out in the night. While drunk, Jim is receptive to an insight he might not have permitted himself if sober. He views the inhabitants of the city as drones in a hive, dwelling in "their solitary cells" and not controlling "their own destinies." His metaphor contains a forceful truth, and his rhetoric is nearly overwhelming:

> And the queen? O City, preparing for what strange, nuptial flight! Having stung her sisters to death, she rises on rapid wing, but when the dead bridegroom has dropped from between her feathery legs she will hurtle down, past the heaped bodies of dead and dying drones. Will not the odor of decay penetrate the royal chamber . . . so that, seeking a cleaner air, she may lead her hive forth in a last flight, in which . . . they will not stop to cull honey from the apple blossom or the rose, but will continue on, an insensate mass, until, dying, falling in a great cloud, they darken with their wings the whole west? (130–31)[22]

Andrew Lytle has examined the city as archetypal symbol, exposing it in this context as a not-so-triumphant example of "the masculine impulse toward the godhead." The city represents man's power to control and shape his world; however, instead of bringing man satisfactory order and encouraging the best in human effort, it creates a deadly pandemonium of souls. Neither Lytle nor McDowell and Cheney, who also discuss the thematic impact of this passage, note that Jim is drunk when he delivers his apostrophe to the city.[23] Although his drunkenness may explain the uninhibited excesses of his

22. Considering Gordon's many allusions to Dante's *Divine Comedy*, she may very well intend in this passage an ironic reference to Canto 31 of *The Paradiso*, in which the angel host is depicted as a swarm of bees moving constantly between the Mystic Rose and God.

23. Lytle, "Historic Image," 584; McDowell, *Gordon*, 31; Cheney, "Gordon's Ontological Quest," 8.

language, it does not detract from the truth of his observation, but emphasizes his usual resistance to the subconscious.

Yet Jim needs to attend to his intuitions, for—Caroline Gordon would agree with Jung—subconscious activity not only compensates for the individual's condition but also offers some cure.[24] A dream that he remembers on his trip to Swan Quarter presents one such prognosis and remedy. After a strange fantasy about a young soldier whom he meets on the train, Jim concludes: "I am going crazy. . . . It is not so much the difficulties of my private life as pressure from without. No, the pressure comes from within. I dreamed the other night that I had swallowed the globe, and the continents, angry at being imprisoned, churned and groaned, rubbing their shores against each other. The pain was so exquisite as to be indescribable. Like childbirth, probably. At any rate it carried its own anodyne, for I have not remembered the dream until this moment . . . It has been coming on a long time, this insanity" (279). If the insanity is a personal disorder, it is also the disease of an age, as Jim's evaluation of his literary friends and as the causes of the Second World War suggest. In the universal search for value, the few who can find a worthy course of action become heroes; those who cannot act or who act only for selfish purposes are less than men.

"There is nothing like war," LeRoy Miller comments to Elsie Manigault, "We are all artists then" (227). An architect, LeRoy has produced nothing since he redesigned Mrs. Manigault's home into another Mount Vernon and became a member of her household. He should well be concerned about rejuvenating his artistic powers. Miller serves in the novel as another failed artist, one whose difficulty in creating is compounded by his homosexuality. In Caroline Gordon's view, Roy's sexual preference is unnatural, and he is associated with Ser Brunetto Latino, who has been condemned to the ring of the sodomites. Reinforcing the imagery of the novel, Catherine Chapman sees Roy as a product of the city: "What was he doing here in this warm, unstirring air? Had the city spewed him and his kind out so that they would roam even these remote fields?" (54). Not only the

---

24. Jung, "Dream-Analysis in Its Practical Application," in his *Modern Man*, 6. Jung calls the "unconscious" what we now usually refer to as the "subconscious."

creature but, in a sense, the creator of the city, Roy brings the estrangement and useless activity of the city dwellers to the country.

Unlike Roy, who seems unable to motivate himself to work and is finally expelled from Big Pond because he seduces the black houseboy, Jim begins to seek significant action to remedy his stagnation and despair. He is regretfully aware that he is too old to join in actual battle: "I was too young for the last war and am too old for this war. But I wish I was one of them, for it is something, in this life, for a man to know where he is going, even if the appointment is with the minotaur" (286). Actually, Jim does arrange to collect some information for the State Department on his forthcoming trip to Italy (271). His responsibilities, however, have not been completely filled by his effort to serve his country. Instinctively he feels this; so, with his travel arrangements completed and ten days remaining before his boat sails, he catches a train to Tennessee, deciding not to notify Catherine of his arrival until the next morning.

Jim's "minotaur" is less tangible than enemy soldiers. As his dream of swallowing the globe suggests, the battle is within. He must fight against those internalized values that make him neglect his soul for the unworthy pursuit of pleasure and commercial success. On the train he meets a young man, Edmund Napier, and becomes engaged in a conversation that again stirs up a swarm of irritating thoughts. Jim is so exasperated at the young man's self-satisfaction that he is outrightly rude to him. At one point he briefly envisions Napier stepping "agilely on to the green, cushioned seat and from there into a plane. . . . The plane ceased to climb. . . . The face grinned as it sped past, but the torso showed a more terrible grin, the wide lips of the disembowelling wound gaping to spray upon the rejected earth Klieg lights, television sets, bomb sights . . ." (279). In this grotesque vision, the technological products of civilization bombard the earth from the disemboweled young man who has "swallowed" so much of his country's ideas and conventions.

Significantly, Jim is becoming increasingly critical of an age that assigns too little value to words and undue worth to selfish consumption of goods. As history professor, he is well equipped to measure the age against others and to call it to task.

Jim is more critical of himself, as well. Only recently has he thought of his affair as adultery, instead of "a diversion, an excursion that anybody might be permitted to make" (280). Jim can now pinpoint the moment that propelled him on his infernal journey; it was the night he became jealous of Catherine, sensing that she could have taken as her lover the painter Koenig, who had been doing her portrait. His suspicions cause him to perceive her as someone completely unknown: "The woman with whom he had been in love, to whom he had been married for years, had disappeared, leaving a stranger in her place. He had regarded the stranger with aversion and had set out to win another woman" (280–81).

Without analyzing his fear that Catherine's feelings towards him could change, that she could prefer another man, Jim refuses the responsibilities of his marriage. He understands the seriousness of that action now in his acute depression, perceiving himself as "suspended precariously over an immense pit" (281). When a marriage is endangered, the individuals whose souls have been committed to that union are menaced too. Jim "strove to realize that he was falling, and could not. She was gone and since then he had been absent from himself. Was the sexual act surrounded with mystery because it was, in essence, magical? Did the woman who once truly received a man become the repository of his real being and thenceforward, witchlike, carry it with her wherever she went?" (281). Previously insisting that he was a scholar, not a gentleman (115), Jim has deliberately divorced his intellectual powers from his emotional and moral self. His impulsive trip to Swan Quarter begins his movement towards psychic reintegration as well as literal reconciliation with his wife. The rebirth that his dream of the continents has prefigured is at hand.

In the country, then, Jim shows himself to be a caring husband whose humility and respect for Catherine indicate his effort to reconcile spirit and mind. Moreover, in realizing what mysterious forces operate within a marriage and within the human soul, Jim taps psychic powers that move him to prophesy, to judge his age and its myths, and to call for love and fresh vision. Yet violence must precede the revelation, for Catherine, in spite of her intuitions and guilty conscience, is stubbornly resistant to reconciliation.

When Jim arrives at the Carthage station near Swan Quarter, he sees Catherine waiting for him and "she seemed to him the embodiment of all that was desirable" (286). This renewed sexual passion signifies Jim's strong urge to be reunited with his wife, but any talk of that is thwarted by Catherine's plans to visit the Manigaults on the way back from the train station. Finally when the estranged couple do arrive at Swan Quarter and Jim learns that Catherine intends for him to sleep in a separate bedroom, he humbly asks her, "Aren't you ever going to forgive me?" His wife rather spitefully confesses that she has been living with Tom Manigault for three weeks, and she challenges her husband with "Do you want me back now?" (299). Jim loses control. He tries to strangle her: "He had taken hold of her because he wanted only one thing, not to be alone in the abyss into which her words had plunged him" (300). Only when her frantic hands tearing at his wrists make him conscious of his action can he break himself out of his trancelike violence.

This near murder is not merely a sign of Jim's strong jealousy; it testifies to his desperation when he sees Catherine abandoning him. Important here is the image of the abyss, prevalent throughout the novel as metaphor for Jim's dangerous psychic condition. Earlier Catherine had intuited that a person with a "broken heart" risked succumbing to a narcissistic self-preoccupation during which other people became like ghosts. By her husband's action, she is nearly plunged into the next world, but the violence of Jim's behavior pulls her out of her ghastly self-absorption. Instead of remaining with Catherine, however, the reader follows Jim outside where he roams alone through "the deep woods" all night long (303).

Jim's wanderings in the woods mark the real resolution of his psychological crisis, just as Dante's meanderings eventually lead him to Virgil, then Beatrice. In this scene Gordon clearly intends no simple contrast between the city and the country as metaphoric homes for the human psyche. Jim himself is his own hell, to borrow a Miltonic formulation. His values and his perceptions determine the estrangement he feels, or they make communion possible. One of the "living dead" like Count Dracula and an estranged wanderer like Cain, Jim has never felt at home in any place because he was searching for the wrong kind of refuge; and in his aimlessness, he unfortunately has preyed on others.

Having nearly killed his wife, Jim flees from the house, insisting, "I do not belong anywhere. There is no place anywhere that is a part of me" (303). Stopped to rest beside a spring, a symbol in Gordon's work of regenerative possibilities, Jim recalls the horror of the last hour, "like the man who, snatched back from a precipice, collapses on the ground for a moment, then tip-toes back and peers over the edge, fathoming the depths of the abyss in order to convince himself that he is safe" (304). As night draws on, he considers, then rejects suicide, but his self-absorption is interrupted by revelatory hallucination. Jim thinks he sees on the opposite bank a man wearing a pack. Surmising this vision to be the image of Irish John Lewis' son, Catherine's forebear who settled the land, Jim addresses him, "I would advise you not to settle. . . . The land is cursed. It is an old land, ruled by a goddess whose limbs were weary with turning before ever Ireland rose from the sea. An ancient goddess whom men have wakened from an evil dream" (306, 308). In the furor of prophecy Jim warns of a homelessness of the spirit: "It is No Man's Land. . . . That is the enchantment. The land will turn brittle and fall away from under your children's feet, they will have no fixed habitation, will hold no one spot dearer than another, will roam as savage as the buffalo that now flees your arquebus" (308). But this pioneer "will not listen." Assuming gigantic stature, the figure—who represents all American pioneers—advances across the stream to find his land. Jim stumbles into some dank spot between two poplars and sleeps.[25]

Jim's prophetic vision corrects the past for its pursuit of a delusory dream, the dream Caroline Gordon defined at greater length in *Green Centuries*, published three years before *The Women on the Porch*. Man cannot re-create Eden either in the wilderness or in the city. He reclaims his spiritual birthright not merely by cultivating his own plot of land or by drudging away in his little cell. He must seek relationship with others and, together, make a pilgrimage through time.

The mundane but highly important gestures of relationship be-

25. The image of the abyss is important in the work of both Gordon and Tate. See Squires, *Allen Tate*, for an analysis of Tate's poetry and fiction. Squires investigates Gordon's use of water as an image of spiritual regeneration in "Underground Stream." Brainard Cheney identifies Cleena, the goddess Jim Chapman addresses in this vision, as a Gaelic goddess "who created the delusion of a land of perpetual youth, a utopia" for those moving westward. See his essay "Gordon's Ontological Quest," 9. That Jim sleeps between two poplars may very well indicate his heroic stature. Robert Graves notes that the black poplar is a tree sacred to heroes and, according to legend, the white poplar or aspen is the tree from which Heracles fashioned a wreath for his head after killing the giant Cacus. See *The White Goddess: A Historical Grammar of Poetic Myth* (2nd ed.; New York, 1966), 105, 193.

tween Jim and Catherine conclude the novel. Joining his wife in making a pot of coffee, Jim perceives that their life is imbued with a significance that makes even small actions meaningful:

> "These old-fashioned pots make excellent coffee," he said.
> "Yes, if you take the time."
> Time, he thought, but what else have we got? . . . It will crush us, and he remembered a day at the beach when they had waded out past the ropes and had stood, waiting for the great, mounting swells to lift them from their feet and rock them like sea gulls on the waves. She had never been a strong swimmer and was always reluctant to bathe in the surf, but he knew that each swell . . . would . . . leave them standing together . . . , and he would take her hand and compel her to stand beside him. (312–13)

Tom Manigault's affair with Catherine does not promise such an enduring commitment, something Catherine has finally acknowledged. We learn that Tom has visited Catherine during the night "to find out what was going on" between the husband and wife (311). Catherine told him nothing—excluding him now from her life with Jim.

At this point in the narrative, Catherine's aunt Willy returns home to report that her stallion Red, which she had been showing at the fair, has been accidentally electrocuted in his stall. Willy, who had turned down the trainer Mr. Shannon's marriage proposal earlier, is now pathetically bereft of hopes for anything but a solitary, unfulfilled life. Scared of intimacy, Willy reacts to Quent Shannon's proposal as she did to the freak show at the fair—where the sight of the man and woman married in a block of ice repelled her (256–57). Ironically, in refusing relationship, Willy has condemned herself to a cold and confining solipsism; thus, her failure in love is a poignant foil to Jim and Catherine's just salvaged intimacy.

Outside in the yard a snake still moves, Caroline Gordon notes, suggesting that temptations and selfish impulses have not been eradicated from the world. However, Jim's gesture—kissing his wife's bare instep—acknowledges his new-felt love and sense of duty towards her. His authority and caring, now revitalized, allow him to speak for both of them: "'Come,' he said and heard all the echoes stir in the sleeping house. 'We will bury him [the stallion], as soon as it's light.

Then we must go'" (316). They will return to the city, where—it is implied—they will work together.

"You must remember it's a circle we're traversing—not necessarily vicious." (22). So Jim Chapman once remarked to Aunt Willy, speaking specifically of "old John Lewis' second childhood." Although one character in the novel, old Catherine, does return to the past in her senility, for the others the circles are more metaphorically the completed patterns of their lives—variously felicitous or unfortunate. The image of the circle suggests again the influence of Dante's *Divine Comedy* on the novel: for some, the circles are rounds in hell, self-created infernos. Others escape—transforming those closed spheres of solipsism into symbols of the eternal, into the spiraling steps towards greater spiritual reality.

The Strange Children

I saw how it was.
—CAROLINE GORDON, *The Strange Children*

Quite appropriately, the dedicatory epigraph to *The Women on the Porch* cautions, "Without doubt no man who sees only with his eyes can know anything of what has been here described."[26] *The Strange Children* (1951) continues Caroline Gordon's interest in knowledge gained not through the eyes alone but through intuition and nonrational experiences. Again the climax of the novel is revelation. Unlike *The Women on the Porch*, however, *The Strange Children* implicitly argues that spiritual insights are best articulated and given form by the Roman Catholic church. Kevin Reardon, a recent convert to Catholicism, profoundly affects the values of the Lewis family, the central characters in the novel.

Noting the effect that Caroline Gordon's conversion had on her fiction, Frederick McDowell remarks, "In her two latest novels [*The Strange Children* and *The Malefactors*] . . . she continued to value an ordered social existence and a sympathetic understanding between

26. Gordon cites the original Greek. This translation is from Hippocrates, "The Art," in W. H. S. Jones (trans.), *Hippocrates*, Loeb Classical Library (1923; rpr. Cambridge, Mass., 1967), II, 209. To preserve some of the Greek play on words, Stuart Curran has suggested to me a more literal translation: "For anyone seeing just with the eyes there is nothing to be known (literally, 'seen') of these questions."

human beings even while she became increasingly Christian in emphasis." Yet, McDowell is quick to point out, "as a writer Miss Gordon is the inquiring moralist even before she is the religious writer."[27] Just as her use of classical myth allows her to disclose archetypal patterns in every age, so Gordon's Christianity gives shape to the universal search for religious meaning and expresses human responses to the ineffable.

Her endorsement of the church, like that of several writers who were her contemporaries, developed from her wish to see embodied in ritual an order that is both social and religious. Tate, who joined the church not long after his wife, shared this desire and, as a man of letters, called for society to admit the same need. Hugh Holman summarizes: "Tate felt that the South should have been Catholic; his essay on religion in *I'll Take My Stand* is an argument with his fellow southerners against establishing an ordered world that lacks a religious frame. . . . The anguish of the soul, he felt, could not be assuaged by the introspective groping of the individual. Yet he was, with the exception of his wife, Caroline Gordon, and Ransom, unique in this persistent cry for a religious structure for his world." Tate's essay in *I'll Take My Stand* (1930) expounds the "whole" view of life in which abstraction, responsible for "the death of religion," is no longer idolatrized, but myth, embodied in concrete particulars, supplies "immediate, direct, overwhelming" images that help discipline the mind and make possible the contemplation of religious truths.[28]

Fittingly, Ashley Brown has emphasized the influence on Gordon's later novels of such religious poets as Dante and T. S. Eliot.[29] The novel, customarily the magnifying glass of the everyday world, when focused to show Gordon's complex view, reveals the spiritual world as it is reflected in the mundane. Her choice of point of view more particularly determines the quality of that image of objective and subjective realities. Perhaps of all of Caroline Gordon's novels in which point of view is so important, *The Strange Children* has been

27. McDowell, *Gordon*, 6, 45.
28. C. Hugh Holman, *The Roots of Southern Writing: Essays on the Literature of the American South* (Athens, Ga., 1972), 184; Allen Tate, "Remarks on the Southern Religion," in Twelve Southerners, *I'll Take My Stand*, 156.
29. Ashley Brown, "Achievement," 287. See also "Novel as Christian Comedy," 161–78, in which Brown thoroughly explores the influence of Dante on *The Malefactors*, noting that the novel was "originally subtitled *A Comedy*" (162).

most scrutinized for the skillful way in which Lucy Lewis, the young daughter of Stephen and Sarah Lewis, functions as third-person limited narrator. Although there have been a number of valuable close readings of the novel, none has examined in detail Lucy's powers of vision or the way that her point of view concentrates the tensions in the novel between enthrallment and freedom.

Lucy's imaginative powers are so great that through her we can see the progress of a soul as it moves from intimations of a supernatural reality to faith and vision. Frederick McDowell has already observed how the fairy tale *Undine*, which Lucy reads over the course of the novel, parallels the action: "Like Undine, Lucy acquires a soul and learns of both the sufferings and the satisfactions which knowledge brings." Through her exposure to the fanatical snake handlers but most of all through her contact with Kevin Reardon, a devoted Catholic, Lucy learns that her conscience—synecdochic for her spiritual life—cannot be ignored. Her lesson suggests in miniature the growth of such adults as Kevin Reardon and Sarah and Stephen Lewis, and contrasts with the failures of Tubby MacCollum, Isabel Reardon, and Uncle Fill Fayerlee.[30]

Lucy, more adult in some ways than her parents and their friends, has the gift for seeing through actions to real intentions and meanings. She also is more empathetic than others and has, in essence, the imaginative ability to project herself beyond her own small vantage point. In her intuitions, truth is often expressed in hallucinatory, dreamlike images, as when, for example, she reflects on her parents' habit of criticizing their friends and imagines them literally tearing people in pieces: "She closed her eyes in order to see more clearly the green sward that surrounded the house littered with the dismembered bodies of visitors: a head tossed into the honeysuckle vines, an arm draped on a stalk of yucca, a pair of legs that had collapsed on the path that went down to the river."[31] Her criticism of adults frequently crystallizes in such concrete images. Thus she perceives the "vicious circle" of the adults' constant drinking as a kind of monster, "lower-

---

30. McDowell, *Gordon*, 35. Robert A. Heilman views Lucy's progress as a "miniature" of the adults' pursuit of truth, in "Schools for Girls," *Sewanee Review*, LX (1952), 302.
31. Caroline Gordon, *The Strange Children* (1951; rpr. New York, 1971), 30, hereinafter cited parenthetically in the text.

ing at her from under beetling brows, its full, voracious mouth twisted a little to one side" (171).

Lucy's perceptions of herself are telling as well. She thinks of herself as a changeling, a word that her mother actually uses jokingly to account for Lucy's physical features, which do not resemble those of either parent (54). Yet Lucy accepts the label because it sets her apart from the adults, just as she habitually insists that she will never be a writer like her parents (90, 173). More importantly, the connotations of the term *changeling* emphasize Lucy's extraordinary ability to understand some people and events better than her parents can. She knows, for instance, far more about the McDonough family (the tenants on the Lewis' land) and their religion than do the intellectual adults. Also, she perceives more about Jenny, the black cook, than her parents, who are usually too busy to think about others. When Lucy imagines herself in Jenny's place, she conjures up an amazingly vivid scene:

> She liked to stand on the little porch and imagine what it would be like to be Jenny. . . . Jenny kept the shades down, night and day. It was always dark inside and smelled of carnations, the flower Jenny loved best. . . . Over in the corner was Jenny's dressing table, covered with blue silk ruffles. On its glass top stood a velvet box that was full of the jewels Jenny's beau, Mr. Stamper, had given her: pearls and diamonds and rubies and garnets and sapphires. Jenny would turn the box on its side so that they all spilled out on the glass, and put the rings on her fingers or drape the necklaces and bracelets over her smooth, dark arm. (70)

Similarly, as Lucy listens to Tubby, Sarah, and Stephen speak of their time together in Paris, she creates a scene, in this instance, imagining a location and objects she has never actually seen: "She had been in Paris then, with her nurse, but when they talked about how after supper they would go out in the bay and, wearing special glasses, dive to look at the flowers that grew on the bottom of the sea, she could see the flowers, too: pink and blue and purple, star-shaped, some of them, others round, like little Banksia roses" (43). Lucy's imagination has nearly magical properties, but her perception of the divine needs strengthening.

Although Lucy can sense unseen forces in the natural world, she does not always distinguish clearly betwen fanciful illusions and truer intuitions. Her changing reactions to Kevin Reardon and Tubby MacCollum map her growth from childish play to a more mature imagination. Before her first meeting with Kevin, Lucy is more interested in fancy. Amusing herself out-of-doors, she sees the crape myrtles lining the walk as "guardians": "In the fading light one of them took the shape of a mediaeval warrior, equipped with sword, shield and streaming plume. A few feet away from him a shorter, stouter warrior half crouched for an upward thrust. The stout warrior was about to throw down his shield! No. Someone passing by had set the crape myrtle boughs shaking" (106). The passer-by is Kevin who, like Tubby, initially seems more responsive to Lucy than her father. More seriously attentive than Tubby, Kevin is also a better guardian: he teaches Lucy moral awareness. Tubby, on the other hand, teases Lucy, paying court to her until his real "Belle Dame," Kevin's wife Isabel, arrives at the Lewis home. Such allusions in the novel to romantic poetry underscore this distinction between enthralling and liberating imaginative play and clarify the dangers of mere romance.

Tubby first calls Lucy "La Belle Dame," and with him she shares her love of the fairy tale *Undine*. Innocently captivated by magic and romance, Lucy identifies very easily with Undine, a bit of make-believe consonant with Tubby's addressing her as Sabrina, the water nymph in *Comus* (17). Notably, Tubby appears just after Lucy has read the description of Huldbrand, a noble knight at first, but one whose selfishness and pleasure-seeking eventually destroy him and his wife Undine. Tubby's identification with Huldbrand becomes more explicit as his deluded infatuation with Isabel, corresponding to Huldbrand's illicit passion for Bertalda, leads him into a fatal adventure. Before the Reardons' arrival, Tubby attends Lucy, who willingly plays with him and leads him to a grove near a waterfall, which Tubby later calls "her elfin grot" (94). In her naïveté, Lucy is flattered by these references to Keats's "La Belle Dame Sans Merci." As she moves through the woods, touching a wand of plum to the leaves about her, she even thinks of herself as *"full beautiful . . . a fairy's child . . ."* (94). However, the mysterious and beautiful lady who charms the knight is also a vampirish seductress who damns him to a death-in-life. The horrible, real "Belle Dame" in the novel is not Lucy, but Isabel Reardon.

In the beginning Lucy is so infatuated with Tubby that when Kevin asks her to show him the woods she tells herself that she will never take anybody to the tree near the waterfall where Tubby carved their initials. During that previous scene, Tubby had also carved the initials of another love, thus anticipating his betrayal of Lucy and his childish obsession with Isabel. When questioned about the other initials, Tubby tells Lucy that the letters stand for Imogene Marie Louise Lointaine, his "little girl's" name (87–88). We learn, of course, that the "I" stands for Isabel. "Lointaine," which is French for "remote" or "far away," signifies Isabel's literal distance from Tubby at that time but also her exotic quality. To Tubby she is a romantic image of the seemingly unattainable and exquisitely desirable lady.

Lucy's enchantment with Tubby actually dulls her imagination, blinding her to all but what she wishes to perceive. For example, she is incredulous of the legend of Saint Martha, which her parents and the Reardons discuss (123), but she has no trouble accepting the equally fantastic story of Undine. At one point, Lucy even tries to imagine what it would be like to be in love with a woman who was a stream (172). Providing another significant insight into her devotion to romance, Lucy hides the crucifix that she steals from Kev behind the volume of the *Morte d'Arthur*, and once the sacred object is out of sight, she tries to forget that she actually stole it.

Her love of romance at first prevents her from attending to a more important reality. Ominously, when Tubby associates Lucy with the Lady of Shalott (194), he invokes the pattern of the Arthurian legends, in which the lady's unrequited love for Lancelot leads to her death and prefigures the kingdom's downfall. Lancelot "was in love with Guinevere," Isabel reminds Tubby; and Tubby, more an erring knight than an errant one, is also preparing to cuckold his lady's husband. However, the traditional links between King Arthur and Christ imply a more hopeful outcome to this love triangle. Arthur's disappearance is balanced by the promise that Camelot will be restored in the future, an analogy to Christ's expected Second Coming. Though apparently undone by his too tolerant love, Arthur eventually will be the greater winner, and likewise, in *The Strange Children*, Kevin is that hero whose faith and love will bring him glorious rewards. Though his greater service is as a tacit spiritual guide to the Lewises, Kevin has already proven his heroism by saving his wife following an automobile accident; in spite of his own severe injuries, Kevin repeatedly crawled to a stream and brought back the water that preserved Isabel's life.

While the fanciful play of a young girl is understandable, Tubby's flirting and scheming with Isabel indicates a profound immaturity. A more romantic figure than Kev, Tubby is no hero. That he later runs away with Isabel, though she is married, would be sign enough of his immoral self-indulgence, but that he has unwittingly eloped with a mad woman shows the extent of his delusion. Like the knight Huldbrand, Tubby is so bent on satisfying his passion that he cannot truly see the object of those desires. What Lucy reads in *Undine* about the knight's search in the Black Valley for his illicit love Bertalda can be applied metaphorically to Tubby's perverse romance. In the "sinister" woods, the knight thinks he sees the form of "a sleeping or swooning woman." Even though it is too dark to see her clearly, he is convinced that he has found his Bertalda and bends to her: "a flash of lightning suddenly illuminated the valley. He saw quite close to him a hideous and wasted countenance, and a dull voice cried: 'Give me a kiss, you love-sick shepherd!'" (233).

If Tubby corresponds to Huldbrand, he also resembles in some unfortunate ways Comus of the masque in which Sabrina appears. A diabolical reveler—Dionysian in his lust for drink and sexual intercourse—Tubby tempts Lucy to romantic enthrallment. The magic potion he proffers is the illusory promise of pleasant fantasy as a way of life. Although Tubby pretends with Lucy that an invisible servant is at his command (23, 67), he is no sorcerer with actual power over the imagination; instead, he is the victim of his own delusion. At the waterfall, this time with both Lucy and Isabel, he quotes "Kubla Khan" without irony: like the potentate of Xanadu, he exalts in his fanciful creations, but since he does not recognize the transitory nature of any "vision in a dream," neither does he appreciate the sublime sources to which the stream can lead him.

Tubby's danger grows as Isabel more and more assumes the role of the Belle Dame. Even before she dresses to look like Lucy—thus revealing her childishness as well as her intention to usurp Lucy as

Tubby's lady—Isabel is an enchanting figure, whom Lucy pictures even before she sees her as nymphlike (32). At her arrival, Isabel greets Tubby, imploring him, "*don't* shut your wild, wild eyes," another ironic echo of the Keats poem (95). Despite her words, Isabel's eyes—not Tubby's—are those of the enchantress: "the color of the periwinkle blossoms that grew in the old graveyard at Merry Point" (95), Isabel's eyes are another sign to the reader of Tubby's doom.

At the waterfall, Isabel coaxes Tubby to take them out in a boat. Instead of suggesting regeneration, the water here becomes the locus of further enchantment. Lucy, looking on or overhearing much of the lovers' play, thinks of her fairy tale, specifically of the episode in which "The false Bertalda had held her golden necklace above the water, to make just such a shimmer, on that voyage that she and Undine and the Knight Huldbrand made down the Danube" (198). Just as this incident marks Undine's betrayal by her knight and the beginning of Huldbrand and Bertalda's troubles, in the novel Tubby and Isabel's sporting in the water shows their increasingly reckless indulgence of their perfidy. Disastrously for Tubby, he forgets the fate of the knight who pursues La Belle Dame. In Keats's poem and, by implication, in *The Strange Children* the deluded man ends up "alone and palely loitering."

More than simply succumbing to his delusions, Tubby actively rejects the vision that could save him. He is responsible for much of the blasphemous talk in the novel, and in the game of charades (in which he insists that Parnell means a priest's mistress and proceeds to act out that etymology), his sacrilege offends Kevin deeply and sends Isabel into a mad fit (145–59). At the end, when Stephen Lewis imagines Tubby "standing at the edge of a desert that he must cross," his friend's face is "featureless, his eye sockets blank" (303). Essentially, Tubby's elopement with Isabel has condemned him to traverse a wasteland on a quest that does not promise salvation. Because of Lucy's earlier description of Tubby watching Isabel, this second image of the death's-head is all the more powerful. Lucy had observed, "The black branch fell straight across his face; his eyes were black holes in what might have been a skull; only the glass that he twirled in his hand gleamed in the light from the window" (282).

Although at first Lucy may think of herself as a changeling, "*not anybody to save*" (84), her identification with Sabrina, the nymph who releases the chaste Lady from Comus' spell, and with that other good spirit Undine indicates that Lucy is finally not the Belle Dame but the creature who gains a soul and thereby salvation. The peculiar lightness that Lucy feels after she has glimpsed Tubby making love with Isabel in the woods marks a transitional state. First, the lightness expresses her sense of belittlement and consequent self-effacement following Tubby's betrayal, and second, it signals her spiritual ascent now that she is freed from the bonds of enchantment and comprehends Tubby's perversity.

When, satyrlike, Tubby gazes at Lucy, it is clear not only that he has no use for the young girl but that he has chosen an empty vision: "The wreathed leaves fell away to reveal the brown, burnished head. Glossy as a new chestnut, the head hung motionless among the softly oscillating green leaves. . . . They [the eyes] had stared straight into hers. But his gaze had merely happened to fall upon her face. . . . And if she and the others had not stood there he would have stared straight before him in the same way, as if he were looking beyond whatever was before him, at something that was not there and never could be there, no matter if you looked all your life" (218, 220). While Lucy may not fully understand what Tubby and Isabel are doing, she knows instinctively that he has betrayed her. Running from the spot, Lucy notices "that her feet felt lighter than usual, and brittle" (218). She imagines herself floating, and when she pricks a finger as she pushes through briars, "the tiny pain seemed to augment the lightness that she still felt in her hands and feet" (219).

This phantomlike lightness reveals Lucy's disorientation as well as a kind of death. She feels unreal, as if her existence is unimportant because Tubby has looked through her. Yet an allusion to Dante's *Divine Comedy* suggests a second meaning. Lucy wonders what her companions Jenny and Lois "would say if she told them that she did not know the way out of the woods. This path they were on did not seem like any path she had ever walked on before" (219–20). Figuratively, Lucy has started on a different course now that Tubby has disappointed her. In *The Paradiso*, Dante's body is lightened as he leaves mortal limitations behind and approaches God through divine revelation. So Lucy has begun a spiritual ascent, though her meanderings in the woods now most resemble Dante's confusion at the start of his pilgrimage.

Tubby's perfidy ends Lucy's enthrallment with romance, but her spiritual maturation is yet to come. When her conscience has moved her to return the stolen crucifix to Kevin and to confess that she lied in implicating Jenny in the theft, Lucy shows that her sense of morality has won over her selfishness and that she now has some knowledge of the crucifix's meaning. Nonetheless, she is still a little girl, whose spiritual growth is limited by the maturity of her intellect and the extent of her experience.

The powerful shift in point of view from Lucy to Stephen at the conclusion of the novel acknowledges the limits of the child's mind, although the reader remains fully appreciative of that childlike blend of emotion, intuition, and reason, the receptivity to knowledge unavailable to the purely rational mind. As Vivienne Koch has outlined, because an omniscient narrator subtly intrudes throughout the novel "when the material becomes unmanageable for a child," the modulation from Lucy to Stephen Lewis' point of view does not jar. In William Stuckey's words, "Part of the author's strategy . . . is to get the reader to identify with Lucy's point of view in order to expose the limitations of mere unaided natural goodness." Yet, most importantly, the shift to her father's consciousness testifies to Stephen's final enlightenment. Frederick McDowell summarizes this point well, pointing out that Stephen "sees that he and all men have desert places to cross and that life is a pilgrimage involving both a progression and an unknown goal. Stephen at last surmounts his intellectual pretensions and his arid way of discounting spiritual experience."[32]

Just as surely as the novel exposes the snares of the undisciplined imagination, it reveals the emptiness of a purely intellectual response to life. Stephen is habitually guilty of cutting himself off from his own spirituality by transforming any such experience into material for footnotes. For example, when Sarah describes Kev's vision of Saint Martha at the car accident, Stephen tries to classify and gloss it: "He is evidently a born mystic. . . . I believe the intellectual or inner vision is regarded as higher than the apparition, which is thought to come to those whose spirits burn with a grosser flame. But there are many records of instantaneous conversion" (227). As Stephen pro-

32. Vivienne Koch, "The Conservatism of Caroline Gordon," in Rubin and Jacobs (eds.), *Southern Renascence*, 333; Stuckey, *Gordon*, 82; McDowell, *Gordon*, 36.

ceeds to tell of the conversion of Saint Margaret of Cortona, Sarah complains, "You know everything, don't you?" During the ensuing argument, she informs her husband that neither one of them has any spiritual life and faults him for resisting her criticism. "Well, you can look up to Kev Reardon now," Stephen retorts (228).

Lucy understands enough of this overheard discussion to think that her parents do not love each other any longer: "It seemed to her that her life up till now had been only a dream, a happy dream." Waking to the reality of a life without spirituality, Lucy envisions the three of them in a prison cell whose key has been thrown away—the kind of nightmare confinement in which Ugolino and his sons met their deaths (229).

A character with a more exaggerated tendency to dissect matters of faith with reason alone is Uncle Fill Fayerlee. The scene in which Uncle Fill strives to dispute theological questions with Stephen, while Tubby and Lucy explore the cave in front of which Uncle Fill sits, is an evocative and structurally important one. This episode, in the penultimate chapter, comes so near the climax of the novel that it almost seems to precipitate what follows. Later that night the Holy Rollers hold the arbor meeting at which Mr. McDonough is bitten by a rattlesnake. Afterwards, during the efforts to save Mr. McDonough's life, the Lewises discover that Tubby and Isabel have eloped; Lucy confesses to Kevin and returns the crucifix; and the action culminates with Stephen's concluding vision. The encounter with Uncle Fill does foreshadow these events by highlighting the spiritual conditions of the major characters and revealing the inadequacy of reason as the sole instrument of the mind.

Uncle Fill is a peculiar sight: the fat man dressed in white sits before a cave from which a stream flows, and a black boy pours buckets of cooling water over him (241–42). He seems oblivious to the symbolic meaning of the water that surrounds him. Similarly, in Tubby's brief excursion into the cave, although he senses the deeper magic of the place, he is not receptive enough to the regenerative powers of the stream: "'Damn it,' Uncle Tubby said, 'I'd turn spelaeologist if I stayed around here. I feel it coming over me now'" (244). Tubby does not delve very far into the cave because he is too bent on playing the cavalier, again addressing Lucy as Belle Dame in Isabel's absence. Like Kubla Khan, Tubby may intuitively recognize the sublimity of the water and the cave, but he does not realize that, in effect, these powers menace his pleasure dome.

Lucy nearly ignores Tubby during this scene. Looking out from inside the cave, she sees her parents and Uncle Fill as if framed. This curious perspective focuses her attention on them so that she overhears her mother telling Uncle Fill that they are going to Mr. Warfleet's to buy a pony, what Lucy has been begging for but has despaired of getting. As yet she does not know that Kevin is planning to buy the animal for her. When she learns this fact, her conscience goads her to return the crucifix.

By refusing to become involved in Uncle Fill's arguments against the Virgin Birth and the prophecies of Christ's birth, Stephen prepares us for his eventual reintegration of spirit and mind. Sarah, trying to be polite to her relative but also trying to suggest the importance of religion, is no match for the old sophist, who declares, "God Almighty gave me my intellect . . . and He expects me to use it. But what does the author of the Gospel of Matthew use *his* intellect for? For glozening and cozening, forsooth!" (249). Once they have all made their escape from the garrulous Uncle Fill, Steve tries to justify his rude silence. Even he cannot "take" Uncle Fill's obsession with rationality, no longer finding such excess amusing, as Tubby does (255).

For all of his litigousness, Uncle Fill raises an important point: "I tell you, the man that can swallow the God of the Old Testament has got a strong stomach. And if we can't put any credence in the Old Testament how we going to put any credence in the New?" (251–52). A God who is both destroyer and savior is ineffable and frightening, difficult for humans to accept. When Robert Heilman examines the significance of the novel's title, he explains that the characters are all "strange" in being "cut off from the spirit"; but he does not fully consider the context of the title, which comes, of course, from Psalm 144.[33] The psalm, a king's prayer for deliverance, asks God to destroy the nation's enemies and then stretch out his hand to David and his people, thus invoking the awesome and awful power of the divine.

The individual's faith must be capable of enduring the inscrutable and the terrible, for a vision of the divine is a violent and disrupting experience. The Holy Rollers, for example, show just how fearsome

33. Heilman, "Schools for Girls," 302.

the powers of God can be and how strong and tensile must be the faith that encounters him. This group of religious fanatics handle snakes during their services because of a literal interpretation of Mark 16:17–18, verses in which the resurrected Christ proclaims how his disciples may be recognized: "And these signs will accompany those who believe: in my name they will cast out demons; they will speak in new tongues; they will pick up serpents, and if they drink any deadly thing, it will not hurt them; they will lay their hands on the sick, and they will recover." Although Caroline Gordon does not necessarily argue for such a literal interpretation of the gospel, she does not question whether the Holy Rollers are responding to real experiences of the supernatural. The speaking in tongues and the visions of these farming people are not satirized. In fact, though Tubby has the advantage of education and culture, his irreverent attitude towards the Holy Rollers as well as his other blasphemies expose him as foolish. As we would expect, Kevin, Sarah, and Stephen are more respectful.

In the final chapter, the four adults and Lucy arrive at the brush arbor meeting in time to hear the testimonies. Characteristically, Tubby slips out early—to run away with Isabel. But the others attend to Mr. McDonough's account of his mysterious and awesome vision of God:

> "I passed under one of the low-swinging boughs and something touched me on the shoulder . . . and says, 'Terence' . . . 'Terence!' it says and I jumped and turned around. But there war'n't nobody there. 'Terence!' it says again and I looked up and there over my head was a million leaves. A million leaves and besides each leaf a tossel raining its golden powder on the ground, and standing there, under that tree, a shirt-tail boy that hadn't been up to nothing but mischief all his life, *I saw how it was. . . . I saw how it was!*" he repeated. "Hit war'n't leaves and tossels. Hit was *God*. God, raining down on the ground! . . . Twenty years ago this March, but it's like I never moved out from under this tree . . ." (291–92)

"PREPARE TO MEET THY GOD!," the message painted on "Holy Roller Rock" in large white letters, is, after all, a fit motto to display near the entrance to the Lewises' land; well might someone be "nervous," as Sarah says, to see those words (14; see also 240).

"The implicit tensions of the book arise from the pull among the varieties of religious experience," Robert Heilman writes. Yet Holy Roller, Roman Catholic, or skeptic may encounter the divine. The preacher in the Holy Roller meeting tells his congregation that Jesus will come to a person after he or she believes; among the assembled Steve recognizes the thought and exclaims, "Good God! . . . he's quoting St. Augustine!" (290). Gordon here insists that experiences of a larger order are essentially the same and are available to all. Some, however, are more receptive than others. Or as Heilman phrases it, "Some see light on the road to Damascus, some don't."[34]

Creativity bent on selfish pleasure-seeking and reason idolatrized to the exclusion of other kinds of knowledge are both imprisoning. When the imagination and the rational mind discipline each other, then the individual can perceive subjective and objective realities clearly. This enlightenment is liberating. Bound, however, by his own egocentricity, Tubby in the final chapter proposes a toast that foreshadows his unfortunate but self-determined end: "'We will drink to the emancipation of all of us,' he said. 'Can't tell when it'll be, but it's bound to come.' He held his glass up and made them all touch glasses with him. 'And to the day and the hour,' he said, 'for when shall we four meet again, in thunder, lightning and in rain . . . ?'" (281). Tubby's echo of the witches in *Macbeth* reminds us of his entrapment by romantic magic, but ironically he also alludes to the time when such perversity will be punished, for his references to the thunder, lightning, and rain recall the traditional accounts of the Last Judgment.

In contrast to Tubby's flippancy is Steve's revelation as he stands in the yard, hugging his daughter against him and watching a Perseid fall: "But the other stars that shone so high and cold would fall, too, like rotten fruit—when the heavens were rolled up like a scroll and the earth reeled to and fro like a drunkard and men called upon the mountains to fall upon them and hide them from the wrath to come" (302–303). The truth of Kevin's vision Stephen has finally accepted, "for all men, it appeared to him now, for the first time, die on the same day: the day on which their appointed task is finished. If that man [McDonough] had made his last journey tonight he would not

34. *Ibid.*, 302, 303.

have gone alone, but companioned by a larger presence, as the friend standing behind him [Kevin] had been companioned when he, too, lay at the point of death, in a strange country and in a desert. But all countries, he told himself wearily, are strange and all countries desert" (303). Unlike that image of Tubby as a walking death's-head crossing a wasteland alone, Kevin and Terence McDonough are aided on their journeys by "a larger presence." Stephen considers now his own pilgrimage, "and he wondered what moment was being prepared for him and for his wife and his child, and he groaned, so loud that the woman and the child stared at him, wondering, too" (303).[35]

Whatever is in store for them, it is clear that Stephen now accepts his responsibility as spiritual guide for his wife and daughter and that, as a family, they may very well have escaped that prison created by excluding spiritual reality from their lives. Nonetheless, the horrible presentiment Lucy had of the three of them locked in a cell forever has been dispelled for no simple pastoral. Like the king who prays for deliverance in Psalm 144, Stephen can only hope that he is worthy of the conflict to come and that ultimately he and his family will find meaning in their arduous journey.

The Malefactors

Sight, sound and flesh Thou leadest from time's realm
As love strikes clear direction for the helm.
—HART CRANE, *The Bridge*

Those artists in *The Strange Children* who have stopped writing or diverted their energies to less demanding literary projects suffer from a loss of vision. The mad woman Isabel has not written a poem in approximately ten years; Stephen does not write poetry any more; and although Tubby has just finished a successful poem about the Civil War and has conceptualized the next one, his immediate plan is to increase his income by writing brief histories of twelve American towns. This commercial scheme undercuts his stature as a

35. Caroline Gordon called attention to Lucy's turning from her mother to her father over the course of the novel and regretted that she did not highlight that development more. See Sally Fitzgerald's "A Master Class," 843.

poet, as does his admission to Isabel that if Steve still wrote poetry, "it would be better than mine" (197). These failures in spiritual perception are also responsible for Stephen's alienation from his wife, as well as Tubby's crazy affair with Isabel.

As in *The Strange Children*, to recover creativity and revitalize relationships the artist in *The Malefactors* (1956) must fully develop his ability as seer. In much of the imagery and in the similarity of Tom Claiborne to Jim Chapman, *The Malefactors* is also closely akin to *The Women on the Porch*. Although the narration is strictly limited to Tom Claiborne's perspective, the techniques in *The Malefactors* resemble those in the two previous novels; they are well suited to reveal an individual's growth towards a more encompassing vision of the world.

With her emphasis on point of view and the visionary—both of which interests are united in her examination of the artist's role—it follows that Caroline Gordon would be intrigued by the relationship between fiction and painting. *The Malefactors* most explicitly lays bare the connections, for Tom's maturing imagination and understanding of the world are compared to the development not only of the poet Horne Watts but also of two actual painters—Carlo Vincent, Tom's now deceased father-in-law, and Max Shull.

Her own predilection for painting, indeed her own gift as a painter, gives Caroline Gordon long and careful practice in recognizing a significant scene and rendering it through well-chosen details. But for Gordon the connections between fiction and painting run deeper. In the preface to *The House of Fiction*, Gordon and Tate call attention to the technical heritage of both fiction writing and painting: "This book differs from other short story anthologies in that it is based on the assumption that fiction is an art closely allied to painting and that, as in painting, there are certain 'constants' or secrets of technique which not only appear in the works of all the masters of the craft but which have been handed down from master to master throughout the ages" (*HF*, ix). Sharing with Jacques Maritain certain assumptions about the affinity of visual art and poetry, Gordon would agree with his analysis of the critical response to a work: "That work will appear to us as infused with the double mystery of the artist's personality and of the reality which has touched his heart. . . . We shall judge the work of art as the living vehicle of a hidden truth to which both the work and we ourselves are together subject, and which is the measure at once of the work and of our mind."[36]

Yet, while art in all its forms can supply us with a kind of knowledge, it does not grant us a complete education, nor can that knowledge exist independent of its structure. Maritain argues against any poetry that "would want to escape from the line of the work-to-be-made in order to turn back upon the soul itself, thinking to fill the soul with pure knowledge and become its absolute." This "perversion," as Maritain terms it, confuses contemplation of the unknown with intellectual forming or creating. "If, freed (or believing itself freed) from the relativities of art, poetry finds a soul which nothing else occupies, nothing confronting it, it is going to develop an appalling appetite to know, which will vampirise all that is metaphysical in man, and all that is carnal as well."[37]

Maritain cites Rimbaud as an example of the debauched poet, one who gave himself over to contemplating his own soul, with the result that he could not produce any work. Thus, while Maritain insists that poetry does respond to metaphysical needs—that is, that it also deals, though in a different way from metaphysics, with the "non-conceptualisable"—poetry as a solely inward-turning quest for spiritual reality becomes damningly narcissistic; the poet needs the outward-turning discipline involved in creating a work of art. Caroline Gordon examines such artistic perversion in the short story "Emmanuele! Emmanuele!" and, more extensively, in *The Malefactors*.[38]

In the novel, Carlo Vincent is surely guilty of this confusion about his proper role as artist. We learn that in the years before his suicide, he painted self-portraits, which Cynthia Vail describes: "In the nude, or mostly in the nude. Sometimes he wears chain armor, sometimes a plumed hat. . . . In one he's St. George fighting the dragon . . . naked" (164). Tom surmises that Carlo himself realized that he "took the wrong turn. . . . or he wouldn't have left orders for those later

36. Maritain, "On Artistic Judgment," in his *Range of Reason*, 19. Gordon comments on her love of painting in an interview with David Ragan: see "Portrait of a Lady Novelist," 18, 19. Mary O'Connor speaks of the importance of Gordon's painting to her writing in "On Caroline Gordon," *Southern Review*, n.s., VII (1971), 465.

37. Maritain, "Concerning Poetic Knowledge," in Maritain and Maritain, *Situation of Poetry*, 52, 53.

38. *Ibid.*, 58, 68; Caroline Gordon, *The Malefactors* (New York, 1956), hereinafter cited parenthetically in the text.

pictures to be burned" (147). Like the writer in "Emmanuele! Emmanuele!" Carlo Vincent's problem is self-absorption. Tom compares the painter's narcissism to looking in a mirror: "The Great Essentist! Got off by himself to show what he could do and all he did was look in the mirror" (281). Revealing Vincent's artistic perversion, this imagery also recalls Guillaume Fäy's habit of writing while facing into a mirror.[39]

Another artist figure in the novel commits suicide when he takes the wrong turn in his writing. Horne Watts, the poet whose career very explicitly parallels that of Hart Crane, is a homosexual whose search for relationship has repeatedly been unsuccessful. When Catherine Pollard tells Tom that a nun, Sister Immaculata, is writing a book about his friend Horne, he scoffs, "I wish Horne could hear that he is being annotated by nuns. . . . Don't they know that he committed suicide? Suicide is a crime against Nature. So is homosexuality. Two major counts against him, according to your categories." Replying that Watts had love, Catherine further explains, "He was trying to find God" (82). Vivienne Koch comments on the view of homosexuality that Gordon presents in this and other episodes, especially Tom's meeting with Sister Immaculata (231–42). Gordon's effort "is to effectively 'place' homosexuality . . . in the context of a larger agony—man's eternal search for wholeness."[40]

Horne's dabbling in magic is further evidence of his misdirected search for the divine, for the power that could make him whole. In her wild days before she joined the Catholic church, Catherine Pollard used to assist Horne and his friend and lover Joe Pastor in their alchemical efforts to tap the sources of creativity. Claiborne remembers, "They put ten quarts of water in a big glass jar . . . and let it stay there awhile and then they poured some wine in. . . . They were supposed to see the Dawn of Creation. . . . Horne always maintained that if they had changed the formula and put a little more wine in they would really have seen something . . ." (73). The old formula, which Sister Immaculata later shows Tom, promises to reveal "The secrets of God" or "what we're all after," as the nun observes (233).

---

39. Caroline Gordon, "Emmanuele! Emmanuele!" in *Old Red and Other Stories* (1963; rpr. New York, 1971), 39.

40. Vivienne Koch, "Companions in the Blood," *Sewanee Review*, LXIV (1956), 649–50.

Tom speculates that Horne Watts had jumped from the deck of a steamer "because his creative energies were failing" (27). Sister Immaculata proposes other motives: "He wrote about the sea all his life and he cast himself into it in the end. We all have our own ways of abandoning ourselves to God's mercy" (242). Neither explanation excludes the other: both associate Horne's poetry with a search for spiritual regeneration. Tom's memories of Horne's own thoughts about art reveal both the obsession and the duty the poet felt: "Some men are born eunuchs, some men are made eunuchs by men, some men become eunuchs for the sake of the Kingdom of God. The words were Jesus Christ's, but they came to him in Horne's voice. When he was drunk enough Horne spoke of himself as a 'holocaust.' The artist must sacrifice everything—including love of women—for the sake of his art, must burn himself up on the Muse's altar. But it was the sea that got Horne in the end, and sharks, not flames, that picked his bones" (121). As devout as he was in his service, Horne sacrificed on the wrong altar. Caroline Gordon patently exposes this kind of error in "Emmanuele! Emmanuele!" where she asserts that "an artist's first duty is the same as any other man's—to serve, praise and worship God."

Tom's dream of Horne Watts and Carlo Vincent links these two figures to his search for renewed creativity. As Tom recounts his dream to his cousin George, the psychiatrist, Tom is slowly making his way back into a dark cave in which Horne and Carlo run before him, when he meets his father sitting beside a cliff to warn him "from going over the edge" (273). Tom looks over the precipice and sees Horne and Carlo lying below, their heads torn off by the fall: "He [Tom's father] showed 'em [the heads] to me and then he gave me a look and he was about to tear his own head off, George, and throw it over the cliff . . . but I couldn't stand that. I woke up screaming" (274). In an image that is drawn from an early Tate poem—two lines of which are later quoted by George (277)—the father's head was transparent so "the skull showed right through the skin and had deep grooves in it—where the worms had been crawling" (273). Tom tells George that if he had not awakened, his father would have torn off Tom's head because it, too, seemed to be full of worms. Correspondingly, in Tate's poem "Homily" (1925), the speaker urges the listener to throw away his "tired unspeaking head":

Why, cut it off, piece after piece,
And throw the tough cortex away,
And when you've marvelled on the wars
That wove their interior smoke its way,
Tear out the close vermiculate crease
Where death crawled angrily at bay.

In his biography of Tate, Radcliffe Squires notes Caroline Gordon's use of the poem in *The Malefactors* and discusses the meaning of the image for Tate, especially in "The Maimed Man": "the headless and footless figure is offered as a premonitive symbol of a life without reason and a life . . . incapable of movement, hence incapable of moral action." Tate's poem begins with an invocation to "Didactic laurel," as Squires explains, a symbol of Apollo and "a poetry located in reason." Escaping reason, Caroline Gordon's protagonist enters the cave in his dream "by pushing aside a growth of laurel."[41]

Usually so dependent on his intellect, Tom finds that in his desperation to restore his creativity he has succumbed to a kind of madness. His repressed subconscious assaults him in dreams and hallucinations, and his reason and emotions appear to be warring. When we first meet him, drinking has already exaggerated Tom's cynical and critical tendencies and encouraged his indulgence in self-pity and depression. His wife Vera does not know how to help him. Shocked when Tom claims to hate his fellow men (100), Vera cannot adequately respond to what really worries him. When he confesses that he has not been able to work for a long time, Vera dismisses the complaint.

Tom has had difficulty writing ever since he and Vera moved into the house twelve years ago; a long poem he had begun then is now hidden in a drawer. For good reason, Tom feels as if most of him has died: "He had sat there [at the desk], day after day, hour after hour, or walked about the room, or stood looking out of the window, or had lain here on this sofa, with his eyes closed as now, sweating, sweating, until it seemed that all the sweat and all the blood had gone out of him and there was left only this dry manikin of skin and bone" (133). Nor has "this dry manikin of skin and bone" been much more

41. Tate, "Homily," in his *Collected Poems, 1919–1976* (New York, 1977), 4; Squires, *Allen Tate*, 204, 203, 204.

successful in his marriage. He resents Vera, complaining that when they married she thought that he "could change the whole world" (25). Yet what really distresses Tom is that Vera in effect abandoned him once she recognized his stagnation. Some time after he has left Vera to live with the poet Cynthia Vail, Tom tells George that it was actually Vera who left him one evening in 1934 because "I haven't been going anywhere in a long time, and my wife knows it" (280). Thus, Tom's lack of direction has prevented them from any real intimacy. The couple has never had a child, nor until George mentions it, has it ever occurred to Tom that his wife might want a family (282). Instead, Vera has diverted her energies to raising cattle, with her prize bull as her surrogate child.

As with Jim Chapman in *The Women on the Porch*, Tom's problems with his wife and his trouble writing are reflected in his distorted perceptions. When we enter Jim's mind the night that he spends drinking in the city, we become aware of realities he ordinarily suppresses: so, too, with Tom. Examining his emerging subconscious, we see the spiritual crisis he must resolve. In nearly every chapter of Part I, which takes place on September 22, 1946, the day of Vera's fair, Tom is taking a drink: to brace himself for what he expects to be a disagreeable meeting, he goes into a bar before he meets Cynthia at the train station; he takes a drink before he visits his bedridden aunt Virginia; he gets drunk at his own dinner party that night, and continues to drink when some of the company go to see Max's studio on the premises. Tom really does seem to hate his fellow men; he attempts to anesthetize himself to any encounter or exchange.

Ironically, by releasing his memories, the drinking reveals the patterns that have shaped his present meaningless life, but the imagery also implies Tom's recovery. Like Jim Chapman in *The Women on the Porch*, Tom feels that he and his acquaintances who suffer the same spiritual crisis are on the edge of a precipice or chasm (68, 274); he conceives of himself in hell (185, 189); and he compares his condition to that of the unhappy poet in the *Pervigilium Veneris* (116). Eventually, however, an awareness of his plight leads Tom to correct it. Further reinforcing our hope for Tom, the imagery of the cave, which was introduced in *The Strange Children*, is developed here. First a symbol of the "deaf unconscious" (281), the cave becomes the locus of insight, as is Plato's cave, and finally a place of worship as the dark chapel of Saint Eustace suggests.

Although Tom resolves to change his condition, he first makes another wrong turn. From a former writer Catherine Pollard—a character Gordon based on Dorothy Day—Tom could learn how to make recompense for his failures. Since Catherine's conversion, she has started a home for vagrants on the Bowery and several communal farms. When she visits Blencker's Brook for Vera's celebration, Tom is drawn to her, intrigued by the changes in her and sensitive to the power that she commands.[42]

As Tom and Catherine prepare to go into the garden to see a statue of Saint Ciannic, "he could not rid himself of the impression that they had agreed to travel together to some other goal, a goal so splendid that he had glimpsed it only in dreams and that not often" (76). Outside, Catherine gazes at Tom, and he senses that she could help him: "He felt as if he had been suddenly plunged into an element hitherto unknown. A voice said: '*Save me! You can!*' He spoke to cover the sound, saying the first thing that came into his head . . ." (80; see also 83).

Frederick McDowell quite accurately identifies Catherine Pollard as "spiritually central to the novel . . . even though the skeptical poet Tom Claiborne is the central intelligence." Indeed, the conflict in the novel is Tom's skeptical resistance to faith: he must acknowledge, as his name suggests, that he is mortal, and to transcend his plight he must accept divine grace. Illustrating this theme, Ashley Brown

---

42. Caroline Gordon also intends a comparison between Catherine Pollard and Saint Catherine of Siena, who ran hospices for the sick and poor. See, for example, *Malefactors*, 39. Brainard Cheney explains that Gordon originally wanted to dedicate the novel to Dorothy Day, but Day did not want to risk having herself and her work identified literally with Catherine Pollard and her charities. See Cheney, "Gordon's *The Malefactors*," 364. Flannery O'Connor also gives an account of Gordon's withdrawing the dedication to Day, in a letter to Sally and Robert Fitzgerald, dated February 6, 1956, in *Habit of Being*, 135. Gordon did, in fact, incorporate a number of details from Dorothy Day's life into the novel. From Day's autobiography *The Long Loneliness*, we learn that Peter Maurin, the man whose theory of a green revolution identifies him with Joseph Tardieu in the novel, compared Dorothy Day to Saint Catherine of Siena in the early 1930s when Maurin and Day were beginning their houses of hospitality and planning a farming commune. For details of their program, see *The Long Loneliness: The Autobiography of Dorothy Day* (New York, 1952).

shows the important parallels between the novel and Dante's *Divine Comedy*, more specifically *The Purgatorio*—both works "with a central intelligence, a character whose perception brings the scenes into focus and thus allows him to arrive at a proper revelation."[43]

However, as Tom's behavior with Catherine exemplifies, he resists his religious impulses so strongly that months pass before he yields to them. In the exchange with Catherine in the garden, we see that Tom knows the way to recovery but habitually suppresses or distorts this knowledge. Catherine recalls how he helped her when she discovered that she had no talent for writing and asked him what she should do:

> "You said, 'Anything! Get drunk. Join the Church. . . .'"
>
> "I spoke metaphorically, using the first words that came into my head."
>
> "I know it," she said, and laughed again. "But that was the first time it had ever occurred to me that *I* could join the Church" (80–81).

Many years ago, as now, Tom could direct a friend to religion but he seems incapable of taking his own advice. By the end of the day of the fair, more accurately at four o'clock the next morning when he suddenly awakes in Vera's bedroom, Tom is already too enthralled with Cynthia Vail to think very long about Catherine's route to salvation. Unfortunately, Tom does not realize the import of his involvement with this other woman whose name associates her with the sinister powers of the moon. Turning his back on his sleeping wife, Tom gazes about the room, perceiving that a "bunch of clothes there on the floor looked like a body, sodden and fallen in some dark encounter. Something curled like a worm lay at a little distance from one limp sleeve" (127).

That wormlike object, the withered spray of lavender that Cynthia had handed to him earlier, as well as the bunched clothes, forebode Tom's undoing. Increasingly preoccupied with Cynthia, he rises from bed and walks out on the balcony: "The moon must just have gone down. Or was that color reflected from the eastern sky? *Was that dawn?* He brought his clenched fist down on the cold iron of the

---

43. McDowell, *Gordon*, 38; Ashley Brown, "Novel as Christian Comedy," 162. Koch, in "Companions," 647, examines the significance of the name "Claiborne."

balustrade. 'They think I'm through,' he said half aloud. 'But I'm not. They'll see. I'm not through yet!' and went back into the house, pausing a second to look down at the sleeping figure he had just left, before he passed into his own room" (127–28). His affair with Cynthia Vail is such a false dawn. Tom attempts to infuse himself with creativity by becoming intimate with this young poet and by associating with other literati—in this specific case, a group of selfish and pretentious intellectuals.

Tom's efforts to revitalize his own potency are grotesquely analogous to the artificial insemination advertized at the fair. At the dinner party the evening of the fête, Tom had voiced his disapproval of such mechanical means of reproduction and accused a neighbor Joe Hess, who endorses all such scientific advances, of being not a farmer but an alchemist—someone who wants "something for nothing" (108, 109). In a sense, Tom also wants something for nothing, but he is as doomed to fail as Horne Watts, who tried to write poetry by getting drunk: "First he [Horne] got boiled, then, while playing a record over and over he laid hold of some line or image for the poem which he would start writing as soon as he recovered from his hangover. Claiborne had sometimes thought, watching Horne's antics, that it was almost as if the poem had a palpable body that floated in the air above Horne's head and that it was only when Horne was intoxicated that he became agile enough to reach up and grasp one of its members" (75). By eluding his conscious self temporarily, Horne could reach creative sources that seemed to have become dissociated from him. Yet this method of composition worked in only a limited way: although it supplied Horne with a few valuable lines for his poems, in the two years before his death he had written just "one short lyric" (75).

Tom experiences a similar splitting of his psyche. As he plunges into madness, he is aware of a voice that generally checks his destructive impulses. When, for example, Tom grows angry at Ed Archer during the dinner party and fantasizes about beating "*the living daylights out of him*," a voice argues with him: "He looked about the table cautiously. They were all madder than he—he had no doubt of that—but it was hardly likely that they heard as many voices, or rather, that they heard one voice so often. It was always one voice" (110). Throughout the novel such incidents are common, and what could be interpreted as internal debate begins to seem more and more like auditory hallucination. In a way, though, Tom is saner than many of his friends. The voice is, at least metaphorically, his subconscious pleading for help—witness, its call in Catherine's presence. It seeks to compensate for Tom's inadequacies and to show him a means of recovery: thus, the importance of his dreams and other extrarational proddings which lead to his eventual reconciliation with Vera and the quieting of his religious conscience.

Tom's uneasiness with religion has been fostered by his father. Until Tom can accept this man whom he has despised so much but emulated nonetheless, he is himself a rather despicable character. Whereas his cousin George, who spent his boyhood summers with Tom, remembers Mr. Claiborne as the foster father who taught him about heroes, Tom calls his father, "A roisterer and a whoremonger . . . [who] never did an honest day's work in his life" (276). George suggests, however, that Tom's problem is not the usual Oedipal conflict (277). Helping him interpret the dream of the cave, George posits, "Maybe your father thinks you're *too* bright. . . . Maybe that's why he wants you to throw your head over the cliff" (281).

Tom's father not only disrespected the women in his life—neglecting his wife and satisfying his sexual passions by frequenting the whorehouse in town or taking up with one of the black women on the estate—he also encouraged Tom to disdain religion. As a child, Tom feared his father's ridicule of church-going: "His father's face always wore the same expression when Aunt Virginia set off for church. 'Virginia and Tom Fayerlee turned Methodist so they could hear themselves talk,' he had said once. . . . One of the stories that people liked to tell about him was of the time he had stumbled into the church, drunk, when they were taking up contributions for foreign missions and, hearing sums of money named, had thought that he was in a poker game and had proceeded to raise" (71). Unawares, Tom is becoming increasingly like the father he could not respect. He is drinking too much and, even worse, leaves his wife to carry on an adulterous affair. Unable to forgive his father for his faults, Tom perpetuates them in his own behavior. Only in the dream of the cave does he realize that his father has always cared for him and is now warning him away from a destructive course.

Tom needs balance. The near madness that throws him into emotional and mental chaos has been caused by an excess of rationality, by an attempt to deny the love and spirituality he needs to nurture his creative, whole self. In urging Tom to seek out Vera at Catherine Pollard's farm, George wisely locates the source of Tom's psychic balance in his relationship with his wife. The union between Vera's emotional, mainly intuitive character and Tom's more cerebral one will be mutually tempering. In the words of the novel's epigraph, "It is for Adam to interpret the voices that Eve hears." As John Simons explains, in its context, this quotation from Jacques Maritain's "The Frontiers of Poetry" means that the human soul must reconcile its reasoning powers with its intuitive ones. Distinguishing between a higher and a lower intuition, Simons describes how the critical intelligence determines "the authenticity of what the soul (Eve) experiences." Thus, Tom must move from delusion to revelation—using his reason as the proper mediator and interpreter of nonrational experience. This reconciliation between the mind and soul takes place on a symbolic level in marriage, especially in such traditional archetypal schemes as Caroline Gordon portrays, in which the woman's intuition and biological fecundity balance the man's rationality and capacity for work.[44]

The one artist whose progress in the novel roughly corresponds to Tom's is Max Shull, another friend and former lover of Horne Watts. Max lives with the Claibornes and, like Tom, has ceased to be productive, though he does not seem anxious about that. As Tom observes, "Now that Max no longer took his painting seriously he wanted a party every day" (20). However, Max's disposition is essentially religious. Despite his initial choice of a shallow and unsatisfying life, there are implications that Max will find his way back, for he seems haunted by religion. For example, in the days when he and Horne were lovers, they both chose patron saints. Max selected Saint Cyprian, the former magician, and named his studio after him. His current studio on the Claibornes' land is also named "St. Cyprian's Oratory" (116–17). Although Max has not painted anything recently, his earlier religious painting of Saint Eustace's conversion is displayed at Vera's fair, which takes place on that saint's day (41–42).

44. John W. Simons, "A Cunning and Curious Dramatization," *Commonweal*, LXIV (April 13, 1956), 55.

These allusions to conversion foreshadow Max's eventual change of behavior. When Tom runs into him again—not having seen Max since he left Vera—Max is coming into Catherine Pollard's flophouse on the Bowery where Tom has just finished talking with Sister Immaculata. Tom learns that Max is working at present on a mural of Saint Eustace for the chapel on Mott Street, which Catherine and her followers are repairing and refurbishing. Max coaxes Tom into the chapel for a look. There, a number of minor characters who have previously been leading selfish and wasteful lives now, perhaps a bit unbelievably for the reader, are happily employed in Catherine's program.

Tom is attracted to all this activity, but most of all to the church itself as a center of spirituality. Yet, once he notices two nuns praying before the altar, Claiborne defensively begins to intellectualize, reciting to himself, "*An altar is a raised structure, or any structure or place, on which sacrifices are offered or incense burned in worship of a deity, ancestor, etc. . . .*" Sensing a mystery here in spite of himself, Tom recalls the story of Jacob's ladder: "*And he took of the stones of that place and put them for his pillows and lay down to sleep and dreamed and behold a ladder set up on the earth, and the top of it reached to heaven: and behold the angels of God ascending and descending upon it, which caused Jacob to wake, trembling, and saying: 'Surely the Lord is in this place . . .'*" (249). Tom fights his intuition; in fact, he is so antagonistic towards the influence he feels in the chapel that he runs out before Catherine Pollard can greet him.

The image of the ladder is related to an important symbol in the novel—the bridge. Like Jacob's ladder, the bridge represents the link between heaven and earth, and in Christian terms, that bridge is Christ who is both God and man. As Sister Immaculata tells Tom: "It's the Humanity of the Word is the bridge between earth and heaven. And it has three steps: the feet that were nailed to the cross, the side that was pierced to reveal the ineffable love of the heart, and the mouth in which gall and vinegar were turned to sweetness. Horne ran to and fro among creatures like a madman, but he ran along the bridge too, else how could he have brought back the stones of virtue that he planted in his garden?" (241–42). Brainard Cheney observes how explicitly Caroline Gordon calls our attention to the life of Hart Crane and to his poetry, not simply to give us insight into this celebrated and sometimes infamous poet whose suicide astounded the literary world, but to dramatize the spiritual quest of the times. Likewise, Ashley Brown holds that the novel is not to be read merely as a *roman à clef*. As in Dante's *Divine Comedy*, the dead characters are made "as important as the living" to show that "the possibilities of saintliness and malefaction have been fully realized in our time as in any other. . . . it is Miss Gordon's intention to place these characters from 'life' in a fictional situation larger than the ones they have actually occupied and thus to make them more than the subject of literary gossip."[45]

To illustrate Gordon's condemnation of such malefaction and contemporary false faiths, Vivienne Koch lists all the camps that are criticized in the novel: science and scientism, Freudian and neo-Freudian thought, aestheticism and fake aestheticism, antihumanism and commercialism, pride of intellect and worldliness, "higher" education and "progressive" higher education. These social or intellectual fads do not provide meaning. Value resides in the archetypal truth of the bridge as symbol. The poet as pontifex—also the title of Horne Watts's volume—builds his own structures of words to direct us towards that meaning. Just so, Hart Crane viewed the bridge, the central image of his important long poem, as "an act of faith besides being a communication."[46]

By the end of the novel, Tom Claiborne, the reborn poet, shows us the bridges between this world and spiritual reality. Through his purging vision of the fire and the dream that later sends him to Catherine for help, Tom is able to become a "bridge-maker"—if not as exalted a leader as the pontifex of the Roman Catholic church, at least a caring husband and a responsible writer. Vision is coupled with proper action, and as in "Atlantis," the final poem of Crane's *The Bridge*, the divine power at work in the mundane world now gives direction to the human soul and body: "Sight, sound and flesh Thou leadest from time's realm / As love strikes clear direction for the helm."[47] A "communication" of an individual's arrival at faith, the

45. Cheney, "Gordon's *The Malefactors*," 369–70; Ashley Brown, "Novel as Christian Comedy," 168.
46. Koch, "Companions," 646–47; Hart Crane to Waldo Frank, June 20, [1926], in Weber (ed.), *Poems and Letters and Prose of Hart Crane*, 231.
47. Weber (ed.), *Poems and Letters and Prose of Hart Crane*, 116.

novel itself points towards a metaphysical truth by enjoining the reader's participation in the "experiential knowledge" of conversion, of renewed creativity and communion.

"Neither way is better. / Both ways are necessary. It is also necessary / To make a choice between them," Reilly informs Celia in T. S. Eliot's play *The Cocktail Party*. Tom's way is not that of Catherine Pollard, truly the namesake of Saint Catherine of Siena. Just as in *The Cocktail Party* where some choose sainthood and some choose to serve God in their workaday lives, in *The Malefactors* there is equal glory to those who perceive in marriage a route towards meaningful action. Yet the "saints" help to guide those who are unsure of their course, for Tom's dream of Catherine finally leads him to his wife.[48] Importantly, it is Horne Watts who points to the woman in the dream (310); earlier, Tom's father warned his son away from a too cerebral, self-preoccupied existence, and now Tom's poetic mentor provides him with a spiritual counselor. When Tom does find Catherine in Saint Eustace's chapel, she admits that she has been praying for him, just as she has been praying for Horne since his suicide. From Catherine, Tom further discovers that Vera was baptized a Catholic and will be obliged to honor the church's teaching "that a wife is subject to her husband, as the Church is subject to Christ" (311). These are the words that send Tom back to Vera.

*

One aspect of Caroline Gordon's fiction that has been noted and sometimes criticized is her scenic development. Yet this technique is related significantly to her concern with vision. Particularly in the later novels, in order to reveal the sublime, Gordon freezes those moments of perception when phenomenal and noumenal realities are fused. Whether through an omniscient narrator or through the consciousness of one of her characters, this stasis is revelation—that is, superimposed and simultaneous perceptions of spiritual truths and the everyday. Therefore, the climactic resolution of *The Women on the Porch* is Jim's vision of the pioneer, whose values have encouraged

48. T. S. Eliot, *The Cocktail Party: A Comedy* (New York, 1950), 141. See Ashley Brown for comparisons of Catherine Pollard to Dante's Matelda and of Vera to Beatrice, in "Novel as Christian Comedy," 177.

spiritual estrangement in the generations inheriting his lust for a new Eden. Similarly, *The Strange Children* ends when Stephen perceives, because of the crises of an evening, that all countries are "strange" to the pilgrim. And *The Malefactors* concludes with Tom's regeneration and his anticipated reunion with his wife. Once the revelation has been received, all subsequent action becomes part of an effort to re-conceive the world in terms of the new meaning.

Many critics feel that this scenic quality weakens characterization and plot development, but it may be helpful to compare the progres-sion in Gordon's novels to the psychological and thematic develop-ment in such collections of short stories as *Dubliners*, which Gordon admired in her critical writings, or even other contemporary volumes such as *Winesburg, Ohio* or *Go Down, Moses*. In each, seemingly dis-crete narratives are linked by similar conflicts and themes; the con-sciousnesses and values of individuals as well as of their communities are explored. Moreover, in *Dubliners* and *Winesburg, Ohio*, there is an artist, or at least a literary man of intelligence and sensibility who perceives around him the many who have failed to find love and meaningful work and who hopes to live differently.

"I wasn't cut out to write short stories," Caroline Gordon once remarked, but in point of fact her short stories have been widely anthologized and of all her work have received the greatest critical scrutiny and appreciation. In actual practice, Gordon tended to con-ceive of her longer fiction in smaller units. Some chapters of her novels were published as short stories in periodicals such as *Southern Review* and *Sewanee Review*. Also, some of the well-known Aleck Maury stories were composed while she was writing the novel, but for one reason or another were not included in the longer work.[49]

Gordon's predisposition for building such discrete scenes is related to her fascination with moments of vision. Her practice bears some

---

49. Baum and Watkins, "'The Captive': An Interview," 450. Some of the chapters of her novels that were published as short stories include "A Morning's Favor," *Southern Review*, I (1935), 271–80, which is taken from *Garden of Adonis*; "The Women on the Battlefield," *Southern Review*, II (1936–37), 515–24, which is from *None Shall Look Back*; and "Cloud Nine," *Sewanee Review*, LXXVII (1969), 591–629, which is the first chapter of *The Glory of Hera*. Vivienne Koch comments on the relationship of many of the stories in *The Forest of the South* to Gordon's novels. See Koch, "*The Forest of the South*," *Sewanee Review*, LIV (1946), 543.

resemblance to her master James Joyce's interest in "epiphanies." Like Joyce, Caroline Gordon strives to convert what he has called "the bread of everyday life" into metaphysical sustenance.[50]

Her emphasis on the revelatory scene also presupposes certain technical connections between the novel and drama. Gordon's high regard for Henry James's fiction has encouraged her own close attention to details of scene, gesture, and speech and to the insights into the growing mind that careful narration provides. In the preface to *The House of Fiction*, she and Tate pay homage to James's technical achievements: "This scheme [Aristotle's scheme of complication, resolution, peripety, and discovery], one of the basic patterns of the human imagination, has acquired a fresh interest in our own time, with Henry James's great technical discovery that 'the same key unlocks both the narrative and dramatic chambers' of 'The House of Fiction'" (*HF*, ix). Thus, Gordon's "photographic habit," which Robert Heilman finds distracting and sometimes ineffective, is, at its best, an indispensable aspect of Gordon's aesthetic and religious vision.[51] Like another southern writer, Eudora Welty, who actually began her career as a photographer, Caroline Gordon is well aware of the significance of the artistically focused, revealing picture; but more than that, she is interested in the mind that constructs the frame and in the completeness of the reality that consciousness seeks to define.

The Glory of Hera

The lower pattern winds serpent-wise.
—CAROLINE GORDON

"We become what we look on longest and most passionately," Tom Claiborne thinks early in *The Malefactors* (38). For her readers, Caroline Gordon consistently presents images of heroic action, whether the heroes are involved in actual battle or in an equally deadly psychomachy. In *The Glory of Hera* (1972), she examines the heroic pattern again, this time in some of its oldest garb—the myth of Heracles. Yet this experimental novel about the Greek demigod

---

50. Stanislaus Joyce, *My Brother's Keeper*, ed. Richard Ellmann (New York, 1958), 103–104.
51. Heilman, "Schools for Girls," 303–304.

provides not only a model of bravery and strength but also a paradigm of the evolving human psyche. "The action," Gordon writes, "takes place on the frontiers of the archetypal conscious mind."[52] The mythic action parallels the growth of the individual towards wholeness, the goal of such modern protagonists as Jim Chapman, Stephen Lewis, and Tom Claiborne.

Whereas *The Women on the Porch*, *The Strange Children*, and *The Malefactors* treat marriage as the metaphor for the union of masculine and feminine principles, in *The Glory of Hera* the individual's maturation is examined in a larger social context. Gordon adapts her style accordingly. Concentrating less on the specific psychological development of Heracles, she focuses on the more general meaning that his actions had for his fellow Greeks and continue to have for moderns. Moreover, Gordon expands her investigation of women, examining the wife and the mother, the prophetess and the priestess, as well as the goddess. The basic story of Heracles' Twelve Labors is enriched by image patterns that interconnect the feminine with prophetic powers and with divinity, in both malevolent and benevolent manifestations. Whether the hero is battling supernatural monsters, consulting a prophetess, or being directly guided by a deity, he encounters divinity in its many inscrutable forms. Furthermore, by a number of allusions to earlier Greek heroes and to Christ, Heracles' action is elevated to the archetypal. Although he is made into a real character, with his own thoughts, emotions, and distinct traits, Heracles is more important as a type, an interpretation reinforced by Gordon's working plan for the novel.

The Glory of Hera was conceived as the first part of a double novel: one volume—"the lower pattern"—was to illustrate mythic, archetypal schemes; the second—"the upper pattern"—was to parallel historical and autobiographical material to those schemes: "The lower pattern winds serpent-wise through the upper pattern of action and deals with the archetypal world which the present day Jungians and the archaic Greeks inform us lies at the very bottom of every human consciousness." While no companion novel was published before Gordon's death, in a sense *The Glory of Hera* serves as the "lower

---

52. "Notes on Contributors," *Sewanee Review*, LXXVII (1969), xiii.

pattern" for all her work. Gordon's earliest novels relied on myth to help develop theme, but *The Glory of Hera* embroiders the fabric of myth itself. Gordon sophisticates the archaic pattern of heroism so that raw myth becomes the story of any man's triumphant confrontation with death. As the template for such modern heroes as Jim Chapman, Stephen Lewis, and Tom Claiborne, Heracles embodies certain essential qualities: he is attuned to spiritual realities; he is strong and courageous enough to battle all monsters—including his own dark self; and he is an unselfish and capable leader.[53]

Although the three novels written after *Green Centuries* give us more hope for man's success, essentially all of Gordon's fiction is concerned with what Brainard Cheney and Thomas Landess have termed an "ontological quest." Historical and mythical allusions often provide ironic commentaries on the characters in the earliest novels: for example, Rion compares himself with the ever-turning constellation of the Greek hunter Orion, feeling caught in a futile search for a new Eden; Rives is a death-wishful Saint George, choosing to fight a doomed battle; and Chance Llewellyn is like Cain, a farmer who murders his brother and loses all that he would save. In *The Women on the Porch*, *The Strange Children*, and *The Malefactors*, literary allusions—especially to Dante's *Divine Comedy*—and references to saints' lives illuminate contemporary searches for meaning.[54]

53. Gordon's scheme for the double novel is quoted in Stanford's "From *Penhally* to 'A Narrow Heart,'" xvi. Before *Glory of Hera*, Gordon was at work on a "chronicle" telling the life stories of members of her family, which she owns "is also the story of my own life." (See "Cock-Crow," 557.) Originally, "A Narrow Heart: The Portrait of a Woman" was the working title for this projected novel, as indicated in those excerpts published in 1960, 1961, and 1965 (see "A Narrow Heart," "The Dragon's Teeth," with Ashley Brown's accompanying note, in *Shenandoah*, XIII (1961), 20–34, as well as "Cock-Crow"). From Ashley Brown's remarks in *Shenandoah*, it seems that Gordon first intended to write one novel, which, like *A Portrait of the Artist As a Young Man*, was to be "'autobiographical,' and consciously based on the action of a myth"—the myth of Heracles (21). Placing her individual life in the context of family history as well as in a larger archetypal pattern apparently became such a large project that she began to conceive of the work as a "double novel," of which *Glory of Hera*, published in 1972, supplies the archetypal theme for the historical and autobiographical variations that were to be developed in the companion novel *Joy of the Mountains*. The complete two-part work was to be entitled *Behold My Trembling Heart*, according to a note in *Southern Review*, n.s., XII (1976), vii.

54. Cheney, "Gordon's Ontological Quest," 3–12; Landess, "Caroline Gordon's Ontological Stories," in Landess (ed.), *Short Fiction*, 53–73.

The possibility of revelation and regeneration makes these quests more hopeful, and yet, as Gordon's method implies, the individual's search for his own spiritual integration is as old as man himself. Thus, Howard Baker investigates Gordon's use of mythic pattern in *The Glory of Hera*. His essay "The Strategems of Caroline Gordon; or, The Art of the Novel and the Novelty of Myth" relies on the work of Claude Lévi-Strauss to compare the fundamentals of mythology to the development of human consciousness. Baker observes that *The Glory of Hera* assumes a number of these parallels and notes that a perceived division between earth and sky designates the beginning of time and consciousness of human mortality; that the stories of heroes who conquer monsters arising from the earth suggest the struggle in individuals to overcome the monstrous part of the self; that mythology also incorporates manners and customs which indicate a growing civilization; and that along with such growth come certain taboos, notably against incest, that encourage people to open up tightly knit groups and form larger communities.[55]

A complement to the scheme Baker discusses is the Jungian "process of individuation," another theory in which the development of the individual psyche recapitulates our human evolution. Although Baker admits that Caroline Gordon would prefer the "simple emotional impact" of Jungian archetypes to Lévi-Strauss's more abstract and general terms, he does not really apply Jungian theory to his argument.[56]

According to Jung and his associates, a person's growth begins with the first approach of the unconscious: this "shadow" self (which is perceived in dreams as the same sex as the dreamer) is composed of "those qualities and impulses [an individual] denies in himself but can plainly see in other people." When that shadow confronts the conscious self and reproaches it, "that is the moment when the ego gets caught, and the result is usually embarrassed silence. Afterward the painful and lengthy work of self-education begins—a work, we might say, that is the psychological equivalent of the labors of Hercules. This unfortunate hero's first task, you will remember, was to

55. Howard Baker, "The Strategems of Caroline Gordon; or, The Art of the Novel and the Novelty of Myth," *Southern Review*, n.s., IX (1973), 546–47.
56. *Ibid.*, 546.

clean up in one day the Augean Stables, in which hundreds of cattle had dropped their dung for many decades—a task so enormous that the ordinary mortal would be overcome by discouragement at the mere thought of it." The labors of the psyche continue when "another 'inner figure' emerges": "If the dreamer is a man, he will discover a female personification of his unconscious; and it will be a male figure in the case of a woman." The "anima" and "animus," respectively, represent female and male principles that must be reconciled with the conscious mind. For a man, the anima "is a personification of all feminine psychological tendencies in a man's psyche, such as vague feelings and moods, prophetic hunches, receptiveness to the irrational, capacity for personal love, feeling for nature, and—last but not least—his relation to the unconscious." If a man is receptive to the urgings of this female principle, then the anima acts as mediator between the ego and what Jung terms the Self—that is, the whole self, conscious and unconscious.[57] Once that totality has been achieved, the individual is led naturally to relationships with others, and thus the process of individuation is finally a social maturation as well.

In Gordon's story of Heracles, the "approach of the unconscious" corresponds to the hero's first intuitions of his own special nature and of the mysterious, larger forces that influence his behavior. For instance, he is not entirely certain why he killed Linus. Through the omniscient narrator who shifts our view to the Olympians, we learn that the two vultures Linus ordered Heracles to shoot were Zeus and Athene. To his foster father Amphitryon, however, it does seem, as Hera so spitefully phrases it, that Heracles' "temper is . . . ungovernable" and that "he will be safer living among beasts."[58] Heracles is sent away from the city.

Purposely, Book I of the novel ends with Heracles' murder of the priest; these first fourteen chapters introduce us to the gods, goddesses, and mortals who will figure in Heracles' history, but it is not until Book II that we enter into the hero's consciousness. In a sense, he has not fully existed until he recognizes his own "shadow"—his rage and violence, which, unchecked, cause his undoing but, disci-

57. M.-L. von Franz, "The Process of Individuation," in Carl Jung *et al.*, *Man and His Symbols* (Garden City, N.Y., 1964), 168, 168–69, 177, 177, 180, 183.
58. Caroline Gordon, *The Glory of Hera* (Garden City, N.Y., 1972), 146, 151, hereinafter cited parenthetically in the text.

plined for higher service, provide courage and strength. When we do enter the demigod's mind, he is tending King Amphitryon's cattle on Mount Cithaeron. As on the day of the games when he struck Linus, Heracles senses a divine presence. This time the goddesses Athene and Aphrodite appear to him, and sagaciously Heracles chooses Athene as his guide. Athene becomes for him a positive aspect of his anima: as Wisdom personified, she helps Heracles through his many labors and trials, whereas Hera, who seemingly is tricked into declaring herself Heracles' foster mother (135), plays the part of the nightmare or bitch goddess while Heracles is on earth. Thus, when Hera drives Heracles into a mad fit, Athene is the one who stops him (231).

The roles these two goddesses play in Heracles' life can be understood in terms of the developing Self. Jungians describe four stages in the evolution of the anima in the male personality: "The first stage is best symbolized by the figure of Eve, which represents purely instinctual and biological relations. The second can be seen in Faust's Helen: She personifies a romantic and aesthetic level that is, however, still characterized by sexual elements. The third is represented, for instance, by the Virgin Mary—a figure who raises love (*eros*) to the heights of spiritual devotion. The fourth type is symbolized by Sapientia, wisdom transcending even the most holy and the most pure."[59] In choosing Athene over Aphrodite, Heracles, in effect, rejects or represses these first two manifestations of the anima. Whenever Hera strikes at him, she attacks his most vulnerable side; as the old witch, La Belle Dame undisguised, she destroys his sexual and familial relationships or, in the case of his birth, interferes with his biological development. Not only does Hera inflict upon him the madness during which he murders his first wife and his three sons, but while he is laboring in penance for King Eurytheus, the Queen of Heaven continues to meddle with his life. For example, she sends the bull of Crete all over the country with Heracles in pursuit (290). Even Eurytheus fits into Hera's plans for Heracles. To thwart her consort's boast that the child born to the house of Perseus by nightfall of a certain day should rule as king of Mycenae, Hera brings the baby

---

59. Von Franz, "Process of Individuation," in Jung *et al.*, *Man and His Symbols*, 185. In "Cock-Crow," Gordon allegorizes Heracles' encounter with the two goddesses as his choosing between Virtue and Pleasure, 566–67.

Eurytheus two months early and delays Heracles' birth (122–23). Without always being actually present, she influences the hero's actions and character from the beginning: it is she who sends the two serpents into Heracles' cradle, and his strangling the creatures is the first indication of his supernatural strength.

With Hera apparently determined to torment and challenge him and with Athene advising him, Heracles is greatly affected by two markedly different female principles. In Jungian theory, the forces the goddesses represent would be termed the malevolent and positive aspects of the anima. Although his terminology is not psychological, Robert Graves describes such complex femininity in *The White Goddess*: "The Goddess is a lovely, slender woman with a hooked nose, deathly pale face, lips red as rowanberries, startlingly blue eyes and long fair hair; she will suddenly transform herself into sow, mare, bitch, vixen, she-ass, weasel, serpent, owl, she-wolf, tigress, mermaid or loathsome hag. Her names and titles are innumerable." This goddess, who plays a central part in the archetypal myth which Graves delineates—"the birth, life, death, and resurrection of the God of the Waxing Year"—is a triple goddess. In the myth, she is "mother, bride, and layer-out" of this god, and her nature is understood symbolically in terms of the moon. Graves explains, "I write of her as the White Goddess because white is her principal colour, the colour of the first member of her moon-trinity, but when Suidas the Byzantine records that Io was a cow that changed her colour from white to rose and then to black he means that the New Moon is the white goddess of birth and growth; the Full Moon, the red goddess of love and battle; the Old Moon, the black goddess of death and divination."[60]

In *The Glory of Hera*, the Queen of Heaven is sometimes accompanied by Athene or Aphrodite, suggesting the trinity of divine female principles they so clearly represent in the story of Paris choosing Aphrodite over Hera and Athene, the event that precipitated the abduction of Helen and the consequent Trojan War. Early in the novel, for example, we see that through the joint efforts of Hera and Athene, Teiresias has been brought up to Olympus for questioning. Although Athene is Zeus's daughter, born from his head, she is "always becoming embroiled in Hera's follies," according to her father

60. Graves, *White Goddess*, 24, 70.

(23). Nor is the Queen of Heaven "above borrowing" from the beautiful Aphrodite the magic girdle that inspires love (19). In addition to her associations with these two lesser deities, Hera herself fulfills each of the roles of the Triple Goddess: at various times, she is a winsome seductress of Zeus, a jealous and spiteful intriguer, and a wise nurturer. Zeus's description of his consort details all these qualities: "Hera was stately of figure, white-armed, golden-haired, with eyes almost as large and as lustrous as those the ox turns upon the priest when he feels the sacrificial knife at his throat. She was also vain, capricious, overbearing, and inordinately fond of her own way" (19–20). Queen of Heaven, Hera is also the guide and inspiration of heroes. The one power Zeus objects to is Hera's ability "to put into the mouths of any of the heroes any words she chose to have him utter! None of the other goddesses possessed this gift. He questioned whether such a gift should be bestowed upon a woman. It made her almost equal to him, the Father of Gods and Men!" (84). From what Hera remarks at the conclusion of the novel, she most certainly considers herself equal. However, the title of the novel refers not only to Hera's personal grandeur but also to her namesake, the hero Heracles—"the glory of Hera" (131).

Zeus's plan—to bridge the abyss between gods and men by creating a demigod who will reign forever (10, 120)—is incomplete without the contributions of the Queen of Heaven. Perhaps because she has been excluded from the inception of this plan, Hera seems to threaten Zeus's design. Yet the father of gods and men never seems completely aware that, in endowing his son with bravery and strength, he has not nurtured the intuition and emotions necessary to build his hero's judgment. Like his father, Heracles is unfortunately slow to acknowledge the importance of those female principles under the direction of Athene and Hera. As both Howard Baker and Janet Lewis imply, Heracles has matured significantly when he finally understands whose namesake he is.[61] Repeatedly he identifies himself as the son of Zeus; and although this is true enough, he fails to give credit to the other deities who shape his character and fate. Only in the conclusion, when Hera actually gives birth to the apotheosized Heracles, is it

---

61. Baker, "Strategems," 546; Janet Lewis, "*The Glory of Hera*," *Sewanee Review*, LXXXI (1973), 189.

clear that his foster mother is his real mother, too: "Zeus, standing between the Queen of Heaven and his latest-born son, smiled upon the younger Olympians. 'Behold our son Heracles!' he cried, and Hera, standing beside Heracles, smiled, too. 'Our son all along,' she murmured, but in a voice so low that only Hermes, who happened to be standing near the dais, heard what she said" (398).

This divine rebirth of the hero at once symbolizes the final matura-tion of the individual psyche as well as a more complete notion of Godhead. Both concepts presuppose the union of masculine and feminine principles. Louise Cowan, who reads Caroline Gordon's later novels as efforts to reconcile "ancient myth and Christian mys-tery," examines the use Gordon makes of these polarities: "Her early novels deal overtly with neither pagan myth nor Christian mystery; but, concerned with the polarities of thinking and feeling, they dra-matize the feminine and masculine principles in a devastated society that cannot surrender itself to love and integration, where death is the overarching enemy." That "union of myth and mystery, nature and grace" that Cowan perceives in the later novels is nowhere so appar-ent as in Heracles' rebirth into Heaven.[62]

Marriage as metaphoric union of the masculine and feminine is the focus in *The Women on the Porch*, *The Strange Children*, and *The Malefactors*; now we see the fruits of that union—a hero of such stat-ure that he becomes a model for other mortals. In his final manifesta-tion, Heracles is a complete being—his anima functioning as media-tor between his subconscious and his conscious Self. For if Hera can be taken to represent the hero's feminine traits, she is ultimately the mother and nurturer of this new being.

The Jungian paradigm of the developing animus—the masculine characteristics within a woman—is analogous to the male's integra-tion. The pattern suggests, in addition, a maturing definition of the masculine. Appearing first "as a personification of mere physical power—for instance, as an athletic champion or 'muscle man'"—the animus next acquires "initiative and the capacity for planned action." "In the third phase, the animus becomes the 'word,' often appear-ing as a professor or clergyman. Finally, in his fourth manifestation,

---

62. Louise Cowan, "Aleck Maury," in Landess (ed.), *Short Fiction*, 10, 11; Cowan's criticism covers Gordon's work through 1965 and the publication of "Cock-Crow."

the animus is the incarnation of *meaning*. On this highest level he becomes (like the anima) a mediator of the religious experience whereby life acquires new meaning."[63]

So Caroline Gordon's description of the hero has grown. At first Heracles is little more than a "muscle man," but guided by his intuitions (and Athene), he becomes a more competent leader. Although he killed Linus in blind anger, Heracles next trains himself for worthier ends: ridding the earth of the monsters that plague mortals. At this stage, Heracles can be compared to heroes in Gordon's early fiction who have physical strength as well as some ability to lead. The protagonist of *Green Centuries*, Rion Outlaw flees his community after ambushing and killing some of the king's soldiers; as a settler in the wilderness, he accepts more responsibility, trying to live peacefully with the Indians and then protecting his family when the Indians decide to attack. Rives Allard in *None Shall Look Back* defends his homeland when Yankee soldiers menace it. Whereas both Rion and Rives are capable of meeting the literal enemies that confront them, they are not prepared for psychological battle. Rives would rather die than try to rebuild a defeated South. Rion becomes less heroic over the course of *Green Centuries* because he cannot respond to the new demands of his family and the growing community.

In the third stage of development, as the struggle within the self is won, the male impulses are directed towards guiding a larger group of individuals by imparting knowledge through the spoken or written word. Heracles becomes a kind of spiritual leader: in fact, the Thebans prematurely set him up to be worshiped as the sea-god Palemon (227). For this hubris, Hera drives him mad. Heracles is more truly a spiritual leader when he takes as his virgin bride Macaria, daughter of King Thespius, and makes her priestess of a temple dedicated to Zeus. In Macaria's first-person account of the ceremony to consecrate the temple, she refers to Heracles only as the Son of Zeus. Indeed, "as priest of the shrine of Zeus the Savior" (196), Heracles has been elevated, at least for the time being, to a purely spiritual role; and when he meets his death many years later, Heracles is officiating at a sacrifice to Zeus.

Similarly, Stephen Lewis, Jim Chapman, and Tom Claiborne be-

---

63. Von Franz, "Process of Individuation," in Jung *et al.*, *Man and His Symbols*, 194.

come prophets of a greater reality. As intelligent men of letters, these modern protagonists seem ready by the end of the novels to serve as better models for their communities—to be like Kevin Reardon in trying to meet the spiritual as well as physical needs of their families and, by implication, in extending their knowledge to their readers and students. However, the conclusion of *The Glory of Hera* permits us to view Heracles in a way that these characters from everyday life cannot be seen. He has literally become god, exalted because of his many glorious deeds. A Christ-like figure, as the many biblical echoes in the novel insist, Heracles is another incarnation, born of a mortal woman and a divine father. Triumphing over death, he is, at this final stage of development, an example of the integrated Self bridging earth and heaven. The physician Podaleirius thus describes Heracles as a kind of savior to Arsippe, the wife of Eurytheus: "Heracles is no ordinary hunter. The beasts which he hunts are those which deal death to mortals. It seems to me that when he slays them he is promising his fellow mortals deliverance from that which formerly threatened death" (283). Heracles conquers death in another way. Like many other archetypal heroes and like Caroline Gordon's modern protagonists who harrow their own infernos, Heracles must descend into hell and confront the terrible forms of despair and meaninglessness before he can reaffirm the value of life.[64]

At the news of Heracles' death on the burning pyre, Zeus informs the other gods: "The serpents that Hera sent to strangle Heracles were burned to ashes in a fire built of oak wood and the male wild olive. On this pyre built of the same woods, my son Heracles will slough off his mortal remains as serpents cast their skins" (396). The serpents—mysterious and deadly powerful—here suggest Heracles' links to Godhead. In the mythic world of *The Glory of Hera*, snakes are not necessarily evil, but they are associated with the inscrutable, which can appear evil because it defeats human rationality and notions of justice. Certainly the snakes that threaten Heracles in his cradle do not seem benevolent creatures; yet they serve Heracles in a

---

64. There are a number of strong allusions in *Glory of Hera* to Heracles' Christ-like service. His mother is compared to Mary (131); Heracles identifies himself with the "Kingdom of Light" (174), acknowledges that his "father's kingdom is not of Thebes" (197), and insists that his "father's business" take precedence over all earthly matters (198). Heracles' concern that "the Father's will was accomplished" during his meeting with Prometheus similarly reminds us of Christ's obedience to his Father's will (365).

curious way. In strangling them he reveals his divine origin. When Teiresias recognizes the portents of divinity, he instructs the Thebans how to dispose of the serpents' bodies and directs Alcmene to change the baby's name from Alcides to Heracles (131).[65]

Agents of the supernatural, serpents can augur good or ill, and a seemingly fatal sign can actually promise good fortune. For instance, Zeus interprets a fisherman's dream of a huge sun with rays that "quivered as if alive," each one having "the head and forked tongue of a serpent," as a good omen that "the hero Perseus is about to return to the earth" (116, 117). The hero, in fact, is Heracles, a descendant of Perseus and the main figure in Zeus's "scheme for the redemption of mankind" (117).

Whereas Athene's son Erechtheus, a reddish-colored serpent, is the "respectable" ruler of the Athenians (23), monsters that destroy crops, livestock, and human lives are malevolent supernatural creatures only a hero can subdue. Even then, destroying a creature linked with divinity is not wholly condoned. Cadmus had to serve eight years for slaying the serpent, a son of Ares, that guarded the grove where he founded Thebes (62). Heracles, in his many wondrous feats, battles a number of monsters that are serpentine or at least, in being descended from the Earth, are the offspring of the great serpent Ophion: the fire-breathing lion of Helicon, the dragon protecting the Garden of Hesperides, and the Hydra of Lerna.

The Hydra—with a body "shaped like that of a huge bitch" and "covered all over with glittering scales ending in a forked tail"—has nine heads set on serpentine necks; the one immortal head "had the face of a woman, but the locks that hung down on each side of the head were serpentine" (273, 274). The Hydra's female face is a reminder of the symbolic connections between serpents and women developed in the Greek creation myth. In the Egyptian temple of Zeus-Ammon, the god instructs Heracles on the nature of women:

> In your dealings with women it would be well to bear in mind
> that they are all more nearly akin to the serpent than we are. One
> and all, they have inherited certain traits from our remote an-

---

65. Bainard Cowan analyzes the serpent motif in some detail, focusing on the transformation of the mysterious powers associated with serpentine symbolism into creative and positive action. See "The Serpent's Coils: How to Read Caroline Gordon's Later Fiction," *Southern Review*, n.s., XVI (1980), 281–98.

cestress Eurynome, the Wide-Wandering One. She was dancing upon the waves in order to separate sea from sky, when the North Wind came past. She engaged him in dalliance to such good purpose that he underwent a metamorphosis in her hands, becoming the great serpent Ophion. Whereupon they domiciled themselves upon Mount Olympus. He coiled about her seven times, and she laid the great Silver Egg, out of which all living creatures tumbled. But when Ophion claimed some share in this achievement, she kicked his teeth out and cast him down into Tartarus. (356)

Zeus is quite conscious of Hera's descent from the great serpent Ophion. Though he and his wife are children of the same father and mother (and so, Zeus is also Ophion's offspring), Zeus admits that Hera is the older deity and seems to be more strongly affected by her serpentine lineage (121).

Hera's frequent rebelliousness indicates her confidence in the power she has inherited. Indeed, Hera and all women command forces stronger and more primal than those the male enlists. Thus, when Apollo slays the dragon of the great earth mother Gaia so that he may claim the oracle of Delphi, Gaia demands as recompense "that the oracles that originated in Apollo's divine mind must be delivered through the lips of a woman, who was called the pythoness in memory of the dragon" (133–34). Perceiving that Apollo is irritated with this arrangement, Zeus reminds the younger deity, "Women are ever in league with the older gods. . . . I see no help for it, my son. The older gods will have their way" (134).

Heracles also senses that women are in contact with the divine powers of creation. Upon meeting Lachesis, one of the Fates, he thinks, "women . . . are all alike, be they goddesses or mortals— concerned only with birth and death, indifferent to what lies in between" (302). Although the hero's thought is an exaggeration, it contains an important observation: women are naturally and traditionally associated with birth and death; and as mothers, midwives, layers-out, and mourners, they participate in the activities and ceremonies that define life's meaning. The attributes of women and of those men who have integrated these qualities sensitize them to spiritual matters. "Receptiveness to the irrational, capacity for personal love, feeling for nature, and . . . relation to the unconscious"—these are the traits the Jungian psychologist von Franz identifies with the feminine. She adds, "It is no mere chance that in olden times priestesses (like the Greek Sibyl) were used to fathom the divine will and to make connection with the gods."[66]

In Gordon's novel, women and the womanly are explicitly linked to oracles and prophecy. The pythoness or Sibyl at Delphi is one such example. Heracles questions her, then steals the sacred tripod upon which she sits when she will not tell him which deity drove him insane (249). The hero's descent into the strange, dark place to consult the cryptic priestess reminds us of Zeus's earlier long pilgrimage to Gaia, then to the oldest daughter of Ocean, and finally to Eurynome—a pilgrimage to the older goddesses who possess the knowledge and the power to help Zeus claim the throne of Olympus.

The seer Teiresias, taking significant part in the action of the novel as well as in the myths of the ancients, has these feminine gifts of intuition and is able to interpret the signs and directives of the deities. Appropriately, he is a hermaphroditic creature. Once changed into a woman for seven years because he struck apart two coupling snakes and killed the female, Teiresias has fully experienced the feminine aspects of his personality. He is like the medicine men and prophets among the Eskimo tribes whom von Franz describes: "Some of these even wear women's clothes, or have breasts depicted on their garments, in order to manifest their inner feminine side— the side that enables them to connect with the 'ghost land' (i.e. what we call the unconscious)."[67]

As the examples of Teiresias and the pythoness show, either the man who acknowledges the female principles within or the woman who is responsive to her own male attributes can have vision. In Jungian theory, as in myth, it is the whole individual who truly sees. The description of the animus at its last stage of evolution is very close to that of the anima at its peak of development: "The animus in his most developed form sometimes connects the woman's mind with the spiritual evolution of her age, and can thereby make her even

---

66. Von Franz, "Process of Individuation," in Jung *et al.*, *Man and His Symbols*, 177. See also Gordon's description of the sibyl in Jungian theory, in "A Narrow Heart," 8.
67. Von Franz, "Process of Individuation," in Jung *et al.*, *Man and His Symbols*, 177.

more receptive than a man to new creative ideas. It is for this reason that in earlier times women were used by many nations as diviners and seers. The creative boldness of their positive animus at times expresses thoughts and ideas that stimulate men to new enter-prises."[68] At maturity, both forces—anima or animus—point to-wards spiritual truths and direct community action.

Not only does the rebirth of Heracles into heaven show the union of those female and male principles that have made his apotheosis possible, but also it designates a more complete notion of Godhead that makes female qualities compatible with those of a patriarchal deity. Again, the findings of Jung reveal a modern correspondence to this insight: "In the manifestations of the unconscious found in our modern Christian culture, whether Protestant or Catholic, Dr. Jung often observed that there is an unconscious tendency at work to round off our trinitarian formula of the Godhead with a fourth ele-ment, which tends to be feminine, dark, and even evil."[69] So too, Robert Graves shows that the primal conceptions of Godhead in-cluded a feminine aspect: the Triple Goddess as mother, bride, and layer-out. Graves's contention is that the patriarchal traditions of our Judeo-Christian culture have repressed our original understanding of the White Goddess.

Although he would have us pay tribute to these feminine powers, Graves does not offer as much hope for individual integration as Carl Jung or Caroline Gordon does. His description of male and female relationships implies perpetual conflict between two unequal princi-ples: Man "is divine not in his single person, but only in his twin-hood. . . . Man is a demi-god: he always has either one foot or the other in the grave; woman is divine because she can keep both her feet always in the same place, whether in the sky, in the underworld, or on this earth. Man envies her and tells himself lies about his own completeness." What Graves advocates—essentially an idolatry of the feminine—is precisely Tubby's problem in *The Malefactors*. Because of his mistaken devotion to Isabel, he neglects his own spirituality. As a paradigm for male behavior, Graves's scheme is an immature one. To an extent, Caroline Gordon would agree with him that the proper

68. *Ibid.*, 194–95.
69. *Ibid.*, 225.

theme of poetry is "the relations of man and woman," for she was concerned in her fiction to reveal the meaning of marriage. Yet in Gordon's fiction it is "relationship"—not merely sexual involvement—that nurtures the growth of the couple. While striving to show the goddess in every woman, Graves belittles the god in every man and, consequently, any mature masculine principle: "Woman worships the male infant, not the grown man: it is evidence of her deity, of man's dependence on her for life." With such disparagement of the male, it is no wonder that Graves does not call for the integration of polarities within a single being.[70]

Admittedly, Hera is a White Goddess, but she is not, finally, the "orgiastic" creature Graves describes. For good reason our last view of her is as the nurturer. Caroline Gordon's larger notion of the individual's psychic growth reconciles mythic patterns with Christian hope and archetypes with social institutions; but Graves holds that the impulses of poetry oppose those of Christianity. According to him, the ascetic doctrine of primitive Christianity revived by the Puritan revolution was responsible for the image of the Virgin Mary, which Graves implies is incomplete: "The cruel, capricious, incontinent White Goddess and the mild, steadfast, chaste Virgin are not to be reconciled except in the Nativity context."[71]

Rather than simply opposing the image of the Virgin with the White Goddess, Gordon insists upon the inscrutable nature of the divine, thereby subsuming both notions in a more complex concept of divinity. As in Jung's theory, the Virgin Mary, or any of the female saints to whom Gordon refers, may serve as an example of a spiritual guide, a Beatrice. The highest level of spirituality, however, is an ineffable reality, which words grasp incompletely but which the mind seeks to contemplate through images.

Discussing twentieth-century perceptions of Godhead, von Franz explains that the dark, feminine, and often evil fourth element has always existed in our culture but has been "separated from the image of God" and has become "his counterpart, in the form of matter itself

---

70. Graves, *White Goddess*, 110, 447. See Caroline Gordon's emphasis on the relationship between the sexes as the subject of all fiction, in *A Good Soldier: A Key to the Novels of Ford Madox Ford* (Davis, Calif., 1963), 3.

71. Graves, *White Goddess*, 458, 425; Gordon criticizes Graves for restricting his Archetypal Woman to one which "deals death" in her *Good Soldier: A Key*, 9.

(or the lord of matter—i.e. the devil)." Our unconscious desire "to reunite these extremes" of good and evil, as von Franz phrases it, is not far from the hope Saint Augustine voices in one of the novel's epigraphs: "And the serpents will be good. . . . Their sting will not be poisonous or harmful. . . . They will pry into the secrets of the temporal world . . . only to catch a glimpse of eternity *as it is known to your creatures*. For these creatures are the servants of reason if they are allowed to be good and are kept from the path that leads to death." But the epilogue, also from Saint Augustine, reminds us how inextricably mixed evil and good appear to us in this world: "My ignorance was so great that these questions troubled me. I did not know that evil is nothing but the removal of good until finally no good remains."[72]

"Myth, let us suppose, is semiconscious wonder. It works with what we know and don't know and invents stories to help us understand the world, by giving truth openings through which it can seep out," comments Howard Baker in his analysis of *The Glory of Hera*.[73] This last novel gives another shape to the dreams and subconscious phenomena that educate the protagonists of *The Women on the Porch*, *The Strange Children*, and *The Malefactors*. Gordon chooses myths that have been crystallized by tradition; they are not merely personal but communal images of truth. Moreover, she structures these inherited legends to show their mysterious relevance, so that the mythic story of the demigod Heracles illustrates the individual's quest to transcend the ordinary, to defy death, which threatens to make life seem meaningless. Like Heracles, the individual who recognizes a human purpose strives to become—given his biological and psychological inheritance—his best and most complete self and a responsible social and religious being.

Calling Caroline Gordon a White Goddess, Mary O'Connor asserts that "writers such as Faulkner, Porter, Flannery O'Connor, Gordon (and I am in no sense rating them in any order of achievement) use their own mythical system, transforming the inherited material of the culture into a self-made account of reality which resolves into sensuous apprehension all the knowledge we have of a place and

72. Von Franz, "Process of Individuation," in Jung *et al.*, *Man and His Symbols*, 225.
73. Baker, "Strategems," 548.

time, and of the folly and tragic dignity of human life. Caroline Gordon makes the burden of heightened consciousness worth carrying and 'the shock of recognition' a healing experience." If she is a White Goddess, Gordon is not Robert Graves's irascible and patronizing creature but a Beatrice who presents her readers with visions, replacing deluded conceptions of life as irreconcilable conflict between such polarities as the corporeal and the noumenal, evil and good, feminine and masculine, intuition and reason, with a more complete and more promising revelation of a physical world imbued with spiritual reality.[74]

74. Mary O'Connor, "On Caroline Gordon," 466.

Epilogue

Ask us, prophet, how we shall call
Our natures forth when that live tongue is all
Dispelled, that glass obscured or broken

In which we have said the rose of our love and the clean
Horse of our courage, in which beheld
The singing locust of the soul unshelled,
And all we mean or wish to mean.

—RICHARD WILBUR, "Advice to a Prophet"

Heracles, according to Caroline Gordon, "fought and vanquished many brave men but his chief 'labors' were his lifelong combat with the monstrous, in whatever guise it showed itself." Yet, in comparison with the Greek hero, "We, today, who can travel faster than sound, keep more at home, so to speak, occupied most of the time, most of us, with watching the dragon coil and uncoil in the 'earth of our own hearts.'" As novelist, Gordon committed herself to a "lifelong study" of "the life and times of the hero," including among those heroic combats the psychomachy of the modern protagonist.[1] In her earliest novels, Gordon examines the ideals in our American past for which men have died, exposing the flaws and the strengths of the values held by the pioneers, by the men who fought the Civil War, and by those who have believed in "progress." While her later work depicts the more private battle of the individual psyche with "the dragon" in the "earth" of his own heart, Gordon's final project, a double novel, was to unite the concerns of all her fiction: *The Glory of Hera* supplies the archetypal pattern of heroism, which the unpublished companion work *Joy of the Mountains* was to develop in its many historical and autobiographical variations.

A member of "the living confraternity" of writers "who pass on by personal instruction to their successors the 'tricks of the trade,'" Caroline Gordon has assumed a place within a distinguished brotherhood of such southern men of letters as Allen Tate, John Crowe Ransom, Robert Penn Warren, and Donald Davidson. Commenting on

---

1. Gordon, "Cock-Crow," 569, 558.

her role in the Agrarian movement, Willard Thorp notes that though Gordon "never signed any manifestoes issued by the Agrarians, she has been present in their councils," and certainly she explored the tenets of Agrarianism in her own fiction. Gordon's generosity, which Thorp sees evidenced in her feeding and lodging the "protégés" of these southern men of letters, extended well beyond the dictates of hospitality; she has, in Thorp's words, "reshaped many a neophyte's prose."[2]

By Gordon's own account, her "secret, conscious life" as a novelist has required a special kind of valor. So Ashley Brown reads the opening chapter from her projected novel "A Narrow Heart: The Portrait of a Woman": "she has already figured herself as somebody chosen for a special role, like Danaë visited by the god in a golden shower. . . . As long as she can walk along her chosen path and retain the sense of the golden light—the sign of her vocation—she can stay the presence of the hovering shadows."[3]

In some ways the novelist's labors are more rigorous than those of Heracles. Both novelist and soldier are committed by their professions, writes Gordon, "to a lifelong study of wars and warriors"; also like the soldier, the novelist struggles arduously and heroically. Calling attention to the trials of Orpheus, Gordon observes, "The Greeks evidently realized that the poet's lot is, in some ways, harder than that of the soldier, since, in his earthly pilgrimage he has for companion his Muse, who is larger than life, capricious in the extreme, incapable of gratitude—'thankless' Milton called her—and, at times, so vengeful that she is bent upon his death." In a letter to a friend, Gordon herself admits to similar artistic struggles: "It is too late for me to turn back now but if anybody had pointed out to me how much harder writing fiction is than the other arts, I am not sure that I'd have had the nerve to go ahead."[4]

Although she admired the Greek seer Tiresias who "saw so clearly what the gods were doing that it was hard for him to fix his attention upon the deeds of any man," Caroline Gordon set for herself, as mod-

2. Tate, "Techniques of Fiction," in his *Essays*, 129; Thorp, "Southern Renaissance," 249.

3. Gordon, "A Narrow Heart," 7; Ashley Brown, "A Note on 'The Dragon's Teeth,'" *Shenandoah*, XIII (1961), 20.

4. Gordon, "Cock-Crow," 558; Gordon, *Good Soldier: A Key*, 6–7; Gordon, "Letters to a Monk," 6.

ern novelist, the difficult tasks of observing human actions closely, as well as discovering on earth the manifestations of divine order:

> A novelist, it is now clear to me, is like those men who wander about in public parks, a huge sack slung over their shoulders, holding in their right hands sticks which have a sharp piece of metal attached to one end. The sharp pointed stick is for impaling any fragments of wastepaper, rags, cigarette butts, any debris that human beings have left lying about under the trees. The capacious sack in which the wanderers stow the litter was handed to them in the early morning and they will have to carry it as long as there is light enough to see what is lying on the grass.[5]

Scrutinizing the physical world, scavenging for the discarded souvenirs of our lives, the novelist fulfills a prophet's function by reading in the commonplace a supernatural message for humanity, a message communicated most effectively and most completely in symbolical language.

Gordon possessed such a vital gift for divining meaning in particulars, as Flannery O'Connor testifies in a letter to her friend "A."; there, O'Connor praises Gordon for rendering the world so concretely that "you walk through her stories like you are walking in a complete real world." "That is real masterly doing," O'Connor concludes, "and nobody does it any better than Caroline."[6]

5. Gordon, "Cock-Crow," 564; Caroline Gordon, "Always Summer," *Southern Review*, n.s. VII (1971), 438.

6. Flannery O'Connor, to "A.," December 11, 1956, in Fitzgerald (ed.), *Habit of Being*, 187.

Bibliography

Fictional Works by Caroline Gordon

Aleck Maury, Sportsman. 1934; rpr. New York, 1971.
Aleck Maury, Sportsman. Afterword by Caroline Gordon. New York, 1934;
      rpr. Carbondale, Il., 1980.
"Always Summer." *Southern Review,* n.s., VII (1971), 430–46.
"Cloud Nine." *Sewanee Review,* LXXVII (1969), 591–629.
"Cock-Crow." *Southern Review,* n.s., I (1965), 554–69.
The Collected Stories of Caroline Gordon. Introduction by Robert Penn Warren.
      New York, 1981.
"The Dragon's Teeth." *Shenandoah,* XIII (1961), 22–34.
"The Feast of St. Eustace." *Kenyon Review,* XVI (1954), 234–56.
The Forest of the South. New York, 1945.
"Frankie and Thomas and Bud Asbury," *Southern Review,* IV (1939), 696–712.
The Garden of Adonis. 1937; rpr. New York, 1971.
The Glory of Hera. Garden City, N.Y., 1972.
Green Centuries. 1941; rpr. New York, 1971.
The Malefactors. New York, 1956.
"A Morning's Favor." *Southern Review,* I (1935), 271–80.
"A Narrow Heart: The Portrait of a Woman." *Transatlantic Review,* n.s., III
      (1960), 7–19.
None Shall Look Back. 1937; rpr. New York, 1971.
Old Red and Other Stories. 1963; rpr. New York, 1971.
"The Olive Garden." *Sewanee Review,* LIII (1945), 532–43.
Penhally. 1931; rpr. New York, 1971.
The Strange Children. 1951; rpr. New York, 1971.
"The Strangest Day in the Life of Captain Meriwether Lewis As Told to His
      Eighth Cousin, Once Removed." *Southern Review,* n.s., XII (1976),
      387–97.
"A Walk with the Accuser." *Southern Review,* n.s., XIII (1977), 597–613.
"A Walk with the Accuser (Who Is the God of this World)." *Transatlantic
      Review,* n.s., XXXI (1969), 96–113.
"The Waterfall." *Sewanee Review,* LVIII (1950), 632–65.
"What Music." *The Magazine,* I (1934), 143–47.

"The Women on the Battlefield." *Southern Review*, II (1936–37), 515–24.
The Women on the Porch. New York, 1944.

Critical Works by Caroline Gordon

"An American Girl." In *The Added Dimension: The Art and Mind of Flannery O'Connor*, edited by Melvin J. Friedman and Lewis A. Lawson. New York, 1966.
"Dedicatory: Letter to Ford Madox Ford." *Transatlantic Review*, n.s., III (1960), 5–6.
"The Elephant." *Sewanee Review*, LXXIV (1966), 856–71.
"Flannery O'Connor: A Tribute." *Esprit*, VIII (Winter, 1964), 28.
"Flannery O'Connor's *Wise Blood*." *Critique*, II (Fall, 1958), 3–10.
Foreword to *Flannery O'Connor: Voice of the Peacock*, by Kathleen Feeley. New Brunswick, N.J., 1972.
A Good Soldier: A Key to the Novels of Ford Madox Ford. Davis, Calif., 1963.
"Heresy in Dixie." *Sewanee Review*, LXXVI (1968), 263–97.
Contribution to "Homage to Ford Madox Ford—A Symposium." In *New Directions in Prose and Poetry*. No. 7. Norfolk, Conn., 1942.
"How I Learned to Write Novels." *Books on Trial*, XV (1956), 111–12, 160–63.
How to Read a Novel. New York, 1957.
"Letters to a Monk." *Ramparts*, III (December, 1964), 4–10.
"Life at Benfolly, 1930–1931: Letters of Caroline Gordon to a Northern Friend, Sally Wood." *Southern Review*, n.s., XVI (1980), 301–36.
"Mr. Faulkner's Southern Saga." Review of *The Portable Faulkner*, edited by Malcolm Cowley. *New York Times Book Review*, May 5, 1946, pp. 1, 45.
"Mr. Verver, Our National Hero." *Sewanee Review*, LXIII (1955), 29–47.
"Notes on Chekhov and Maugham." *Sewanee Review*, LVII (1949), 401–410.
"Notes on Faulkner and Flaubert." *Hudson Review*, I (1948), 222–31.
"Notes on Hemingway and Kafka." *Sewanee Review*, LVII (1949), 215–26.
"The Novels of Brainard Cheney." *Sewanee Review*, LXVII (1959), 322–30.
"Rebels and Revolutionaries: The New American Scene." *Flannery O'Connor Bulletin*, III (1974), 40–56.
Review of *Robber Rocks: Letters and Memories of Hart Crane*, by Susan Jenkins Brown. *Southern Review*, n.s., VI (1970), 481–87.
"Some Readings and Misreadings." *Sewanee Review*, LXI (1953), 384–407. Reprinted in *Joyce's Portrait: Criticism and Critiques*, edited by Thomas E. Connolly. New York, 1963.
"Stephen Crane." *Accent*, IX (1949), 153–57.
"The Story of Ford Madox Ford." In *Highlights of Modern Literature: A Permanent Collection of Memorable Essays from the "New York Times Book Review,"* edited by Francis Brown. New York, 1954.
"A Virginian in Prairie Country." *New York Times Book Review*, March 8, 1953, pp. 1, 31.
"With a Glitter of Evil." *New York Times Book Review*, June 12, 1955, p. 5.

Gordon, Caroline, *et al.* "Panel Discussion." *Flannery O'Connor Bulletin*, III (1974), 57–78.

Gordon, Caroline, and Jeanne Richardson. "Flies in Their Eyes? A Note on Joseph Heller's *Catch 22.*" *Southern Review*, n.s., III (1967), 96–105.

Gordon, Caroline, and Allen Tate, eds. *The House of Fiction: An Anthology of the Short Story with Commentary.* New York, 1950.

———, eds. *The House of Fiction: An Anthology of the Short Story with Commentary.* 2nd ed. New York, 1960.

Secondary Works on Caroline Gordon

Allen, Walter. *The Modern Novel in Britain and the United States.* New York, 1964.

Alvis, John. "The Miltonic Argument in Caroline Gordon's *The Glory of Hera.*" *Southern Review*, n.s., XVI (1980), 560–73.

Baker, Howard. "The Strategems of Caroline Gordon; or, The Art of the Novel and the Novelty of Myth." *Southern Review*, n.s., IX (1973), 523–49.

Baum, Catherine B., and Floyd C. Watkins. "Caroline Gordon and 'The Captive': An Interview." *Southern Review*, n.s., VII (1971), 447–62.

Bittner, William. "For the Ladies." *Saturday Review*, November 16, 1957, pp. 20–21.

Blum, Morgan. "The Shifting Point of View: Joyce's 'The Dead' and Gordon's 'Old Red.'" *Critique*, I (Winter, 1956), 45–66.

Bradbury, John M. *Renaissance in the South: A Critical History of the Literature, 1920–1960.* Chapel Hill, 1963.

Bradford, M. E. "Quest for a Hero." *National Review*, August 18, 1972, pp. 906–907.

Brooks, Cleanth, *et al.*, comps. *American Literature: The Makers and the Making.* Vol. II of 2 vols. New York, 1973.

Brown, Ashley. "The Achievement of Caroline Gordon." *Southern Humanities Review*, II (1968), 279–90.

———. "*None Shall Look Back*: The Novel as History." *Southern Review*, n.s., VII (1971), 480–94.

———. "A Note on 'The Dragon's Teeth.'" *Shenandoah*, XIII (1961), 20–21.

———. "The Novel as Christian Comedy." In *Reality and Myth: Essays in American Literature in Honor of Richard Croom Beatty*, edited by William E. Walker and Robert L. Welker. Nashville, 1964.

Brown, Jane Gibson. "The Early Novels of Caroline Gordon: The Confluence of Myth and History as a Fictional Technique." Ph.D. dissertation, University of Dallas, 1975.

———. "The Early Novels of Caroline Gordon: Myth and History as a Fictional Technique." *Southern Review*, n.s., XIII (1977), 289–98.

"Caroline Gordon." *Wilson Library Bulletin*, XII (September, 1937), 10.

"Caroline Gordon, Novelist, Critic and Short-Story Writer, 86, Dies." *New York Times*, April 14, 1981, Sec. B, p. 18.

"Caroline Gordon, Novelist and Critic, Dies in Mexico." Chicago *Tribune*, April 15, 1981, Sec. 4, p. 11.

Charles, Norman, ed. "Recent Southern Fiction: A Panel Discussion." *Bulletin of Wesleyan College*, XLI (1961).

Cheney, Brainard. "Caroline Gordon's Ontological Quest." *Renascence*, XVI (1963), 3–12.

———. "Caroline Gordon's *The Malefactors*." *Sewanee Review*, LXXIX (1971), 360–72.

Cowan, Bainard. "The Serpent's Coils: How to Read Caroline Gordon's Later Fiction." *Southern Review*, n.s., XVI (1980), 281–98.

Cowan, Louise. "Nature and Grace in Caroline Gordon." *Critique*, I (Winter, 1956), 11–27.

Cowley, Malcolm. "The Meriwether Connection." *Southern Review*, n.s., I (1965), 46–56.

———. "Two Winters with Hart Crane." *Sewanee Review*, LXVII (1959), 547–56.

Davis, Robert Gorham. "Inside the Short Story." *New York Times Book Review*, July 30, 1950, p. 4.

———. "It Isn't Life That Counts." Review of *How to Read a Novel*. *New York Times Book Review*, October 27, 1957, p. 6.

Eisinger, Chester E. "Caroline Gordon: The Logic of Conservatism." In his *Fiction of the Forties*. Chicago, 1964.

Fitzgerald, Sally, ed. "A Master Class: From the Correspondence of Caroline Gordon and Flannery O'Connor." *Georgia Review*, XXXIII (1979), 827–46.

Fletcher, Marie. "The Fate of Women in a Changing South: A Persistent Theme in the Fiction of Caroline Gordon." *Mississippi Quarterly*, XXI (1968), 17–28.

Ford, Ford Madox. "A Stage in American Literature." *Bookman*, LXXIV (1931), 371–76.

Review of *A Good Soldier: A Key to the Novels of Ford Madox Ford*. *Times Literary Supplement*, October 4, 1963, p. 794.

Gray, Richard. "Acts of Darkness, Ceremonies of the Brave: Caroline Gordon." In his *The Literature of Memory: Modern Writers of the American South*. Baltimore, 1977.

Hartman, Carl. "Charades at Benfolly." Review of *The Strange Children*. *Western Review*, XVI (1952), 322–24.

Heilman, Robert B. "Schools for Girls." *Sewanee Review*, LX (1952), 299–309.

Hoffman, Frederick J. *The Art of Southern Fiction: A Study of Some Modern Novelists*. Carbondale, Il., 1967.

———. "Caroline Gordon: The Special Yield." *Critique*, I (Winter, 1956), 29–35.

Jacobs, Robert D. "Best of Its Kind." *Hopkins Review*, IV (Spring, 1951), 59–60.

King, Lawrence T. "The Novels of Caroline Gordon." *Catholic World*, CLXXXI (1955), 274–79.

Koch, Vivienne. "Companions in the Blood." *Sewanee Review*, LXIV (1956), 645–51.

———. "*The Forest of the South.*" *Sewanee Review*, LIV (1946), 543–48.

Landess, Thomas H. "The Function of Ritual in Caroline Gordon's *Green Centuries.*" *Southern Review*, n.s., VII (1971), 495–508.

———, ed. *The Short Fiction of Caroline Gordon: A Critical Symposium.* Irving, Tex., 1972.

Lewis, Janet. "*The Glory of Hera.*" *Sewanee Review*, LXXXI (1973), 185–94.

Lowell, Robert. "Visiting the Tates." *Sewanee Review*, LXVII (1959), 557–59.

Lytle, Andrew N. "Caroline Gordon and the Historic Image." *Sewanee Review*, LVII (1949), 560–86.

———. "*The Forest of the South.*" *Critique*, I (Winter, 1956), 3–9.

McDowell, Frederick P. W. *Caroline Gordon.* Minneapolis, 1966.

O'Connor, Mary. "On Caroline Gordon." *Southern Review*, n.s., VII (1971), 463–66.

O'Connor, William Van. *The Grotesque: An American Genre and Other Essays.* Carbondale, Il., 1962.

———. "The Novel of Experience." *Critique*, I (Winter, 1956), 37–44.

Paterson, Katherine. "Caroline Gordon's House of Fiction." *Washington Post Book World*, April 19, 1981, pp. 1, 2, 6.

Peden, William. "From Poe to Welty." *Saturday Review of Literature*, June 17, 1950, pp. 18, 26.

Porter, Katherine Anne. "Dulce et Decorum Est." Review of *None Shall Look Back. New Republic*, March 31, 1937, pp. 244–45.

Ragan, David. "Portrait of a Lady Novelist: Caroline Gordon." *Mark Twain Quarterly*, VIII (1947), 18–20.

Rocks, James E. "The Christian Myth as Salvation: Caroline Gordon's *The Strange Children.*" *Tulane Studies in English*, XVI (1968), 149–60.

———. "The Mind and Art of Caroline Gordon." *Mississippi Quarterly*, XXI (1968), 1–16.

Rosenberger, Coleman. "Artists, Writers, and Their Problems in Miss Gordon's Comedy of Manners." *New York Herald Tribune Book Review*, March 25, 1956, p. 3.

Ross, Danforth. "Caroline Gordon's Golden Ball." *Critique*, I (Winter, 1956), 67–73.

Rubin, Louis D., Jr. "The Image of an Army: The Civil War in Southern Fiction." In *Southern Writers: Appraisals in Our Time*, edited by R. C. Simonini, Jr. Charlottesville, 1964.

Rubin, Louis D., Jr., and Robert D. Jacobs, eds. *Southern Renascence: The Literature of the Modern South.* Baltimore, 1953.

Simons, John W. "A Cunning and Curious Dramatization." *Commonweal*, LXIV (April 13, 1956), 54–56.

Squires, Radcliffe. "The Underground Stream: A Note on Caroline Gordon's Fiction." *Southern Review*, n.s., VII (1971), 467–79.

Stanford, Donald E. "Caroline Gordon." *Southern Review*, n.s., XVII (1981), 459–60.

————. "Caroline Gordon: From *Penhally* to 'A Narrow Heart.'" *Southern Review*, n.s., VII (1971), xv–xx.

————. "The Fiction of Caroline Gordon: A Reissue." *Southern Review*, n.s., VIII (1972), 458.

————. Review of *The Glory of Hera*. *Michigan Quarterly Review*, XII (1973), 89–90.

Stuckey, William J. *Caroline Gordon*. New York, 1972.

Thorp, Willard. "Southern Renaissance." In his *American Writing in the Twentieth Century*. Cambridge, Mass., 1960.

————. "The Way Back and the Way Up: The Novels of Caroline Gordon." *Bucknell Review*, VI (December, 1956), 1–15.

Toledano, Ben C. "Savannah Writers' Conference—1939." *Georgia Review*, XXII (1968), 145–59.

Tyler, Anne. "The South Without the Scent of Lavender." *New York Times Book Review*, April 19, 1981, pp. 6, 15.

Van Doren, Mark. "Fiction of the Quarter." *Southern Review*, III (1937), 159–82.

Warren, Robert Penn. "The Fiction of Caroline Gordon." *Southwest Review*, XX (January, 1935), 5–10.

West, Ray B., Jr. "The Craft of the Short Story: 1951." *Western Review*, XV (1951), 84, 86, 157–60.

Bibliographical Sources on Caroline Gordon

Bradford, M. E. "Caroline Gordon: A Working Bibliography, 1957–1972." In *The Short Fiction of Caroline Gordon: A Critical Symposium*, edited by Thomas H. Landess. Irving, Tex., 1972.

Golden, Robert E., and Mary C. Sullivan. *Flannery O'Connor and Caroline Gordon: A Reference Guide*. Boston, 1977.

Griscom, Joan. "Bibliography of Caroline Gordon." *Critique*, I (Winter, 1956), 74–78.

Kinsman, Clare D., and Mary Ann Tennenhouse, eds. *Contemporary Authors: A Bio-bibliographical Guide to Current Authors and Their Works*. Permanent Series. Vol. I of 2 vols. Detroit, 1974.

Rubin, Louis D., Jr., ed. *A Bibliographical Guide to the Study of Southern Literature*. Baton Rouge, 1969.

Spiller, Robert E., *et al.*, eds. *Literary History of the United States*. 4th ed., rev. Vol. II of 2 vols. New York, 1974.

Related Background Material

Abrams, M. H. *Natural Supernaturalism: Tradition and Revolution in Romantic Literature*. New York, 1971.

Blackmur, R. P. "San Giovanni in Venere: Allen Tate as Man of Letters." *Sewanee Review*, LXVII (1959), 614–31.

Booth, Wayne C. *The Rhetoric of Fiction*. Chicago, 1961.

Brooks, Cleanth, Jr., and Robert Penn Warren. *Understanding Fiction*. New York, 1943.

———. *Understanding Poetry*. 3rd ed. New York, 1960.

Butcher, Samuel Henry, ed. *Aristotle's Theory of Poetry and Fine Art, with a Critical Text and Translation of the "Poetics."* 4th ed. London, 1923.

Carlyle, Thomas. *On Heroes, Hero-Worship, and the Heroic in History*. London, 1841; rpr. New York, 1974. Vol. V of *The Works of Thomas Carlyle*, edited by H. D. Traill. 30 vols.

Chase, Richard. *The American Novel and Its Tradition*. Garden City, N.Y., 1957.

Chattanooga *News*, January 1, 1920—May 24, 1921.

Core, George, ed. *Southern Fiction Today: Renascence and Beyond*. Athens, Ga., 1969.

Cowan, Louise. *The Fugitive Group: A Literary History*. Baton Rouge, 1959.

Dante Alighieri. *The Divine Comedy*. Translated by John Ciardi. New York, 1977.

Dante Alighieri. *The Inferno*. Translated by John Ciardi. New Brunswick, N.J., 1954.

Davidson, Donald. *Southern Writers in the Modern World*. Athens, Ga., 1958.

Day, Dorothy. *The Long Loneliness: The Autobiography of Dorothy Day*. New York, 1952.

Eliot, T. S. *The Cocktail Party: A Comedy*. New York, 1950.

———. *The Sacred Wood: Essays on Poetry and Criticism*. London, 1920.

———. "Ulysses, Order and Myth." *Dial*, LXXV (1923), 480—83.

———. *The Waste Land: A Facsimile and Transcript of the Original Drafts Including the Annotations of Ezra Pound*. Edited by Valerie Eliot. London, 1922; facs. and rpr. New York, 1971.

Fain, John Tyree, and Thomas Daniel Young, eds. *The Literary Correspondence of Donald Davidson and Allen Tate*. Athens, Ga., 1974.

Fitzgerald, Sally, ed. *The Habit of Being: Letters of Flannery O'Connor*. New York, 1979.

Ford, Ford Madox [Hueffer]. *A Call: The Tale of Two Passions*. London, 1910; facs. Ann Arbor, 1967.

———. "Techniques." *Southern Review*, I (1935), 20—35.

Glasgow, Ellen. *A Certain Measure: An Interpretation of Prose Fiction*. New York, 1938.

Graves, Robert. *The White Goddess: A Historical Grammar of Poetic Myth*. 2nd ed. New York, 1966.

Gross, John. *The Rise and Fall of the Man of Letters: A Study of the Idiosyncratic and the Humane in Modern Literature*. [New York], 1969.

Heilman, Robert B. "Baton Rouge and LSU Forty Years After." *Sewanee Review*, LXXXVIII (1980), 126—43.

Holman, C. Hugh. *The Roots of Southern Writing: Essays on the Literature of the American South*. Athens, Ga., 1972.

James, Henry. "The Art of Fiction." In *The Art of Fiction and Other Essays*, edited by Morris Roberts. New York, 1948.

————. Preface to *The Portrait of a Lady*. Edited by Leon Edel. New York, 1881; rpr. Boston, 1963.

Jones, W. H. S., trans. *Hippocrates*, Loeb Classical Library. Vol. II of 4 vols. 1923; rpr. Cambridge, Mass., 1967.

Joyce, Stanislaus. *My Brother's Keeper*. Edited by Richard Ellmann. New York, 1958.

Jung, Carl G. *Modern Man in Search of a Soul*. Translated by W. S. Dell and Cary F. Baynes. New York, 1933.

Jung, Carl G., *et al.*, *Man and His Symbols*. Garden City, N.Y., 1964.

Kreiger, Murray. *The New Apologists for Poetry*. Minneapolis, 1956.

————. *The Tragic Vision*. New York, 1960.

La Motte-Fouqué, Friedrich Heinrich Karl, Freiherr de. "Undine," translated by Edmund Gosse. In *Undine and Other Stories*. London, 1932.

Levernier, James Arthur. "Indian Captivity Narratives: Their Functions and Forms." Ph.D. dissertation, University of Pennsylvania, 1975.

Lubbock, Percy. *The Craft of Fiction*. London, 1921; rpr. New York, 1955.

McCarthy, Mary. "Settling the Colonel's Hash." In her *On the Contrary*. New York, 1961.

MacLeish, Archibald. *The Irresponsibles: A Declaration*. New York, 1940.

Maritain, Jacques. *Art and Scholasticism and the Frontiers of Poetry*. Translated by Joseph W. Evans. New York, 1962.

————. *Creative Intuition in Art and Poetry*. New York, 1953.

————. *The Range of Reason*. New York, 1952.

Maritain, Jacques, and Raïssa Maritain. *The Situation of Poetry: Four Essays on the Relations Between Poetry, Mysticism, Magic, and Knowledge*. Translated by Marshall Suther. New York, 1955.

Michaux, F. A. [François André]. *Travels to the Westward of the Allegany Mountains . . . with Lower Louisiana*. Translated by B. Lambert. London, 1805.

O'Connor, Flannery. *Mystery and Manners: Occasional Prose*. Edited by Sally Fitzgerald and Robert Fitzgerald. New York, 1969.

Ransom, John Crowe. *Selected Poems*. 3rd ed. New York, 1969.

Rubin, Louis D., Jr. *The Wary Fugitives: Four Poets and the South*. Baton Rouge, 1978.

Schorer, Mark. "Technique as Discovery." *Hudson Review*, I (1948), 67–87.

Simpson, Lewis P. *The Man of Letters in New England and the South: Essays on the History of the Literary Vocation in America*. Baton Rouge, 1973.

————. "The South's Reaction to Modernism: A Problem in the Study of Southern Letters." In *Southern Literary Study: Problems and Possibilities*, edited by Louis D. Rubin, Jr., and C. Hugh Holman. Chapel Hill, 1975.

Sophocles. *The Oedipus Cycle: An English Version*. Translated by Dudley Fitts and Robert Fitzgerald. New York, 1949.

Squires, Radcliffe. *Allen Tate: A Literary Biography*. New York, 1971.

Stewart, John L. *The Burden of Time: The Fugitives and Agrarians*. Princeton, 1965.

Tate, Allen. *Collected Poems, 1919–1976.* New York, 1977.
———, ed. *The Collected Poems of John Peale Bishop.* New York, 1948 and 1976.
———. *Essays of Four Decades.* Chicago, 1968.
———. *The Fathers and Other Fiction.* New York, 1938; rpr. Baton Rouge, 1977.
———. "*The Fugitive*, 1922–1925: A Personal Recollection Twenty Years After." *Princeton University Library Chronicle*, III (April, 1942), 75–84.
———. Contribution to "Homage to Ford Madox Ford—A Symposium." In *New Directions in Prose and Poetry*. No. 7. Norfolk, Conn., 1942.
———. "The Post of Observation in Fiction." *Maryland Quarterly*, I (1944), 61–64.
———. "Three Commentaries: Poe, James, and Joyce." *Sewanee Review*, LVIII (1950), 1–15.
Taylor, Peter. Contribution to "Comments on Neglected Books of the Past Twenty-five Years." *American Scholar*, XXXIX (1970), 345.
Thorp, Willard. "The Writer as Pariah in the Old South." In *The Dilemma of the Southern Writer*, edited by Richard K. Meeker. Farmville, Va.: Longwood College, 1961.
Thucydides. *The History of the Peloponnesian War.* Edited in translation by Sir Richard Livingstone. London, 1943; rpr. New York, 1972.
Twelve Southerners. *I'll Take My Stand: The South and the Agrarian Tradition.* New York, 1930; rpr. Baton Rouge, 1977.
Vivas, Eliseo. "Allen Tate as Man of Letters." *Sewanee Review*, LXII (1954), 131–43.
———. "Literature and Knowledge." *Sewanee Review*, LX (1952), 561–92.
Warren, Robert Penn. *Brother to Dragons: A Tale in Verse and Voices: A New Version.* Rev. ed. New York, 1979.
———. *Selected Poems, 1923–1975.* New York, 1976.
Watt, Ian. *The Rise of the Novel: Studies in Defoe, Richardson, and Fielding.* Berkeley, 1957.
Weber, Brom, ed. *The Complete Poems and Selected Letters and Prose of Hart Crane.* New York, 1966.
———, ed. *The Letters of Hart Crane, 1916–1932.* New York, 1952.
Welty, Eudora. "Place in Fiction." *South Atlantic Quarterly*, LV (1956), 57–72.
Wilbur, Richard. *Advice to a Prophet, and Other Poems.* New York, 1961.
Wimsatt, W. K., Jr. *The Verbal Icon: Studies in the Meaning of Poetry.* [Louisville, Ky.], 1954.
Young, Thomas Daniel. "A Prescription to Live By: Ransom and the Agrarian Debates." *Southern Review*, n.s., XII (1976), 608–21.

Index

Abrams, M. H., 25
Agrarianism: influence on Gordon, 2, 35, 84–85, 166–67; beginnings of Agrarians, 6–7; as literary image, 7–8; as program of reform, 8; and man of letters tradition, 34. *See also* Davidson, Donald; Gordon, Caroline; Ransom, John Crowe; Tate, Allen; Warren, Robert Penn
Anderson, Sherwood, 147
Aristotle, 31, 39, 148
Arnold, Matthew, 1–2, 9
Arthurian legends, 123–24

The Ballad of the Sad Café, 100
Baudelaire, Charles, 11, 13, 27
Bernanos, Georges, 23
Bishop, John Peale, 43–44, 45, 54
Booth, Wayne, 14, 16–17, 33
Brooks, Cleanth, Jr., 26

Capote, Truman, 15, 24, 33
Carlyle, Thomas, 10
Chattanooga *News. See* Gordon, Caroline
Chekhov, Anton, 13
Coleridge, Samuel Taylor, 124, 128–29
Conrad, Joseph, 26
Cowley, Malcolm, 6, 34
Crane, Hart: friendship with the Tates, 6, 18; poetry introduced to Fugitives by Tate, 6; on science vs. poetry, 18; model for Gordon's characters, 97, 135, 144–45; in *Women on the Porch*, 110; *The Bridge*, 145–46
Crane, Stephen, 14

Dante Alighieri: in *House of Fiction*, 11–12; and "symbolical imagination," 12; influence on Gordon, 19, 24, 98, 119, 139–40, 145; allusions in Gordon's fiction, 98, 104–109 *passim*, 112, 115, 118, 126, 128, 132, 150; Beatrice, 163, 165
Davidson, Donald: as man of letters, 1, 35, 166; contribution to Southern Renaissance, 4–5; as Fugitive poet, 6; as

Agrarian, 6–8, 35; "The Southern Writer and the Modern University," 34–35; friendship with the Tates, 35
Day, Dorothy, 139

Eliot, T. S.: influence on Tate, 1–2, 7, 8, 10; influence on Gordon, 3, 19, 39, 40–41, 85, 98, 119; poetry introduced to Fugitives by Tate, 6; *The Waste Land*, 7, 40–41, 48, 85, 86, 94; *The Sacred Wood*, 9; "Tradition and the Individual Talent," 9, 17, 39; "convention," 17; "dissociation of sensibility," 54; "mythical method," 85; *The Cocktail Party*, 146
Expatriates, 6

Faulkner, William: and agrarianism, 5, 8; verisimilitude, 15, 23; poetic qualities in fiction, 19; *Sanctuary*, 100; *Go Down, Moses*, 147; mentioned, 39, 164
Flaubert, Gustave: influence on Gordon, 3, 26, 29, 40; Impressionist tradition, 13, 15; use of point of view, 14; compared to Faulkner, 19; poetic qualities in fiction, 20; Gordon directs Flannery O'Connor to, 28; quoted in *Green Centuries*, 48
Ford, Ford Madox: as man of letters, 2; influence on Gordon, 2, 3, 15–16, 26, 30, 75–76; Impressionist tradition, 3, 15; *A Call*, 15–16; poetic qualities in fiction, 19; Gordon's *A Good Soldier*, 33; review of *Penhally*, 55
Frazer, James, Sir, 85
Freud, Sigmund, 99
Fugitive magazine, 3, 7, 17
Fugitive poets, 2–6 *passim*, 25

Glasgow, Ellen, 5, 7
Gluck, Christoph, 103–104
Gordon, Caroline: as writer not as critic, 1, 26; as critic, 2, 3; as teacher, 2, 3, 13, 26–35, 167; early newspaper work, 3–4; and expatriates, 6; conversion to Catholicism, 22, 25, 83, 118; as White God-